The Design

of

Real Time Applications

The Design
of
Real Time Applications

M. Blackman

Arthur Andersen & Co.

A Wiley–Interscience Publication

JOHN WILEY & SONS
London · New York · Sydney · Toronto

Library of Congress Cataloging in Publication Data:

Blackman, Maurice.
The design of real time applications.

'A Wiley–Interscience publication.'
Includes bibliographical references.
1. Real-time data processing. I. Title.
QA76.54.B55   1975   001.6'44'04   74–26960

ISBN 0 471 07770 4

Preface

My intention in writing this book is to add to the literature of computing, a guide for analysts, project leaders and managers who are designing and installing real time applications. In my experience, the literature available on real time concentrates on technical matters of software and equipment. In contrast, I have set out to indicate where to start, and how to proceed, to design an application which uses the real time mode of processing. My intention is to fill a gap in the literature concerning the activity of the application designer.

There are two components to the book. The first is a method for organizing the content of a transaction driven system into a hierarchy of system units. It starts with the entire application and ends with the program unit which processes one function for one type of entered message. The second is a scheme of documentation which formally describes each member of each set of system units at each level of subdivision. The attributes described at each level are chosen to ensure early and thorough consideration of the important issues in the real time mode of processing. These are identified early in the book from a study of the unique aspects of real time systems.

I do not wish to claim this book as a complete study of real time commercial computing. I have tried not to duplicate existing literature, particularly in the areas of sizing hardware and designing general software. However, I have had to consider the reader for whom this may be a first contact with real time. There are therefore introductory chapters on types of real time system and a description of one particular system. This system provides the source material for all the worked examples later in the book.

There are also chapters on the topics of planning system design and implementation since I could not assume a shared understanding of the meaning of such terms as preliminary design, detailed design, economic evaluation, etcetera. The really new material is therefore diluted with some recapitulation but still this is not an attempt to present a thorough study of all facets of real time.

The ideas presented have many sources. My first step was made when I needed to describe concisely the logic of the use of a series of terminal entries to accomplish the check in of a passenger during the processing of an aircraft departure. A flowchart showing the decisions governing the use of the available entries was prepared. On reflection it appeared that the design process would have been much better directed had such charts been prepared in advance to identify the entries needed to suit each system function. Thus the concept of a system unit which linked a series of entries into one function was born. To this concept was added work habits of disciplined and formal documentation developed in batch systems design. My basic knowledge of real time and its unique characteristics was gained from experience of various manufacturers and from the writings of James Martin. The end result, my contribution, is to bring the formality of good batch design practice to real time systems in a way which recognizes and harnesses their unique features.

The methods presented have been used to assist in the design and installation of a number of systems with which I have been associated. The methods are therefore presented as a fully developed scheme of work and documentation. However I am sure that improvements and changes can and will be made. I would ask everyone using the book to think critically about its proposals, and tailor them to suit the scope of his own applications. I would welcome correspondence about successes, failures and adaptations of the methods.

In another respect, it would be naive of me to think that these proposals are the last word in systems methods. Real time use of computers is rapidly developing and advances in both hardware and software are making the work of the programmer less extensive. For all but high performance systems, packaged solutions will become more and more acceptable. The amount of design and implementation work may well reduce to the point where the more detailed levels of documentation will not be necessary. However, in the interim, I believe that the methods proposed are relevant and their use improves the quality of application design.

In recent months, I have noticed a tendency for batch systems development to change. Applications on which I have worked, which have involved processing many different kinds of batched transactions through common programs, have been usefully described by reference to their transactions rather than their programs. IBM have introduced 'structured programming' which includes among its innovations, transaction oriented descriptions of processing logic. I believe that the reader will find some affinities between the methods in this book and these new developments. It may be that the next few years will see the emergence of a method of design and documentation which will suit both batch and real time systems, by virtue of a common concern in both with the transaction as the impetus for processing. I hope that this book will therefore prove to be in the mainstream of general commercial computing.

ACKNOWLEDGEMENTS

For the development of my thoughts on real time I must thank my colleagues and friends at the then separate airlines of BOAC and BEA, in particular Alan Jacobs, the late Bill Devereaux and John Cutting (BOAC), Mark Haegele, John Morcom, Daphne Harris and the other members of the Transaction Utility Study Group (BEA) and Roger Townsend. Help and advice has also vii

been received from many other people with whom I have had the pleasure of working in the past few years.

Finally I am indebted to the devotion and care with which the typing and illustration work was done. Many people were involved over a period of time working under the direction of Mary Curley, Linda Jeffries and Terry Gannon. Without their help, the book would never have been fit for publication.

October 1974   MAURICE BLACKMAN

Contents

PART I

The Nature of Real Time

Chapter 1

An Invoice Payments System

INTRODUCTION

Why should management methods alter when a computer project has a real time element to it? The building blocks are still programs and files. Why the difference?

The first part of this book will attempt to convey the differences between real time and batch systems. The differences originate in the method of use of computer facilities so this will be examined first. Their consequences in systems design and installation will be traced so as to establish that there are new problems for the project leader or data processing manager to solve. The rest of the book offers suggestions for their solution.

If each reader had the opportunity to sit in front of a computer terminal and use it in a business environment, the sense of the difference would be very quickly established. As a second best, this chapter describes and illustrates an invoice payments system in operation. The full sequence of activities would be tedious to describe but a selection made to show one business event is presented to try to convey an experience of the difference. Once the difference has been felt the rest of the book should make some sense even to someone who has yet to participate in his first real time project.

For both the newcomer and the real time practitioner, the system described in Chapter 1 provides the source material for the illustrations throughout the book. Even if the fact of difference is accepted, this chapter should still be read so that the background to the illustrations is appreciated.

Our story opens, with a brief description of the general design of the illustrative system.

DESCRIPTION OF USER SITUATION

The Firm and its Policy

The firm concerned is in retailing. It has many hundreds of branches, sells many thousands of different items bought from thousands of suppliers. Orders are requested by each branch for the items it requires. These are recorded centrally and placed with appropriate suppliers. Goods are delivered to the stores and invoices are sent to the central office for payment. A computer system is used to control payments and a real time system is the means of capturing payments data.

Both orders and invoices relate to the supply of goods to a single store. When invoices are received, there are likely to be many from each supplier. The invoices can therefore be batched by supplier for control. This operation is performed before the invoices are passed to the data entry clerks.

The data entry operation is performed in a central office. The data is entered through visual display units (VDU). Many clerks work in the same office on a variety of data entry jobs of which invoice entry is only one. When they receive the work it has already been batched and controlled so their working situation is very similar to that of punched card clerks. The difference is that their machines are linked directly to a computer which has been programmed to participate in the data entry process.

The link with a computer is used for two prime purposes. The first is to reduce drastically the number of characters entered, the second is to provide immediate validation. The reduction of key strokes is achieved by utilizing data already filed and by implying data from data previously entered.

Outline of Method

Invoices are typically received from suppliers before the stores have notified central office of the receipt of goods. Therefore the data capture operation has two phases. First the receipt of the invoice and its total is registered, then after several days the invoice is recalled and matched against goods received. This matching process is performed to ensure that the totals originally entered are correct. The goods received are priced from the product file, extended and totalled. The total is checked against the invoice total. Mismatches between transactions and product file are referred for further details to be entered. The matching of files is performed offline during the delay period between the two outline activities.

When the delay period expires, a clerk in the data entry office recalls batches one by one for checking.. Those with errors are examined further. The corresponding Goods Received data for an invoice whose total does not match the total calculated on goods received, is displayed. The clerk can match item for item and enter discrepancies or alter the total on the invoice. Discrepancies are entered not to amend the Goods Received data but to record a difference. The difference will eventually result in a claim or credit note. At the end of this process an accurate reproduction of the invoice will be recorded in the system.

That briefly is the context of the example. How does it work in practice? We will follow a batch of invoices through the real time part of the system.

THE FIRST DAY

First Entry

On Wednesday 13th March, VDU operator Mary Clarke received a batch of invoices which she transcribed onto the blank form set up on her screen. Her

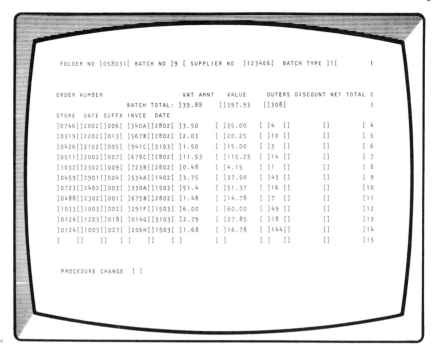

Figure 1.1. Invoice entry record

entry is shown in Figure 1.1. The data that Mary entered is in the fields marked by square brackets][. This is a feature of the particular terminal used that it has protected space over which the operator cannot enter data. The space where data can be entered is marked by these brackets. When a field has been entered, Mary can press a TAB key to position on the next unprotected field.

The first line entered is to identify the batch of invoices, the supplier and the batch type (prepaid or not). The second line contains the total value of the batch and the total number of outers (the units in which items are despatched—outer packaging as opposed to the item's individual packaging). On the third and subsequent lines she enters data for each invoice in the batch. This is store number, date of order (in a day-month form) and the order serial number; invoice number (supplier's reference) and date; tax and value of invoice; number of outers; any discount and consequent net amount. When all invoices in the batch are recorded, Mary can indicate whether she is going to change the type of work she is doing. On this occasion she is not. She can therefore signal the end of message and transmit the data accumulated in terminal storage to the computer.

The entry that she has made is described as a form-filling or formatted entry. To make it, she needed a blank form to be displayed on the screen. This was produced initially when she started to use the terminal in the morning. At that time she entered her own coded identity and the type of work she had been assigned. The computer responded with a blank form suited to that type of work. As we saw above, she has the opportunity to change her work type on subsequent entries. Until she does so the computer will go on returning blank forms for her to fill in. Unless, that is, she makes an error.

First Response

The computer has detected a possible error in the data that Mary has submitted. Figure 1.2 shows the response. Below the data that she has entered

```
    FOLDER NO ]058031[ BATCH NO ]1 [ SUPPLIER NO  ]1234E6[  BATCH TYPE ]1[          1


    ORDER NUMBER                      VAT AMNT   VALUE     OUTERS DISCOUNT NET TOTAL 2
                       BATCH TOTAL: ]39.88    []397.93   []308[                     3
    STORE  DATE SUFFX INVCE  DATE
    ]0746[]2002[]006[ ]340A[]2802[ ]3.50    [ ]35.00   [ ]4  []        []      [ 4
    ]0319[]2202[]013[ ]567B[]2802[ ]2.03    [ ]20.25   [ ]10 []        []      [ 5
    ]0426[]2102[]005[ ]941C[]3103[ ]1.50    [ ]15.00   [ ]3  []        []      [ 6
    ]0511[]2002[]007[ ]678C[]2802[ ]11.53   [ ]115.25  [ ]14 []        []      [ 7
    ]1032[]2302[]009[ ]723B[]2802[ ]0.48    [ ]4.15    [ ]1  []        []      [ 8
    ]0459[]2901[]004[ ]534A[]1402[ ]3.75    [ ]37.50   [ ]43 []        []      [ 9
    ]0723[]2402[]003[ ]330A[]1503[ ]▶1.4    [◦]51.37   [ ]16 []        []      [10
    ]0488[]2302[]001[ ]675B[]2802[ ]1.48    [ ]14.78   [ ]7  []        []      [11
    ]1033[]1003[]002[ ]291F[]1503[ ]6.00    [ ]60.00   [ ]49 []        []      [12
    ]0124[]1203[]018[ ]014G[]3103[ ]2.79    [ ]27.85   [ ]18 []        []      [13
    ]0124[]1003[]027[ ]206H[]1503[ ]1.68    [ ]16.78   [ ]144[]        []      [14
    ]     []    []    [ ]    []   [ ]        [ ]        [ ]  []        []      [15



    PROCEDURE CHANGE  ] [

    ERROR: LINE 10 - INVALID VAT AMOUNT - DECIMAL POINT NOT ALIGNED
```

Figure 1.2. Error response

the computer has added a message notifying her that an error exists, describing whereabouts it is on the display and the probable nature of the error. In the body of the display, the computer has added further information—placing an asterisk after the field in error and setting the cursor and start of message symbol on the first character of the field.

The cursor is a symbol which shows the operator at all times whereabouts the next character will be placed when entered. It can be moved around the screen by pressing control keys on the terminal keyboard. The 'start of message' symbol as its name implies marks the beginning of the screen space which will be transmitted when the next message is sent.

Second Entry

Figure 1.3 shows the correction which Mary has made. She has substituted £5·14 for the amount originally entered. In this case the computer has correctly located and diagnosed the error but it could have been diagnosed wrongly. It

Figure 1.3. Corrected entry

made a test that there were two digits after the decimal point of VAT amount. When it found that there were not, it reported 'DECIMAL POINT NOT ALIGNED' while the error could have been that a digit had been omitted. The programmer cannot know which will occur when he selects the error text for that particular condition. He has chosen a meaningful message which might on another occasion be an incorrect definition of the error.

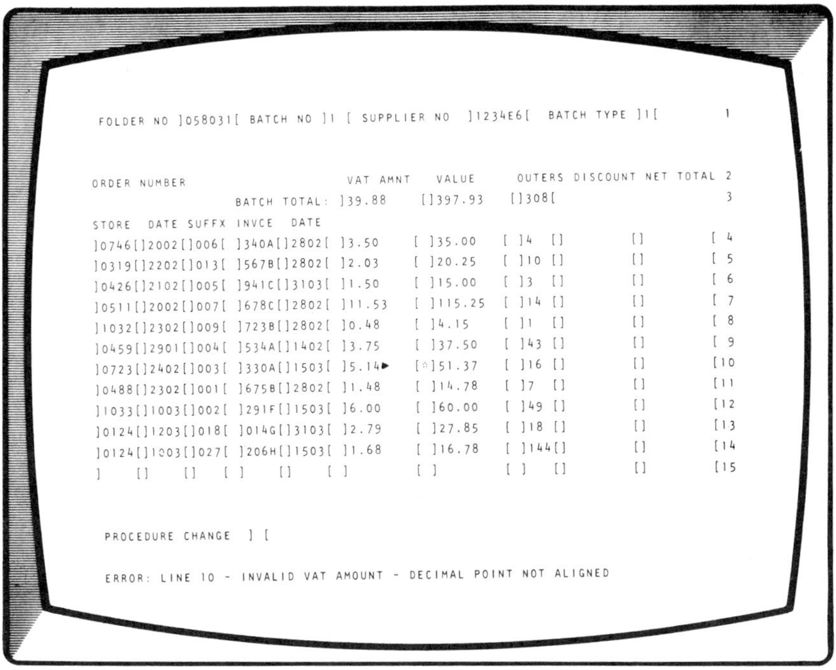

Second Response

This time all is well. The response is an empty form ready for the next batch to be entered (see Figure 1.4). This shows Mary that her previous batch has been accepted. Had there been several format errors in the batch, each would have been presented in turn until the batch was clean.

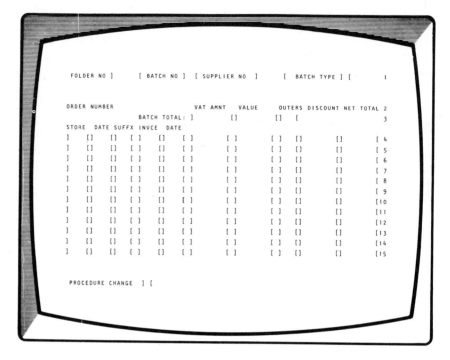

Figure 1.4. Blank format

Associated Response

However, unknown to Mary, the computer program has detected an error in the batch control. It is in the process of producing the associated response shown in Figure 1.5. This response appears on a printer well away from Mary.

RPT OPR02		INVOICE BATCH TOTALS ERROR LISTING				13/03/75 PAGE 37	
		- - - - - ORDER NUMBER - - - - -					
FOLDER NO/BATCH NO	SUPPLIER	STORE	DATE	SUFFX	VAT AMNT	OUTERS	
058031/09	1234E/6	0746	2002	006	3.50	4	
		0319	2202	013	2.03	10	
		0426	2102	005	1.50	3	
		0511	2002	007	11.53	14	
		1032	2302	009	0.48	1	
		0459	2901	004	3.75	43	
		0723	2402	003	5.14	16	
		0488	2302	001	1.48	7	
		1033	1003	002	6.00	49	
		0124	1203	018	2.79	18	
		0124	1003	027	1.68	144	
					- - - - -	- - - -	
			BATCH TOTALS		39.88	308	
						****	

Figure 1.5. Error printout

This is not a characteristic of real time systems generally—only of this one. To save disturbing the rhythm of data entry and so keep up Mary's keying speed, only simple errors are returned to her. Complex errors such as this one are referred for subsequent correction.

This error will be investigated offline by any of the clerks on correction duty and the printed response will be marked with appropriate correction. This and the batch will then be filed for nine or ten days.

THE BATCH PROCESSING PHASE

In this interval, the goods which are the subject of the invoice should have reached the store. The store will mark up a copy of the original order with the quantities received for each item ordered or substituted. This document serves as a Goods Received Note (GRN) which is sent in turn to the central office. Another data entry procedure will capture the GRN which will then be associated with the original order by batch methods. This is perhaps four days after receipt of the invoice. Additional days are allowed to lapse to take care of unusual postal delays. On an appointed day in this system cycle, Thursday 21st March, the batch processing system processes an invoice in the batch that Mary entered. With the order identity as a key, the invoice is matched with the corresponding Goods Received Note. It is found to be different in that the invoice total entered does not match a total calculated by pricing the goods received. There could be several reasons for this, one of which being that Mary entered the invoice value incorrectly. Another might be that the supplier made a mistake in his calculations or changed his prices without informing our company. Whichever is the reason it will have to be investigated, identified and maybe corrected.

On Monday 25th March, the processing cycle has progressed to the point when it is time to complete the data entry process.

THE FINAL DAY

Third Entry

Janet Thomson is on correction duty. At some point during her day she reaches folder 058031 and asks whether there are any corrections pending for any of its batches or the invoices within them. Figure 1.6 shows the entry she makes. It is also of the form-filling type though the form is a simple one. The blank form was made available to her because she has registered with the computer for correction duty.

Third Response

The computer system examines each batch in this folder to detect the presence of errors yet to be corrected. Only batch 9 has problems. The

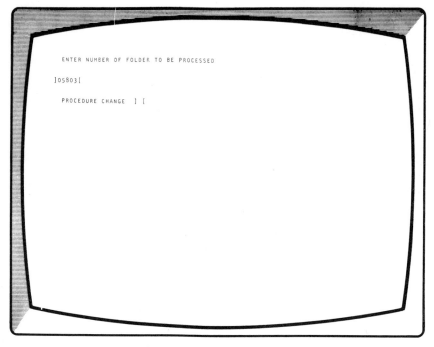

```
ENTER NUMBER OF FOLDER TO BE PROCESSED

]05803[

PROCEDURE CHANGE   ]  [
```

Figure 1.6. Correction request

```
FOLDER/BATCH NO   SUPPLIER NO    ORDER NUMBER      VAT AMNT   OUTERS
058031/09          1234E/6        0746 2002 006    ]3.50     [ ]4  [
                                  0319 2202 013    ]2.03     [ ]10 [
                                  0426 2102 005    ]1.50     [ ]3  [
                                  0511 2002 007    ]11.53    [ ]14 [
                                  1032 2302 009    ]0.48     [ ]1  [
                                  0459 2901 004    ]3.75     [ ]43 [
                                  0723 2402 003    ]5.14     [ ]16 [
                                  0488 2302 001    ]1.48     [ ]7  [
                                  1033 1003 002    ]6.00     [ ]49 [
                                  0124 1203 018    ]2.79     [ ]18 [
                                  0124 1003 027    ]1.68     [ ]144[
ENTER 1 IF INVOICE OMITTED         BATCH TOTALS ]39.88     [ ]308[
      2 IF BATCH ABANDONED   ]  [                          ♦♦♦
```

Figure 1.7. Response to correction request

response shown in Figure 1.7 alerts Janet that she has corrections to make. From the data on her screen she can see that batch 9 has the problem. She examines the forms in folder 058031 and finds that batch 9 has attached to it the printed report which we saw earlier. One of Janet's colleagues has checked through the documents in batch 9 and found the error. It was simply a listing error. The 'Outers' count for order 009 on 22nd February at store 1032 had been omitted from the batch total.

Fourth Entry

Janet can quickly correct that. Her cursor is already positioned on the first field which she might enter—the VAT amount on the first invoice. She uses her NEWLINE key to position herself at the batch totals line then TAB to skip to the correct field. She then overwrites 308 with 309 and depresses END to transmit the entry (see Figure 1.8). The opportunity to alter apparently correct

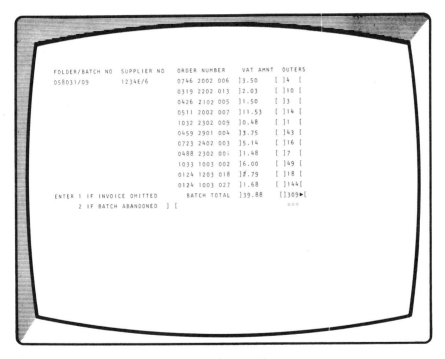

Figure 1.8. Corrected entry

data is provided in case compensating errors occur. Then the detail and total might match and both be wrong.

Fourth Response

A computer program quickly verifies that the batch now matches. Satisfied with that, it then examines each invoice to determine whether the invoice

```
FOLDER/BATCH NO  SUPPLIER NO  ORDER NUMBER
058031/09        ]1234E6[       ]0124[]1003[]027[

ITEM DESCRIPTION                    QTY  UNIT      PRICE    DISCNT     VALUE
TOTAL ENTERED                                                        ]124.20  [

B957 MULTI ADAPTOR WHITE EMP     ]4   [ DOZ] [ ]4.50    [ ]     [  18.00

580 APP CONN-WHITE-BRIT          ]16  [ DOZ] [ ]2.80    [ ]     [  44.80

229 PLUG-13A-BROWN-EMP           ]2   [ DOZ] [ ]1.20    [ ]     [  2.40

227 PLUG-13A-3/PIN-WHITE-BRIT    ]8   [ DOZ] [ ]3.60    [ ]     [  28.80

246 SOCKET-5A-2/PIN-WHITE-BRIT   ]8   [ DOZ] [ ]2.80    [ ]     [  22.40

251W PLUG WHITE BRITISH          ]1   [ DOZ] [ ]6.00    [ ]     [  6.00

NEW ITEM CODE ]     [            ]    [        ]        [ ]     [

NEW ITEM CODE ]     [            ]    [        ]        [ ]     [


NO MORE PAGES
```

Figure 1.9. Incorrect invoice

```
FOLDER/BATCH NO  SUPPLIER NO  ORDER NUMBER
058031/09        ]1234E6[       ]0124[]1003[]027[

ITEM DESCRIPTION                    QTY  UNIT      PRICE    DISCNT     VALUE
TOTAL ENTERED                                                        ]124.20  [

B957 MULTI ADAPTOR WHITE EMP     ]4   [ DOZ] [ ]4.50    [ ]     [  18.00

580 APP CONN-WHITE-BRIT          ]16  [ DOZ] [ ]2.80    [ ]     [  44.80

229 PLUG-13A-BROWN-EMP           ]2   [ DOZ] [ ]1.20    [ ]     [  2.40

227 PLUG-13A-3/PIN-WHITE-BRIT    ]8   [ DOZ] [ ]3.60    [ ]     [  28.80

246 SOCKET-5A-2/PIN-WHITE-BRIT   ]8   [ DOZ] [ ]2.80    [ ]     [  22.40

251W PLUG WHITE BRITISH          ]0   [ DOZ] [ ]6.00    [ ]     [  6.00

NEW ITEM CODE ]341W [            ]1   [        ]7.80    [ ]     [

NEW ITEM CODE ]     [            ]    [        ]        [ ]     [
```

Figure 1.10. Corrected invoice

matched the order or at least, the goods received. In fact one invoice does not match. Its total value £124·20 should have been £122·40 according to the goods received (see Figure 1.9). The details known about the order and receipt are displayed to Janet by combining data from the original order with amendments made from the GRN (see Figure 1.10).

Fifth Entry

Janet can now compare data on the invoice line by line with that on the GRN. She sees the difference, the WHITE BRITISH PLUG has not been invoiced. Instead a different plug at a higher price has been substituted. Whether or not they were received, and it looks as though the ordered items were received correctly, Janet must now make the correction. In doing this she is not altering the GRN, she is altering the stored invoice whose data she has otherwise not had to enter. Her action will eventually generate an investigation with the store manager in an attempt to reconcile GRN and invoice.

SUMMARY

That has been a representative illustration of a simple data capture real time system. We will return to it repeatedly as the techniques described in this book are discussed.

It is of course only one example out of many hundreds of systems each with its own individual features. What our example has in common with other real time systems will be more interesting than the differences at this time.

This system was one needing access to a large central computer only part of the time. The series of entries for the first day had need of logic to a limited extent only. The contribution made by the computer was simple enough. The computer's size would have been dictated by the volume of transactions and the convenience of having all terminals controlled by one processor. On the final day, more facilities were required, since data had to be retrieved from storage. Since the distribution of work was not known in advance the data had to be equally accessible to all terminals.

What of the logical features of this system which distinguish it from a batch system? The most obvious is the interaction between the operators and the computer. This will be discussed more fully in the next chapter. Less obvious is the activity within the computer to support that interaction. The individual interactions of entry and response are not separate and random, there is a larger unit which connects a sequence of interactions. This requires an ability to carry forward data from one entry to another and maintain its connection with the same operator. Another facet of the same situation is that the existence of the larger pattern makes it possible to interpret the meaning of later entries in the context of earlier ones. Mary, the first operator, made a particularly cryptic second entry which would have been received in the computer as:

$$\alpha\ 5\cdot14\ \Omega$$

where α represents the start of message symbol and Ω the end of message. The meaning of that message could only be deduced from the context established by the first message. Its meaning in turn was originally established when Mary chose her procedure at the beginning of her shift. The procedures and position reached must be maintained separately for every operator since the operators are not synchronized.

Another less obvious quality of the system is the interaction between the operators. Mary's work on the first day was accessible to Janet on the final day. Other real time systems, such as airline reservation systems and online stock control, make the results of one operator's work immediately available to all, through shared central files maintained online.

Finally the adoption of online techniques permits the employment of uniquely human attributes in those parts of the work with which we are better qualified to deal. The well designed system delegates work requiring speed and accuracy to the computer leaving judgement and aesthetics to people. Mary had to show judgement when diagnosing the error reported to her and Janet had to identify the change between the goods received and invoiced data.

The next chapter considers the unique features of real time systems more analytically and then the consequences of these differences for the designer and programmer.

Chapter 2
Real Time Characteristics

PURPOSE

Effects are Subject of Book

This chapter contains the reasoning for the existence of this book and the shape that it has taken. The argument is that the techniques which will be proposed are a response to certain inherent characteristics of real time data processing. This chapter first of all indentifies a number of properties of real time applications and traces their consequences in altered system development objectives. The methods proposed to handle these objectives will be explored in detail in the latter parts of the book.

Properties of Real Time Projects

The variety in real time systems will be described in the next chapter but there are a number of characteristics which they have in common and which set them apart from batch. Taken together the characteristics classify systems as real time. There are others which relate to the more complex systems but five are common to all. The first is the direct contact between the beneficiary and the system. Secondly, that contact results in immediate processing on the part of the system even if processing is incomplete. Thirdly, a real time system will have the potential to serve several users at apparently the same time and fourthly, the demand for service will be unpredictable. Finally, the systems employ the technology of teleprocessing.

These characteristics and the problems that they raise are inevitable companions of a real time project but the problems can be as successfully overcome as those of the earlier batch systems. The chapter will discuss each property in turn and identify its consequential problems and their effect on project development.

DIRECT CONTACT

Primary Purpose of Real Time

Many real time systems will realize tangible benefits through the property of direct contact with their users. The lengthy data preparation, submission, error detection, correction and resubmission cycles are cut out by enabling the originator of data to record it directly into the computer system. This approach saves elapsed time and avoids many system complexities needed to control error submission and resubmission. If the originators of data also enter it, they will understand its meaning better than data preparation staff and computer operators. Consequently they will make less mistakes in entering data and the system can refer to them for adjudication on feasibility violations. There is an opportunity for programs to suspend processing until doubtful data is clean rather than make unfounded assumptions simply to avoid a programmed halt. Error detection and subsequent processing becomes conversational, with computer contributions made in time to assist in the execution of a live task.

No Buffer between User and System

The reverse of this particular coin is that the usual obscurity afforded to the computer by a data preparation cycle is no longer present and the behaviour of the system is fully exposed. The appearance of the system therefore becomes of more serious concern to the development team and the system's users. Every entry and response must be carefully designed for use by persons not familiar with computer programming. The system will be more intricately related to the manual operations carried out. A successful system must be easy and natural to use or it will become a constant irritation. If the users have a related manual procedure—for instance for collecting orders—the chances are that it will be subject to its own changes in the course of the development of the real time system. Designers and users must therefore be in close communication throughout the development period and then a significant effort must be devoted to the training of users. This aspect cannot be stressed enough.

Security is Important in Design

The loss of the data preparation stages removes a number of opportunities for exercising control over the use of the system. A real time system must therefore include security features within the computer programs. There are three aspects to be incorporated: security of access to facilities, security of data files and the audit trail. The first involves the employment of techniques to ensure that unauthorized persons are not able to use the system, in total or in part. The second implies the protection of data which is personally or commercially private. The third is concerned with maintaining a record of what actions have been carried out. Provision of an audit trail is particularly important if the terminals used make no automatic record of activity in a permanent form.

Integrity, Fallback and Recovery

In a real time system, the computer contribution is intricately interwoven into the procedures of a using department. When the computer breaks down, the real world—which those procedures are recording—does not. This fact has far-reaching consequences for hardware and software design. A breakdown on a computer running batch work is accommodated and overcome by rerunning the job in hand and rescheduling the subsequent jobs into the slack period left for that purpose. Program design is affected only in arranging the structure of runs to minimize the problem or by adding a recovery routine if a program must restart partway through. A significant proportion of the design effort for a sensitive and extensive real time system might well be devoted to coping with failure. Adequate treatment of recovery and restart might be more important and difficult than the design of the direct application logic. The effects of failure show in three areas of design—integrity, fallback and recovery. Features designed to prevent failure from becoming apparent are classed as 'integrity'. If the system fails, fallback procedures carry on the work of the system in a more or less degraded fashion. Recovery is the process of bringing the computer system back to full production.

Of these, integrity will be considered by the users to be most important since failure can be extremely disruptive. Too many failures may destroy confidence in the system before they actually damage the operation. The methods adopted for integrity can be physical or logical but will add expense to the project. This expense may not be justified if the users can tolerate failures—as might be the case in an inquiry system. The tolerance can often be increased if the procedures used during fallback are carefully thought out. In one airline system for instance, terminals are controlled by small computers which are themselves programmed to continue to collect data when the main computer breaks down. The service offered is degraded in that little validation or processing can be done but failure is not total. A careful approach to fallback and integrity will aim to offer only the service which is justified and cost effective.

Recovery processes involve the restoration of computer conditions as near as possible to those obtaining before the breakdown. Any facets of the pre-breakdown situation which cannot be restored must be completely erased and the affected users informed. Thus any partly completed activities must not leave traces in the form of updated records if the activity cannot be continued. Another, secondary, aspect of recovery is the subsequent recording in the computer system of all activity which has taken place during the fallback period. Special facilities may have to be included in the system to accelerate this process.

Conversion must be Planned

The interdependence of computer system and user which makes failure so important will also affect conversion. Batch systems conversion can be difficult, with new procedures to be learnt and data to be transcribed, but there at least the computer is out of sight. Conversion of real time systems adds to those the extra problem of the physical installation of terminals into the working area. Each terminal will need an area the size of an average desk with cabling, control units and modems adding to the space required. As with failure, the real world cannot stop during conversion and the existing procedures must continue.

Conversion can be made less disruptive if it is staggered. There are a number of ways of doing this which can be used alone or in combination. The project can be introduced in stages, making additional facilities available at weekly or monthly intervals. The terminals to be installed might be of different types. Each type could be introduced singly. The project might serve a number of departments or geographical locations. They can be brought online at different times.

Topics are Considered Earlier

The enhanced importance of system integrity, fallback, recovery, conversion and security means that these topics must be considered earlier in the design process than is usual in designing batch systems. The design features included to cover them are a significant proportion of the total and are impossible to add on successfully to the application at a late stage of design. Successful solutions to these problems will frequently need additional terminal entries and responses, different file access techniques and different record layouts. Their late consideration will put the project at risk.

If for no other reason, early consideration is important since these topics are responsible for much of the project's costs. Their effect on cost must be known before the project can be realistically evaluated. In batch work, decisions on restart points and file positioning have been left to programmers. In real time these matters must be the concern of senior analysts early in the project.

Testing is More Rigorous

Finally, direct contact between user and system means that program errors will be evident to users even before they are known to computer operators. Integrity features, such as duplicated equipment can mitigate equipment failures but system failures must be minimized by testing. Testing has always had an important place in the development of batch systems but in real time systems, lip service must be replaced by genuine action to ensure that no errors remain which can be removed by careful testing. The effort devoted to testing is increased in two ways: the testing is more carefully done, and there is more of it. Additional care is expressed by prior planning and subsequent review. Additional content means extra stages. Batch programs are individually tested and then system tested. Programs in a big real time system are put through as many as nine different stages of testing each of which is planned, reviewed, executed and reviewed again. The success and convenience of so much testing depends on good test software without which the burden of this necessary work would be too much.

IMMEDIATE PROCESSING

Analogies

The difference between batch and real time systems in this respect can best be illustrated by an analogy. A similar difference exists between telephone calls and letters. Telephone calls are unpredictable and must be dealt with when they occur. Usually all the steps for dealing with the call must be taken in sequence, at once and for that call alone. The effect is that there is little scope for the economies of shared 'set up' time in batching but on the other hand the unproductive time spent by batches between operations is avoided. The net effect is that processing effort for a telephone call and a real time task is greater but duration is very much reduced—to seconds instead of hours.

Although in a commercial situation a telephone call may be dealt with by asking the caller to call again or await a return call, the call is more usually processed straight away. The same can be said of entries to a real time system. Processing is immediate and any updated records are available to any other user (with the appropriate authority). The justification of many real time systems is that the effect of a single user's activity is immediately available throughout the system and business opportunities are not lost irretrievably and unnecessarily through lack of information.

Relationship between Program and Transaction is Reversed

A batch program controls transactions. It calls them one after another and processes all of them before passing control over the transaction file to the next program. This control relationship is reversed in a real time system. There a transaction enters the system and calls each program module that it needs for processing, in turn. The effect can be imagined by considering a string of programs in a batch system acting upon a batch of one. Since there is only one member of the batch, the work areas and buffers which one program sets up will be exactly duplicated by the next and the intervening 'write' and 'read' of the transaction become redundant. The transaction can be said to control the programs and not vice-versa. See Figure 2.1.

Complex Interfaces

An interface between batch programs is composed in principle of simple filed records. The effect of one program's processing is stored within the records and that is the sole means of communication between two programs in respect of each individual transaction. The interface between two real time programs can be much more elaborate. This opportunity arises because no other transactions intervene before processing is continued by a following program. Work areas, register contents and part processed records can be handed on from one program to the other in core.

20

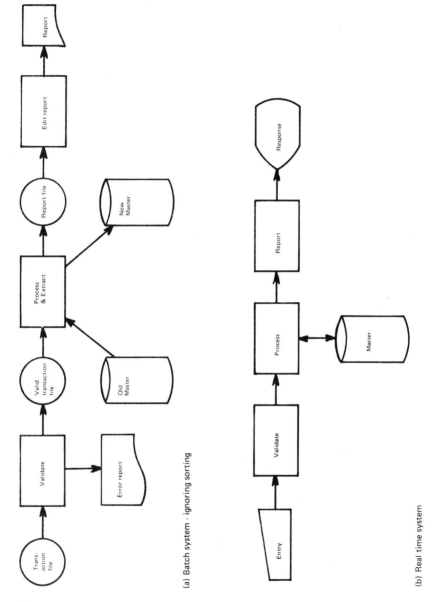

(a) Batch system - ignoring sorting

(b) Real time system

Figure 2.1. Changed relationship between program and transaction

The consequence of immediate processing is thus an increase in the complexity of interfaces between programs. The successful execution of strings of programs depends upon a shared understanding of these interfaces between the programmers concerned. The interfaces can be simplified by adopting formal methods of transfer of data and be made explicit by careful and complete definition. Common understanding must be finally confirmed by testing the links between programs—the link testing phase.

Database Techniques are Applicable

The multiplicity of programs in the strings appropriate to each entry type requires another change from batch practice. There will hardly ever be an occasion when a record design is private to one program. Data file structure, record and work area layout are therefore defined independently of programs in order to ensure that each program uses common definitions. Logical definitions are given physical form by building a compiler library file to enforce the inclusion of identical definitions in each program.

Another feature of data base practice is the employment of file structures designed to facilitate the retrieval of single records rather than a large number in sequence. The serial access methods familiar with tape and simple direct access systems are replaced by the index, randomizing formula or chain otherwise employed only in advanced batch applications. The objective of the file designer with respect to time is to reduce access time for a single record rather than to optimize arm movements of a disc head. This is not to say that the 'seek' component is not important but that less can be done to minimize movement between records. The dedication of a device to a single file will rarely be possible so there can be no certainty about the position of the read-write head on a moving head device. What can be done is to take advantage of any hierarchy of permitted access time to match device speed. Files can be spread across several devices to provide more read heads and channels and reduce queueing for records of the same file. The opportunities for tuning the file system are quite extensive and make advisable the separation of physical storage space management from program logic. If application programs simply use GET and PUT commands for logical units of data then the arrangement of physical data can be adjusted without interfering with application logic. The scope of the real time system can be allowed to grow by extending the uses of current data or adding new files without recording existing programs.

Unpredictable Combinations of Events will Occur

The immediacy of processing means that the activities occurring in the computer system when processing is requested cannot be arranged in advance. The availability of free storage space and the contents of occupied space will be different on every occasion that a particular activity is run. Different activities and different occurrences of each will have need for different proportions of coding and work space. Optimum performance will be achieved if the location of storage space is as unrestricted as possible and space is released as soon as possible. These considerations argue for the dynamic allocation of immediate access storage, the relocatability of programs and the adoption of segmentation for programs. The transfer of control between programs must therefore be effected by software.

If a high level language and an advanced operating system is used, the ability of the program to work in unpredictable surroundings can be almost automatically achieved. Otherwise, testing must prove a program's ability to operate in this unpredictable environment. This feature is best tested by arranging for each activity to be initiated in many different combinations during the testing of sequences of activities.

Testing Needs Software

The handover of data between programs in core, program modularity and the employment of database techniques, which are the consequences of the property of immediate processing, make program testing more demanding of software. The interdependence of programs means that any one program will assume the presence of many supporting programs. If those supports are also being developed then they cannot be assumed during testing of a specific program. Instead, test programs and software are employed to simulate the missing parts of the environment. This software is inserted between the application program and the run time software so that calls for data access or transfers of control between programs can be trapped and serviced according to instructions in the test job stream. The test software also simulates the terminals to give hard copy of test results and to allow tests to be repeatable.

CONCURRENT EXECUTION

Differs from Multi-programming

Real time transactions which refer to files or backing storage must suffer delays during data transfers. Serial batch systems can overlap input-output operations of earlier or subsequent data records with the processing of the current one. In a real time system a transaction must wait for data retrieval. The need for any other than the current record cannot be satisfied in advance. It is therefore useful to cause several activities to proceed in parallel to improve performance and make best use of the CPU. This can be done by sharing with background batch jobs in a multi-programming environment, but if the real time system has any volume, several real time activities can be made to overlap.

This technique is known as multi-threading and differs from multi-programming in that not only are the CPU and channels shared, but the data files, programs and peripherals are shared as well. As discussed in the previous section, there is an argument for making core utilization as flexible as possible, so the prior separation of core into partitions is not usual in multi-threading.

Tasks Contend for Data and Programs

Programs and data will be very intimately shared between concurrent tasks. They may very well be referring to the same record and may require the same programs to service them. A system can achieve program sharing by using more than one physical copy of the program in core but the more usual technique is to make the programs re-entrant. A re-entrant program is one which can be used by more than one activity almost concurrently. Thus if task A activates the program but has to wait for data before completing, task B can take control and overtake task A in its use of a later sequence of code without any harmful effect. To achieve this property, such a program must not be modified in any way during execution.

If two tasks wish to refer to the same data, there will only be a problem if updating is contemplated. If both tasks read the record and both update it and write back the updated copy, the effect of the first update will be obliterated by the second. That eventuality must therefore be prevented. The sequence of updates is not material, only the fact that the effect of each is recorded.

Tasks must be Separated

Taking this section with those preceding it, a picture of potential confusion of dynamic core, relocatable and re-entrant programs must be clarified. The key to the confusion is the primacy of the transaction over the program. The unique entity is the transaction. If an area of storage is set aside for each current transaction to hold control data in a standard format, the confusion disappears. The transaction currently in control is identified by pointing at its control area. Typical of its contents are the addresses of work areas in core, the identity of the current program being used by the task, the relative position reached in that program, values of index registers when the task was last interrupted and areas for transferring parameters needed by service routines. Its function is analogous to that of a job card which accompanies a piece of work around an engineering factory.

Program re-entrance is achieved by keeping all switches, modifiable addresses and intermediate processing results out of the program and in the private work area where they are addressable via its base address.

Tasks must be Supervised

The success of concurrent execution relies upon the imposition of a discipline over the use of any shared resources. The discipline is imposed by requiring that requests for core, programs or data transfer must be executed indirectly by software. Thus an overall supervisor program regains control at frequent intervals and is able to schedule the execution of tasks in a disciplined manner. Requests for each shared resource must be queued. Task requiring core or data channels are forced to join a queue and once their requests are serviced they must join another queue to regain control of the CPU to execute more code.

Apart from the points at which the task in control deliberately suspends itself for its own purposes, it can be interrupted at any time by the usual hardware interrupts which accompany the overlap of I/O with processing. Also the hardware can include a timing device which generates 'spurious' interrupts after a pre-set elapsed time. Every interrupt is an opportunity for the control program to check all its queues and decide which task may next have control. If it cannot find anything to do, it can relinquish control in a shared system to the multi-programming executive to permit a batch job to have a turn.

Program Modularity is Desirable

The applications and software programs operating in this environment will give less trouble if their functions are clearly defined and independent of each other. The interfaces between software functions must be kept as simple as possible. Their use should not depend upon knowledge of their methods.

Adopting the disciplines of modular programming for application programs will also pay. Many application programs will be used in a variety of combinations to perform different tasks. If their initial set up conditions are simple and they perform single functions, then the opportunities for misusing them are reduced and the testing needed to link several together will be relatively easy. Each module can be thought of as a 'black box' as can strings of modules assembled to synthesize a larger function.

Concurrency must be Tested

One of the recommended stages of testing would have the proving of multi-threading as its objective. This is best simulated through software rather than attempting to achieve it with terminals. A multi-threading test simulator can be made to exercise the programs of a complete system. Entries can be made up on cards and read directly or after transcription to magnetic tape. The simulator software then reads them in as if they had come from the communications software and presents them to the real time program. Thereafter, until the responses are ready for sending, the system will behave exactly as it would under live conditions. The development of such a simulator takes significant effort. Collaboration between several users of a particular type of equipment is recommended either via a proprietary software package or shared development of a purpose built routine.

LESS PREDICTABLE DEMAND

Predictability is Limited

Though most commercial organizations can predict demand for their services and hence their data processing by season or even by time of day, they cannot predict from minute to minute. This is not important in batch systems since the act of batching and scheduling makes processing entirely predictable.

Real time processing must be supplied on demand and its unpredictability means that the system must be ready to respond at any time during the 'real time day'. From minute to minute the arrival rate is random.

The immediate processing characteristic means that reasonable variations in demand must be accommodated by the system. There is no scope for matching machine capacity to average demand since machine time in a real time system is not a storable resource. Like airline seats or hotel rooms, if it is not used it cannot be stored for later overloads. Classic queueing theory demonstrates that if service is provided to match average demand, queues will form and grow (see for example, Sasieni and Ackoff, *Fundamentals of Operations Research*, John Wiley & Sons, 1968). On the other hand to provide capacity to serve maximum demand will ensure that service resources are lying idle for uneconomic periods. In order to perform the analysis necessary for the best balance, the system designer must know the response times required and the processing needed by each entry.

Task Identities are Unknown

Also random within similar limits is the nature of processing required. Each entry type will have its own frequency distribution, but again, from minute to minute, the system must be ready to respond to any permitted entry type.

The first task of the system must therefore be to discover the identity of the entry and hence the program first required for processing. The identity of the originating terminal will be known since the executive system will have had it to trigger transmission. In a simple system this may be enough to identify the entry, but normally an examination of the content of the message will be required. Since this will have to be applied to every entry, a general purpose facility is justified.

The System Contains many Queues

Our earlier discussion of the consequences of concurrent processing identified many different queues within the system. The queues are adopted to control access to resources—core, channels and processing time. The analysis of necessary resource levels must therefore treat each of those resources separately. From a knowledge of the distribution of entries and the demands that each type makes, it is possible to construct demand distributions for the different services. Then a service level can be set for each and the necessary amount determined by queueing theory. Instead of just one queue, a real time system is a series of linked queues. The different resources must be balanced for acceptable levels of performance.

Even then peak loads cannot always be serviced and a check must be kept on resource use to prevent its exhaustion and a consequent system failure. If danger levels are reached, the system must briefly refuse to accept further demands. In other words, a queue is formed outside the system.

Demand is Investigated Early

It is a fact of queueing situations that service is purchased by adding resources, so to set performance criteria too high costs money. The system design period should therefore establish maximum permissible response times rather than desirable values. Further, entry types will differ in their need for fast response, so a blanket '5 second response' will mean unjustified cost if 50 seconds can be allowed for some responses.

The demand for services will be derived from increasingly detailed appreciation of the system. First, the frequency of different jobs done by the users—and therefore the transactions they will use—will be established by observation and review in the manner familiar from batch systems analysis. The different entries which service one transaction will occur with different frequencies. Each entry type will make different demands on the available resource types. An investigation sufficiently detailed to reveal the data needed for a full analysis requires a considerable knowledge of system logic. To be useful it must be done before equipment selection. Such a level of detail is rarely achieved as early in batch design.

NOVEL TECHNOLOGY

Terminals and Communications

The equipment which typifies real time applications for most people is the display terminal—the heir of the radar screen and oscilloscope. This has been in use for commercial data processing since the early 1960s. Contrast this with the typical batch peripheral—the punched card reader—which dates back to the last years of the nineteenth century.

The other component of many real time configurations, new to commercial users, is the communications equipment. Everyone is familiar with the telephone, but its application to the transmission of data is less widely understood. There seem to be more parts to understand and more choices to make—modems, terminal control units, communications control units, multi-drop lines, duplex or half duplex. There are also more suppliers involved in the installation—at least the telephone company is added and maybe a terminal manufacturer as well.

In fact the unfamiliarity is not too important provided it does not engender fright and loss of judgement. It can be corrected by training, available from the telephone company or equipment manufacturers. This training has to be planned and costed, but is available. More important is the new range of choices to be made and the increase in possible combinations.

Terminals vary from a simple teleprinter working at 10 characters per second, through to a small computer acting as the terminal for a much larger machine. There are printers, displays, voice units, badge readers and light pens. They can stand alone or operate in clusters, by themselves programmable, or controlled by a programmable unit. Telecommunications lines can be simplex, half duplex or full duplex, working at speeds from 100 bits per second to 50,000, private or using the switched public network. The only sure way through this maze is the development of a clear statement of the requirements of the applications before attempting to select any equipment. The designer will need an appreciation of the options available so that the requirements are not expressed in terms which prejudge the solution. Armed with a statement of the needs of the different applications and locations to be served, the analyst can invite suppliers to offer their products for evaluation.

Technology is Developing

The single most important fact about a novel technology is that it is prone to rapid development. The equipment purchased today can seem out of date before it is installed. Development occurs in both the performance of the equipment and in its cost. New companies enter the market, as engineers see new ways of dealing with problems or cheaper methods of production. This fluid situation means that the systems employing today's equipment must be capable of adapting readily to tomorrow's—or even to yesterday's if today's supplier goes out of business.

Protection by Logical Terminals

The strategy for protecting application programs from the effects of terminal development is to make them independent of any particular physical terminal. Application programs should receive from and send to 'logical terminals'. This is to say that no part of the message processed or constructed should depend upon the physical characteristics of a particular physical terminal type. The test of this quality of a system is whether terminals can be changed from one type to another without reprogramming any part of the application. Another benefit of 'logical terminals' is that in the event of a single terminal failure or the loss of a line, back-up arrangements can include the switching of messages to other terminals in the network. Then the alternatives need not even be of the same type since it will frequently be convenient to print a display message or vice-versa. The definition of a logical terminal is made by the system designer and will specify a list of features which can be assumed to be operative, and the means of invoking them. The software must convert the standard representation of each feature, such as cursor movement, into the form accepted by the actual terminal being addressed. If the actual terminal has no equivalent hardware feature then its simulation is a further task for the software.

Equipment Selection Considerations

With the dispersion of peripheral devices to locations remote from the computer room, the concept of standby equipment changes. Standby to a batch installation was (in theory) another installation of similar configuration to which operators took tapes, cards or disc packs and carried out runs as if at home. The task of switching a widespread telecommunications network to another computer is even less practical. For systems which must have uninterrupted service, the standby must be a second machine on site or a multiprocessor configuration. The applications which justify this approach are very few. Equipment which is reliable enough for effective real time systems rarely breaks down and even then is rapidly repaired by the substitution of new parts. More sensitive is the non-computer equipment such as air conditioning or power supply whose failure can lead to a computer shut down. Duplicate equipment for those components may well be worth investigation.

The rapid advances in terminal technology, which can be expected to continue for some time yet, have one other implication for the data processing manager. The contractual arrangements for equipment should usually include rental rather than purchase of terminals since changes in equipment can be effected as technology changes.

SUMMARY

Consequences in Systems Design

The five major differences considered in the chapter have been shown to have many consequences in the conduct of a real time installation or project. The consequences show up in many ways—in design techniques, in sequence and content of familiar work steps, in software for operations and for development and in documentation. Figure 2.2 lists the topics just discussed and their treatment. Each strategy named there is a statement of good intention. It is the aim of this book to offer practical methods by which those intentions can be embodied in good practice.

DIFFERENCE AND CONSEQUENCE	STRATEGY
Direct Contact	
—interface between user and system is more important	Early and continuous user involvement in design
—inclusion of security features	Early consideration of security
—intolerance of breakdown	Early consideration of integrity, fallback and recovery Thorough testing
—potential disruption during conversion	Early planning Conversion in stages
—greater proportion of design effort needed for these topics	As much consideration in design as application logic

Immediate Processing
—transactions call programs

Careful interface definition and maintenance
Formal data transfer mechanisms
Additional testing stages

—increased sharing of files between programs

Separate data definition

—retrieval of single records

Additional data access methods
Separation of logical and physical data

—unpredictable combinations of events

Dynamic core allocation
Relocatable programs
Software control transfers
Additional testing
Test software

Concurrent Execution
—multi-threading

Compilers which generate re-entrant code
Private work space for each transaction
Additional testing

—overlapping data updates

Data management software

—competition for resources

Resource queues and control software
Interruption of tasks
Application program modularity

Less Predictable Demand
—random arrival rates

Careful investigation of demand

—random activity identities

Message recognition software

—complex queueing system

Statistical and simulation techniques
Early design of system logic
Individual response times

Novel Technology
—equipment more complex

Designer training

—extended choices

Prior definition of requirements

—equipment obsolescence

Logical terminal concept
Separate communications software

—fixed location of the connection between the teleprocessing network and the central computer

Careful study of the justification for standby equipment
Careful planning of fallback procedures

Figure 2.2. Consequences of differences between real time and batch systems

The list divides roughly evenly between strategies which can be effected by software and those which are the concern of project management. It is with the latter that this book is mainly concerned.

Chapter 3
Variety in Real Time Systems

PURPOSE

Variety must be Acknowledged

'Response time' is a term learnt early in considering real time systems. Some applications included under the term 'real time' will have response times measured in milliseconds. Many of the military systems concerned with guidance exhibit that characteristic. Other commercial applications have response times between one and five seconds, a pace suitable for conversational interaction between machine and user. Information retrieval systems can take minutes to respond with abstracts or summaries and still be useful. Response time is only one characteristic in which systems can vary and still be real time.

Variety in Many Characteristics

There are in fact so many characteristics by which systems can vary that characteristic classes can be identified. There are the physically apparent configuration features, such as number and type of terminal, location with respect to the computer, degree of terminal clustering, etc. There are logical features apparent on examination of the controlling software such as extent of dedication of the processor to real time, variety of the incoming message types handled, and ability to handle concurrent messages. There are user characteristics such as the effect of breakdown on the user's ability to continue his business functions.

Classification

All of these characteristics and many others provide means of classifying real time systems by function. Classification is useful since the accurate location of a particular application in a class will enable predictions to be made about its demands on hardware, software and methods. In this book, classification is useful since the methods proposed are intended to be 'classless' so that if they can be shown to apply to all members of a reasonable classification system their 'classless' quality is demonstrated.

The functional types which will be identified are five:

> Enquiry
> Message Switching
> Data Capture
> File Update, including permanent and
>   temporary (memo) updating
> Process Control

The remainder of this chapter is devoted to describing each type briefly so that later in the book, reference can be made to a system type without further explanation.

ENQUIRY SYSTEM

General Description

The key feature of a pure enquiry system is that the state of the system at the end of the day is the same as at the beginning. No files are changed, no transactions captured. All that happens is that a terminal is used to look at data. Figure 3.1 illustrates such a system. Two master files containing fixed data held on a direct access medium are online to a computer. Two classes of user wish to locate records and review key fields. The first user is a salesman wishing to

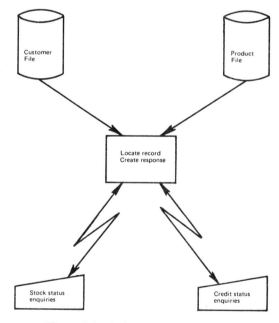

Figure 3.1. A simple enquiry system

check whether a product is in stock and if not what other product is a suitable substitute. The second user is a credit clerk wishing to check whether a new order for a customer will cause his indebtedness to exceed his credit limit.

The functions of the application programs are to distinguish the two types of query, to locate the relevant record, possibly after changing an uncoded identification into a file address, then to format a suitable response to the query.

An enquiry system can service a large number of users spread around the world. It can encompass a much larger variety of message types, it could perform calculations to derive new fields from those on file or included in the message. It could access more files.

For a system to qualify as 'enquiry', the essential features of not changing existing data or capturing new data must be observed. The data accessed is therefore maintained by regular batch computing and the system is not especially vulnerable to breakdown, except in the loss of its files. For this purpose, the output of the batch system will usually be duplicated, either physically or logically, by means of a serial version of the direct access reference files. If a direct access file fails it can be recreated.

Justification

The justification lies in the value of information, the speed of response and the timeliness of communicating the results of the most recent update to the inquiring users. An evaluation should consider:

(a) what decisions have to be taken?
(b) how is decision making performance measured?
(c) how does good performance show in company results?
(d) how could performance be improved by better information?
(e) how much is improvement worth?
(f) is it greater in value than the investment?

The characteristics of situations likely to produce a positive answer to the evaluation process are:

(a) a multiplicity of locations where similar inquiries can be made
(b) difficulties in keeping printed files current such as might arise from fast moving stock or a large product or customer list, although printed files might still be produced at intervals for fallback
(c) a keenly competitive market where good customer service can be repaid by increased orders
(d) volatile customers—or some other euphemism for clients who have a habit of defaulting
(e) an undercapitalized business where the penalty for receivables is high in terms of interest on borrowings to finance them
(f) possible staff savings if file look-up is a laborious process.

These ideas are only offered as clues to help recognize situations worth evaluating. The list is not exhaustive and is certainly not a substitute for evaluation. The manner of evaluating computer projects is a major subject in itself and is not considered in this book.

Key Design Decisions

Enquiry systems represent a major portion of the real time applications currently in existence so any design methodology must be able to accommodate them. The key decisions which have to be taken during design are as follows.

(a) RESPONSE TIME

Response time in an enquiry system represents the length of time that elapses from when the terminal operator transmits an enquiry to when the response is received at the terminal. An acceptable response time may be only a few seconds. Since response times are usually improved by increased CPU power, the length of the response times will be an important factor in all aspects of the design phase.

(b) FILE DESIGN

If rapid response times are required and a large number of terminals are included in the system, the file design becomes increasingly important. It may be necessary to develop a tailored access method if the software supplier's method of retrieving the requested data adversely affects the response times.

Another important consideration in file design is the amount of time allowed to restore any lost data in the file. A tailored file structure, rather than the traditional structures offered by the computer manufacturer, may be necessary to satisfy this requirement.

(c) ENTRY TYPES

The number of entry types, and the degree of complexity associated with each type, has a significant impact on the design and installation work. A system with a limited number of simple enquiries against one master file requires far less effort than a system with a wide range of enquiries, each possibly involving several responses from multiple files to satisfy the enquiry.

MESSAGE SWITCHING

General Description

The application pattern is that one user makes an entry at his terminal and attaches an address to it. The entry may be in plain language or coded in some way understood by the recipient. The message is not interpreted by any computer program so its form is chosen only for considerations of convenience and transmission load. At the receiving terminal, the message will be received as sent, with some indication of its origin. The configuration is illustrated conceptually in Figure 3.2.

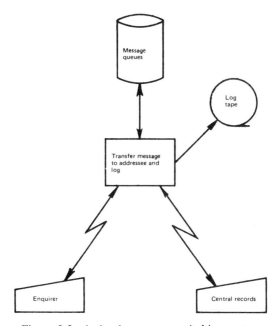

Figure 3.2. A simple message switching system

The central task of the computer program appears to be relatively simple. The address included as part of the message 'envelope' (that part of the received string which is not the 'text' of the message) must be translated into a hardware address of the device to receive the message. The text is then passed on in a new 'envelope' which includes the origin in a form recognized by the user.

Complications set in if the traffic load is heavy since the receiving terminal or line may be busy. A program will be needed to control message queues and to keep lines as busy as possible so that performance is good. The sequence of forwarding messages will therefore be determined by two conditions, sequence of receipt and the availability of a communication path to the receiving terminal. Traffic may be heavy enough to justify storing queued messages on a direct access device.

As a terminal comes free, the queue handler will ask whether there is a message waiting. If so, all the messages so far accumulated for the terminal will be sent in sequence. To achieve this effect there may well be a sophisticated program for controlling available storage space, issuing space as required and receiving it back again when the message is called into core for transmission.

Other program functions may be concerned with resending messages on request from the receiving terminal and controlling the transmission of messages too long for storage in single buffers. The problems of recovery and restart after machine failure need attention to ensure that messages are not lost. This service might well be performed by a log tape which permits lost messages to be reconstituted.

The demand for core and CPU time is relatively low. This feature can be recognized in two ways, either the application is serviced by a small foreground partition in a largely batch machine or the application is relegated to a 'mini' computer of modest core and speed. Some manufacturers produce machines especially for such applications, capable of high throughput but little processing. Some specialize in such configurations and will provide software packages which enable the data processing department to ignore real time altogether. If the installation does not intend to venture further into real time then such an approach would be appropriate.

Another feature worth considering is to provide some intelligent program for taking decisions on addressing. The simplest is whether to repeat messages to more than one destination. This might be useful in a stock enquiry situation where products are held at more than one location. The program can be made to use a product code to look up a simple file for the relevant addresses, or it can simply repeat the message to all locations.

Apart from this extension though, the application exhibits the following characteristics:

(a) simple programming and little of it
(b) no programs to interpret message content
(c) any number of terminals—but likely to be high rather than low.

Justification

The characteristics of situations which might justify this configuration are:

(a) an international spread of locations
(b) many locations for possible answers to enquiries
(c) a high return from being able to get answers quickly—such as high value or perishable products
(d) a short file combined with these other characteristics rendering a full inquiry system unnecessary
(e) a need for a hard copy record of inquiries.

Even so, there is little difference between this and the public switched telegraph system. Any decision to invest in a private version should be readily made on simple cost comparisons. The only other advantages of a private system will be speed in achieving answers—minutes rather than hours and the chance for simple data capture.

Key Design Decisions

The major design considerations for a message switching system are as follows.

(a) TURNROUND TIME

The turnround time is measured from the transmission of the message from the sending location to the completion of the message transmission at the receiving location. The length of this time interval is dependent upon several factors: terminal speed, type of communication line, size of message, availability of the receiving line and terminal, number of terminals, etc. The length of the turnround time that is established as acceptable for a system will largely dictate the degree of sophistication and complexity of the design phase. It is rarely necessary for the turnround time to be less than five minutes since the receiving operator is not waiting for an expected response and usually has other duties.

(b) FILE DESIGN

There could be one very important design task if there are a significant number of terminals in the system and the messages are long. Normally, the messages will be of sufficient size to require the temporary storage of the message on a direct access device. If the message must be segmented to be stored temporarily, the file structure must provide for chaining the segments together. This requirement may significantly affect the amount of file time, which in turn directly affects the throughput of the system. Therefore, extreme care must be taken to make sure that the file approach adopted is capable of handling the projected volumes of data within the time limit established.

(c) RECOVERY

The effort required to design recovery facilities for message switching is usually much more extensive than for an enquiry system. Since several messages may be in various stages of processing at any point in time, it may be necessary to develop elaborate controls reflecting the status of all messages at each step of the operation. The design effort to minimize the loss of data in the event of a failure in many cases exceeds the effort to design the regular processing of the messages.

DATA CAPTURE

General Description

Figure 3.3 shows a data capture system applied to the common business function of order processing. Instead of writing order forms or punching cards, the order clerks enter data through a terminal. The use of the terminal and the computer permits both validation of the orders and a reduction of keystrokes by means of access to files.

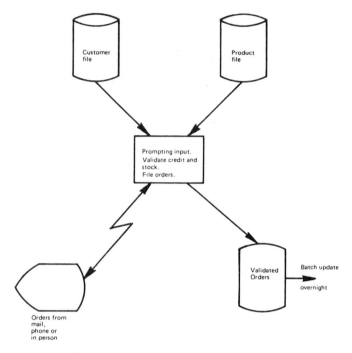

Figure 3.3. A simple data entry system

The system may use different modes of data entry—the user will either enter data in a form specified by the computer on the screen or he may make free form entries. The essential difference is whether the entry is prompted, by forms or instructions, or is unprompted. If prompted, the meaning of incoming data is already apparent to the computer program. Unprompted messages on the other hand must be recognized and interpreted by program.

Once the incoming message is recognized and interpreted, the processing will generally continue with validation. Validation will comprise both format validation and feasibility checks, against standing files as well as for value ranges and other features. In accessing standing files, the system obviously shares features with enquiry systems. If validation checks are failed, the program may invite user participation on an exception basis by referring doubtful cases for adjudication by the order entry clerk. He in turn may be able to refer to the customer for clarification. The direct contact between an experienced clerk and the firm's files permits human judgement to be allied with the speed and accuracy of the computer to form a combination more powerful than either alone.

The valid transaction is added to a transaction file after acceptance. This may be a simple serial file to interface with an earlier batch processing system or it may be filed in a complex network structure on a direct access device. In the latter case associations between orders from the same customer or for the same product or by the same salesman, may be formed online to permit more efficient processing in the subsequent batch system.

If the application has been made extensive enough to concern all data sources in an order processing application, then the variety of message types will be large. Large enough in fact, to support attempts at generalizing the message analysis process.

At least during 'the real time day' the traffic volume could be enough to justify the dedication of the CPU to the real time activity. The effect of multi-programming is then created by multi-threading—the concurrent processing of more than one real time activity accessing the same data files. In a multi-threading environment, core utilization can be improved by adopting programming techniques which produce 're-entrant' code.

The increased number of terminals associated with this and the previous class makes the permanent allocation of an area of core to each terminal an uneconomic proposition. Instead, the core not occupied by control programs and resident project coding, system wide constants and some small tables, is treated as an allocatable pool. A program to manage core is introduced which services requests for fixed or variable length segments and makes core released by a completed task available for use. This function can be simple or complex depending on how widely core segment sizes are allowed to vary.

The function of message queue control was described briefly in the message switching application. There the queue effectively decoupled incoming messages from their destination terminals since message processing terminated with an 'output to queue' rather than a 'transmit to terminal'. At some arbitrary later time determined by transmission line availability the queue was emptied. In the data entry system, traffic rates and consequent competition for resources are likely to lead to the decoupling of the three activities of message reception, processing and dispatch using two queues instead of one. The purpose is to permit the choice of priority between these three activities. The scheduling of any one of them is the task of a message control program. As in message switching, good performance is assisted by first keeping transmission lines as busy as possible. The line control software takes a message into a buffer and activates the message control program. It attaches the message to its 'waiting to process' queue, then checks the 'waiting to send' queue for responses whose processing is complete and for which a line is available. Having despatched as many responses as possible, it will then return to its 'ready to process' queue and take a message from there to pass to the message recognition program.

In summary, then, the project programs will not be substantially different from enquiry application programs. The supporting services though, are more likely to resemble and extend those of message switching. They are likely to be available in a package. The functions are:

(a) message queue control
(b) core management
(c) program management
(d) message recognition.

Justification

This technique is being increasingly employed and there are very real benefits to be gained, provided the scope of the application is carefully reviewed and restricted to features which show a return.

Since a data entry system has all the features of an enquiry system, the characteristics which justify it will apply to this case also:

(a) multiple access to centralized files
(b) fast moving files difficult to communicate to many locations
(c) good customer service
(d) reduced inventory
(e) reduced receivables by prompt billing and recording of receipts.

Tangible savings in staff time can be made if the data needed to record an order is complex or is presented in a variety of forms. Either situation can lead to a transcription operation to permit the data preparation staff to deal with clean source data. Either situation is a breeding ground for errors which lead to error reports, batch balancing problems, contra-entries, suspense files and long correction cycles which cause a disproportionate expense. Online data capture permits the correction of errors while the origin of the data is readily at hand.

Not only are errors corrected but their incidence and the cost of their correction is reduced. The entire data preparation department with its control clerks, record keeping space, equipment, floor area and personnel overheads can frequently be saved. The cost of data capture equipment and programs must be set against this but the equation will increasingly favour the online system.

A further small advantage is available from the ability to involve the clerk directly in validation. The validation of data by range or feasibility checks can be improved by setting tighter limits to acceptable values. A violation is not however rejected, but referred to the clerk for confirmation. Limits can be made a function of customer or product history since spurious errors will be overridden.

The online system provides data preparation staff with the opportunity for increased job satisfaction if their management accepts the opportunity to train them for the more responsible work of data origination. Where data preparation demands dexterity and speed, data entry can give an opportunity to exercise discretion and judgement in interpreting quite high level company policy.

In the example of order processing, the foreshortening of the procedure between order taking and validation may provide benefit to the company through improved performance as well as reduced cost. More sensitive credit and stock policies can be implemented. Orders which would previously have been refused through incomplete knowledge of stock or credit positions, can be filled. Orders can be filled with substitute products.

Key Design Decisions

Compared to the two applications discussed so far, this one is more likely to be serviced by display terminals. The higher degree of interaction will demand a faster effective response time than a printer can give. If a form-filling approach is used for entering data, a CRT terminal becomes virtually indispensible.

The real time activity of the system will definitely be broken up since at intervals the master files available for enquiry and validation need to be refreshed. The online files are copies of the results of the most recent batch processing run, so following each updating cycle, the online files will be overwritten with new versions. By this means the data concerning recent transactions is made available.

Particularly relevant in this context is the matter of adding and deleting file records. Since by definition no file updating occurs, there can be no record of customers or products added to their files since the last update. Customers and products will only be added when activity on their records is expected. Hence short batch cycles are preferred if record turnover is significant. Conversely, customer and products may be deleted precisely so as to prevent activity on their records. Either way, the requirement for short cycles arises.

Because the online files are regularly refreshed, the storage equipment can be fixed rather than exchangeable. There is no need for elaborate file control to ensure the security of the dismounted packs and an opportunity remains to use the magnetic drums or fixed discs still offered by some manufacturers. These offer high performance and no investment in the removable packs. High performance is particularly important when the system is highly interactive.

Data capture with offline batch updating offers an opportunity for a simple solution to the fallback problem. The online system can generate a log file which resembles card images and the batch system can be programmed to accept transactions from the log of the data capture system and from cards. Then fallback consists simply of switching over to cards or rather to punching sheets when the online system fails. The cards produced during downtime are then transcribed to tape with a standard utility program. The batch system must be capable of accepting multi-reel files or the direct access device equivalent, but such a feature should be included in the operating system. Of course, the transactions represented by the cards are not subject to the validation checks of the online system and the batch system must provide for all the usual error detection, reporting and recycling. However, their frequency will be slight and easily handled. The convenience of this approach must not obscure the fact that loss of service is inconvenient and costly.

The amount of effort to design a recovery system so that lost service can be easily restored, can represent a major portion of design. For this reason the problem must be considered early. Recovery facilities needed include the ability to protect the collected data and restart the system as close as possible to the same status that existed at the time of failure. In this way lost effort is kept to a minimum. The solutions involve file duplication and transaction logs among others. For our purpose, the key lesson is the early recognition of the need for restart provisions and their integration with the main stream of design.

Data capture systems need more elaborate security arrangements than enquiry systems in order to prevent fraudulent transactions from being introduced into the files. The security and control normally built into a batch system will still be necessary in the batch component of the combined system and should stop any fraud from an online entry as well as it does for cards. By providing for human intervention, though, the type of fraud arising from giving preferential treatment should be detectable if a log of overrides of feasibility checks is made. Also, a delinquent client can place a series of orders whose total value exceeds his credit limitations since the credit remaining is not changed in the online system as each order is received. Whether or not this is important will depend upon the system for authorizing the physical despatch of goods. If this is subject to the results of the batch processing system then there should be no problem, but if not, then some protection must be designed, such as a limit to the value of orders per client per day.

The time required to access data will be important when the process is interactive. For this reason the system may need special file access techniques such as randomizing, to give better performance than indexed access.

FILE UPDATE

General Description

Airline reservation systems are those most likely to come to mind as examples of file updating systems. The actions which cause the use of the system are reflected immediately in real company files—unsold seats are reduced, passenger records are created, passenger names are added to the list of intending passengers for a flight. A system used by intercontinental airlines will be available for 24 hours a day so no 'overnight' batch processing can take place. In the more advanced systems the computer program will participate to the extent of preparing business documents (airline tickets) in the course of the transaction.

This mode of processing is illustrated in Figure 3.4. The application of order processing is used again to show how the system has changed from that of data capture, although the use of such an elaborate system for this work is unlikely. Now the master files online are subject to updating and the flow of transactions is captured direct onto the open item business files of Accounts Receivable and Open Orders. Further, the transactions result in the output of business documents in the shape of delivery notes, packing slips, invoices and receipts directly at the appropriate location. The functions of stock checking and credit checking of the original enquiry system are included as part of the order validation process. Message switching of orders from the order taker to the despatcher in the storeroom is included and data is certainly captured in order for it to be acted upon.

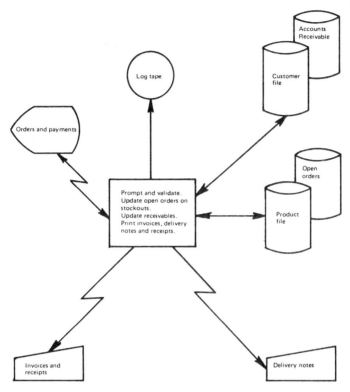

Figure 3.4. A simple file updating system

The features of queueing, core management, program management, multi-threading and generalized message analysis, found in the large data capture system all exist here. The new features are security and file processing.

Security encompasses physical and logical security. Physical security can be regarded as including protection of the system against both corruption and breakdown while logical security is more concerned with the problem of preventing unauthorized access to functions or data. These features may be important in the simpler systems already covered but they are vital here.

The factors which justify a full scale real time updating system are the very ones which dictate that long periods without processing ability can be extremely serious. Consequently such designs emphasize features to protect the system against breakdown and to speed recovery when it does occur. These features must be integral in the design from the beginning because to add them later can result in unsatisfactory solutions and serious underestimates of the work needed to develop the project.

Externally, the system may exhibit features such as duplicated processing units and storage devices. The system design must maintain duplicated files, must dump files and core contents periodically, must reconcile files against each other from time to time and must check for authority of a user to carry out functions or access data. Special routines must be incorporated to be run after a period of down time in order to lose as little processing as possible and to assist the entry of data accumulated while no computer service was available.

File processing becomes more complex because filed records are being amended and inserted as well as simply accessed. Amending files online raises the problem of controlling the simultaneous processing of a record by more than one transaction. A product could easily be the subject of two simultaneous orders and the system must be protected against both transactions retrieving an identical record of the current amount on hand to which a deduction is applied. The potential result is best illustrated by example. Product X has 20 items on hand; order 1 is for 8 while order 2 is for 13. In servicing order 1, $20 - 8 = 12$ giving a residual value in the record written back to file. For order 2, the same original record was retrieved since order 1 was still in process so $20 - 13 = 7$, also written back but overwriting the result of processing order 1. Obviously order 2 must be held up until order 1 is completed but supposing the customer placing order 1 starts by only wishing to make an enquiry. The delay for customer 2 may be many minutes. The system must distinguish retrieval of data for enquiry from that for update and in the event of an enquiry followed by an update, the record in question will have to be retrieved twice to preserve the distinction. Not only that, but in the case of a stock record in the example, the validation of quantity available against order quantity will need to be repeated before updating since the balance could change in between retrievals.

The possibility of adding records raises the question of overflow and file organization. The frequently-used indexed sequential method will not be appropriate since overflows are not always handled in a method suited to real time processing. The single index could also be inadequate since records may have to be retrieved by various keys. For credit checking, order lines must be associated with a customer; for stock checking with a product, for despatch with a route, for commission with a salesman. The data needs to be associated in various ways logically without recording in various sequences physically. The technique of associative addressing may therefore be introduced. This implies linking associated records with an owner record either by storing the address of a record in its neighbour in the chain or by forming a short temporary index in the owner record (see Figure 3.5). (For further discussion of file organization, see Dodd, George G., Elements of Data Management Systems, *Computing Surveys*, **1**, 2, 1969. Lefkovitz, D., *File Structures for Online Systems*, Macmillan, London, 1969.)

Related to both security and file processing is the maintenance of an audit trail of transactions, when no record except the effect of the transactions on files, exists. To audit such a system successfully, the auditor must understand the concepts of real time and the penalties imposed on a fast response system if additional reporting is built into it. The use of a transaction log file with transactions automatically 'stamped' with time and date on receipt, the association of a user identity with the transaction and the production of confirmatory documents are possible additional system functions to guard against fraud and error.

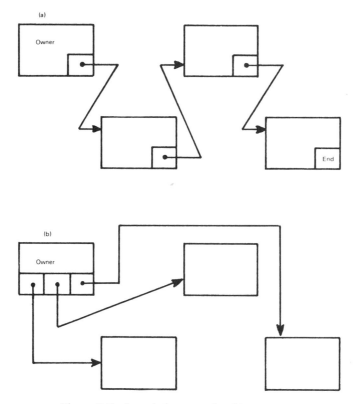

Figure 3.5. Associating records with an owner

Finally a comprehensive online updating system is likely to have more variety in its terminal types than the others so far discussed. The data entry features will still be best served by display terminals while the online processing will need to be recorded on some permanent medium. The printer terminals developed from telegraph devices will therefore have a use as well. Some applications may call for even more types, such as badge readers, card machines, line printers or specially built devices. This variety of terminal types must be interfaced with the hardware and the system. An interfacing program or terminal handler is usually employed to permit processing programs to be independent of the source and destination of the processing activity.

Justification

The additional equipment and the processing necessary to secure the system to maintain online file control and to service unusual access techniques, might suggest that an online updating application will usually not justify the significant investment leap. However online file updating systems have been successfully introduced, and there are situations which justify them.

The first applications were to military tasks related to process control. Obviously flight data collected to compute control surface settings cannot be subjected to a 24 hour batch processing cycle. So when results of processing are required in much less than any feasible batch cycle time, there is no alternative. Such cases must still be carefully reviewed especially if some similar function has been undertaken before by batch or manual methods. A clear performance gain must be demonstrated to justify the investment.

Performance gains, having an easily computed financial value, could be demonstrated in the case of airline reservation systems. The distinct end to the life of the airline's product once a flight has departed, coupled with the product's high value, made the sale of an extra 2-5% of seats extremely worthwhile. A gain of £50 per flight on several thousand flights per year is a conservative estimate of the return. Many other industries have products similar to an airline trip—hotel rooms, investment opportunities for finance companies, theatre seats, advertising space—which all share the same characteristics of transience, and high value. When coupled with high volume, such situations are worth the evaluation of a real time solution.

Key Design Decisions

A file updating system can include features from all three of the previous system types.

Their design decisions of response time, file design, variety of transaction types, management of the communications network, recovery and security are all of continuing importance. To these must be added the design of a fallback system and the added importance of recovery, security and file design. When a real time system is as comprehensive as is suggested above then the user company may have real difficulties in continuing to trade if the computer system fails in any respect. The early consideration of these design topics is essential to the success of the system and, as will later become apparent, the methods proposed in this book are intended for exactly that purpose.

MEMO UPDATE

General Description

The full scale file update system is comparatively rare in commercial computing. Much more common is the 'memo' update system which is partway between a data capture and a file update system. It is described after the less likely and more complex file update since its nature is more easily appreciated by contrasting the two.

The 'memo' name is given since the major files are changed by real time transactions but not permanently. Certain key fields such as stock balance are changed but the online file copy is not the permanent business file. At the end of the real time day the online file is scratched and the captured transactions are passed against the real master file in a batch system.

Memo updating has the advantage over full online updating that the control over accounting information still resides in the batch system. Control and audit techniques in batch systems are well developed and understood. The processing and equipment overhead necessary to exercise control is then incurred in the batch system where it does not affect online system performance. The company employing memo update has a ready-made back up system in the event of failure in the real time component.

The scope of such a system can vary widely. In the order processing situation used previously for examples a common variation would be that new customers cannot be added in the real time system. Another area for variety is in the data which is updated. Certainly, stock balances will be changed but outstanding order value on a customer record may not be. Decisions on scope are best guided by clearly defining why the updating feature is being used. Usually the purpose will be to improve validation of transactions.

Justification

The 'memo' feature can be justified in two ways: as an extension of scope in the validation aspects of a data capture system or as a means of reducing exposure to security and recovery problems in a file update system. In either case the main justifications have already been discussed. The only topic to be considered is the incremental justification for the update feature.

The update will usually be added to improve customer service. In the order processing situation, there is an advantage in being able to detect all out of stock conditions and either save later disappointment or permit a substitution, perhaps while the customer's participation can be invited. However, there remain the problems of updating files online: simultaneous enquiries giving misleading results on a few occasions, recovery of updated records after a file failure and the design of a fallback system. The gains arise by avoiding the problems of data security and control.

PROCESS CONTROL

One other frequently encountered class of system which fairly deserves to be called real time can be generally entitled process control. Another name used is 'sensor based' systems.

In such systems, the events which provoke processing are not reported to the system by user staff through keyboards but rather they are detected and reported automatically by instruments. The responses of the system are not addressed to human senses by displays or reports but are signals used to activate tools or controls to cause changes in the process being controlled. The processes may be military, industrial or commercial. Guidance systems for aircraft, continuous process chemical plant, medical monitoring systems are all examples.

The techniques and decisions of design applicable to the commercial systems discussed earlier will be similar in most respects. Response time will be critical though not necessarily shorter. Protection against and recovery from failure will be as important. Fallback solutions will probably be different but the concept remains valid. All the features of the controlling software, such as detection of message type, multi-threading, program management, core management, etc., will be exhibited.

However to save spending unnecessary space justifying a contention that this book is relevant for process control systems design, no such claim will be made. Readers concerned with such systems are invited to form their own judgement as to the applicability of the techniques presented.

SUMMARY

The point has been made in discussing file update systems that they commonly contain traces of the simpler systems discussed first. In fact the general point can be made that actual systems will usually exhibit features of more than one system type. They have been discussed separately to identify their consequences in design activity. The consequences overlap those identified in the previous chapter from a consideration of the five major differences between real time and batch. In this chapter, we have seen again why real time systems design is so concerned with security, fallback, recovery, file processing and response time.

In the next chapter, the key concepts which underlie the remainder of the book will be introduced. The rest of the book will then elaborate an approach to the design process which uses those concepts to attack the problems of ensuring that the key design decisions are soundly based, by forcing their consideration at the appropriate time in the design activity. The methods are intended to be equally suited to any of the levels of systems complexity introduced in this chapter. There is a common pattern to these system types which derives from the interactive and event-driven features found in all.

Chapter 4

Conversations and Exchanges

COMPUTER SYSTEMS DESIGN TASKS

Batch Systems

As a prelude to describing the principles of design and documentation which this book is propounding, the method used by the author for batch systems design will be reviewed.

There is a general pattern. It starts with the recognition of an information processing problem. A number of solutions may be considered which differ from each other in terms of their outputs, namely the reports and documents to be generated by the system. These solutions are described to the users of the system by means of illustrative reports and a general estimate of the differences in cost. The most promising is selected and the outputs which characterize it are defined more precisely and approved.

Once the reporting system is defined and the methods of using the reports are agreed, the processing system which will produce them can be specified. Specification will identify and define:

(a) the inputs to the system, i.e. sources of data to be processed,
(b) the files which will be used to supplement the source data, i.e. master files holding data which does not change regularly,

and finally,

(c) the computer programs which will accept source data, maintain files, extract and edit reports.

This simplified account illustrates the sequential process by which the tangible results of systems design are achieved. These are:

(a) report specifications
(b) source document specifications
(c) file definitions
(d) system flowchart showing how programs link the other sets of entities together
(e) program specifications.

A system may be composed of a number of program strings or suites concerned with different reporting functions. Most often these occur when different reports are produced at different intervals. For example an order processing system may have daily runs concerned with preparing deliveries, weekly runs for sales management reports, monthly runs for statements and top management statistics and yearly runs for financial reporting. It is rare though for a system to have more than a few different strings of programs.

Real Time System Design Difference

A real time system, or the real time part of a combined system, has similar components. It comprises a number of computer runs, each of which has source data, refers to files and produces output. Figure 2.1 shows the similarity. Figure 2.1 also shows the first clue to the differences in that the different processing functions of a batch system are separated from each other by files which form the interface between programs.

The analogous functions of a real time system flow do not have as clean an interface. Real time programs pass data from one to the other in a variety of ways implying complex interfaces in core. The other important difference is that a similar chart exists for each different type of entry permitted in a real time system. Each is presented to the computer system independently and at random so that a complete system flowchart for a real time system comprises many times the number of charts for an equivalent batch system.

The consequence is that the type of system flowchart shown in Figure 2.1 is not at a sufficiently high level to be the starting point of system design. Instead, additional design levels must be interposed between the identification of the problem and the programs to process its solutions.

EXCHANGES AND CONVERSATIONS

The Exchange Concept

If the programs which process an entry are too small a unit to convey the system design, the next level of abstraction must be the group of programs taken as a unit. Instead of looking into the charts let us look at the chart as one unit. This unit could be considered to comprise the entry which provokes the processing, the processing itself and the possible responses which might result. Externally the user will experience it as an *exchange* of information between himself and the computer. This is the name we will use.

An EXCHANGE is defined to be the system unit which links together a single entry type with its possible responses. An ENTRY is a string of characters sent from a terminal to the computer while a RESPONSE is a string of characters sent from the computer to a terminal. An entry and a response together with the processing programs which link them form an exchange.

The Conversation Concept

The exchange concept allows us to step back one level from the programs and files of the system flowchart. The next step is to organize the process of identifying the component exchanges of a real time system. This step relies on another common characteristic of real time systems—that its exchanges are related in sequences. Exchanges do not occur entirely at random at a terminal. Very frequently sequences are used to effect a particular function. These sequences can be thought of as *conversations* between the terminal user and the computer. A CONVERSATION is defined as a series of exchanges linked together by the common purpose of achieving some business function.

These definitions of entry, response, exchange and conversation are put forward as units in a scheme for organizing the process of real time systems design. A system can be considered as sets of these entities, like reports, source documents and program strings in a batch system, around which the design and installation process can be organized.

The illustration of real time processing with which this book opened can be analysed into conversations and exchanges. The exchanges are clearly the entry-response pairs. The conversations can be identified in this instance as the sequences of exchanges to perform two distinctly separate jobs—one to enter the notification of receipt of invoices, the other to carry out corrections to reconcile the invoice with the goods received or ordered.

Procedures

For the moment we will leave consideration of the conversation and return to the topic of designing the real time system.

A conversation between a terminal user and the computer takes place as part of a larger procedure of carrying out some business function with a combination of manual and computer actions. The conversation is a tool employed in the execution of some higher duty which forms part of the job definition of the user. An airline reservation clerk uses his computer terminal to check that seats are available and to record a reservation, but the procedure of making a reservation includes questioning the customer, looking up reference manuals and perhaps writing a ticket. The invoice entry procedure illustrated in Chapter 1 includes receiving and batching the invoices before and filing them after, the first computer conversation. A particular procedure might include more than one computer conversation. The whole invoice entry example in fact includes two: entry and correction.

So the next step back in our withdrawal from the detail of traditional system flowcharts is the identification of procedures which will contain computer conversations. This level is of significance since procedures are the units which have meaning to users and are the units by which the installation of the new system may be most conveniently managed. The conversion of a real time system can be thought of as the installation of procedures. These are the units in which business activity is organized and they exist independently of the computer system. Their design must allow for failure because business activity will go on whether or not the computer system is available.

Stages of Real Time Design

The concepts of procedure, conversation and exchange give a structure to the process of system design for real time systems. As with batch systems, this process occurs after careful study of existing systems and the identification of changes necessary to improve on its performance in respect of the problem being studied. The process consists of the following steps which may be executed sequentially or reiterated to improve design:

(a) identification of conversations which will aid in the execution of current or new tasks
(b) definition of procedures embodying those conversations
(c) definition of conversations in detail
(d) identification of exchanges necessary to realize the approved conversations
(e) specification of files and programs required to effect the changes.

This last step brings us to the point from which we started since those files and programs form the system flowcharts illustrated in Figure 2.1.

THE EFFECT OF THE CONVERSATION CONCEPT

Abbreviation of Messages

The essential characteristic of human conversation is that it creates a context within which individual exchanges are given meaning. The word 'yes' taken out of context has very limited significance. It is a general indication of agreement, but to what? Only the context of the conversation in which it is used will give it more meaning. However, in that context no additional words are necessary to give it that extra meaning because the context has been established and is shared between the participants.

The conversation concept, in an interaction between computer and terminal user, has similar power. It permits entries to be abbreviated so that a single key depression conveys all the information that 'yes' can convey in context. Information established in earlier exchanges of the conversation is available to add meaning and so significantly reduce the amount of keying to be done.

Conversation Control Record

The concept of providing a context for exchanges can be physically realized by providing a record to store the effective information between exchanges. As we have said, the context must be shared to enable it to endow successive entries with extra significance. The computer will only retain the context if stored space is set aside for it. This space is here called a Conversation Control Record (CCR).

The CCR is a stored record since by definition it exists beyond the lifetime of single exchanges. While it could be kept in core, space limitations and other drawbacks will usually make that impractical.

A CCR could exist in theory only for the lifetime of a conversation and then be destroyed. In practice however a single terminal or a single terminal user will only carry on one conversation at a time. It is therefore usually convenient to associate a single CCR either with each terminal or with each user. It is most often the terminal which is selected since this eases the problem of retrieving the CCR. Each entry is usually tagged automatically with its terminal of origin by software. The terminal identity can then be used as a key to retrieve the relevant CCR.

However, in a system where users move around between terminals, they may wish to have access to their own CCR to continue a conversation from whichever terminal they are near. Then some means of automatically establishing user identity, such as a badge reader, will make that a convenient key for CCR retrieval. A system where many users share one terminal would have similar characteristics.

The CCR is used to collect and store data which must survive longer than an exchange. It will probably hold a user identity, the type of conversation currently in progress and data identifying records being used in the conversation in addition to purely application data.

Permitted Next Entries

The existence of a record which provides a context for individual entries permits the exploitation of another similarity between human and machine conversation. At any point in a conversation, the next utterance type is fairly predictable—if the conversation is directed to a single purpose. The set of probable next utterances is very much smaller than the infinite set of possible utterances in the language. This is most easily illustrated when answering questions. For example, Shopkeeper: 'Good morning madam, what can I get for you today?' Customer: 'To be or not to be, that is the question?' Shopkeeper: 'Pardon?' The customer's reply would convey no meaning in that context however meaningful it would be at other times. The shopkeeper expects a reply specifying stock items and quantities—however obscured by introductory remarks on other matters.

Of course, in human conversation, the brain is so powerful that apparently irrelevant responses can be given meaning and unexpected responses are not rejected out of hand. Different responses can be thought of as graded on a probability scale with the most expected responses able to convey information more succinctly since they have to make least alteration to the context so far established.

A crude approximation to this characteristic can be built into a computer system using the Conversation Control Record. Once a context has been established with an opening entry which identifies the conversation, the successive entries will be drawn from a small range of entries permitted in that conversation. As the conversation develops, the range of permitted next entries will change but the existence of a table of them will help to identify the particular entry made. When the conversation is completed, the list of entries will become those which will identify any conversations which that user is now permitted in the context of the application.

Entry Recognition

The use of a permitted next entry table in the CCR will help to make the entry recognition function fast and accurate. The entry recognition program must know the structure of the CCR so that it can refer to the permitted next entry table. As each exchange is completed, its final program will update the table to reflect the current status of the conversation.

The significance of this table to entry recognition is that the population of possible entries is very much reduced and the sequence of entries in the table might be adjusted to reflect the probability that entries would occur. Thus the number of trials to match an entry would be reduced.

The method used to define an entry's identity can vary. The initial entries of conversations are likely to be identified with literal codes since the number of those entries which is possible between conversations is likely to be much higher than the number of entry types permitted once a conversation is in process. In principal the use of a literal need be considered only as a special case of recognition by format.

There can be a benefit in reduced keystrokes derived from this use of the CCR, since fewer entries need to be identified by codes. Since the number of entry types permitted at any time is small, recognition by entry format becomes possible at the cost of a penalty in processing time. This may not be of significance in many projects but if entries are short enough so that their format is easily recognized, and used with high frequency, the saving in keystrokes from eliminating redundant characters could be significant. Discussion of entry recognition is continued in Part III.

One other factor has a bearing on the topic of entry recognition. Users of a project may vary in their security clearance to use certain facilities. The range of permitted entries can also be modified to recognize this factor if user status is stored in the CCR. This implies that it is included in the user's sign-on entry or in some table of master information which can be accessed by user identity.

The Context Hierarchy

The CCR is one of a series of records which aids the processing of an individual entry. Many proprietary real time control programs recognize a record which we will call in this book an Exchange Control Record (ECR). The ECR is equivalent to the IBM CICS Task Control Area, the ICL DRIVER Task Administration Block and the Univac CONTCRTS Transdata. This is a transient record which exists in core for the life of a particular exchange. It provides space for holding control and application data which is of general interest of the software and user programs in the exchange. It also provides a method of passing parameters between programs. In effect it acts as a work order which stays with the entry in its progress through the computer system. It is the embodiment of the exchange since the original message from the terminal may be very quickly destroyed, well before the processing activity is complete. An inquiry to display certain fields of a filed record for instance, may be discarded as soon as the retrieval parameters have been extracted from it. The ECR remains live until the response has been constructed, edited and dispatched.

To the CCR and ECR a third area can be added to complete the hierarchy of work space which can be built for a real time system. The third is the program work area (PWA) which contains data of interest to a single program only. This program is suitable for such data as accumulators and intermediate results which do not need to be passed on from one program to another.

Thus a hierarchy of space is available for processing, organized according to the expected life of the data items concerned. At the bottom, for data of interest to a single program, is the PWA. Next, for data relevant to more than one program but no more than one exchange, is the ECR, then comes the CCR for data of interest beyond one exchange. Finally for data of interest to different conversations conducted by different people at different times, there is the permanent storage of the application data files and a general system work area.

Relevance to Installation

The concepts of procedure, conversation and exchange have relevance to the phase subsequent to design, that of installation. The major activities of that phase are programming, testing and conversion. The concepts have relevance to programming since the programmer will need to be confident in the distinction between them to know how to classify particular data items into the work space hierarchy.

More significantly however, the entities of exchange and conversation are convenient for the organization of both testing and conversion. Testing, as has already been discussed, is of particular importance in real time systems. Once program testing is completed, the exchange is a suitable unit for testing groups of programs together. This is analogous to the batch testing phase of program strings or runs. Once exchanges are functioning properly, they can be linked to form conversations and so on. Testing is thus the reverse process to system definition.

We have already introduced the thought that conversion is the installation of procedures rather than whole systems. Frequently, a real time system can be installed by cutting over conversations. This is an elaboration of the conversion principle of cutting over by function. This is likely to lead to an easier conversion process because the drama of program deadlines and user preparation can be lessened if conversion is spread out in this way.

Once a system is installed, the exchange concept may be of relevance to the maintenance process. Exchanges can be thought of as system modules and provided the interface between an exchange and its conversation is maintained, an exchange 'module' can be replaced or modified. This process should be as convenient as the modification of a program module in a properly modularized system.

EFFECT ON DESIGN EFFORT

Common Exchanges

A product of conversation specification is the identification of the exchanges which comprise each conversation. The mechanism for this work will be considered later. However the work is done, the end result will be a population of exchanges organized by conversation. Since the conversations are related by virtue of being part of the same project they are likely to deal with similar data. There is a high probability that some exchanges from different conversations will have a similar purpose. There might, for example, be a number of conversations which use an exchange to enter customer identity for the purpose of displaying a customer record. In one, this might be to answer inquiries; in another, as a prelude to making an amendment or executing a transaction.

The recognition of the separate entities of conversation and exchange provide for a definite stage of reviewing the range of exchanges proposed to effect conversations. This stage has the purpose of deliberately seeking out opportunities to combine similar exchanges with the object of reducing installation effort. The success of this stage reduces subsequent design effort, programming and testing.

Common Programs

An exactly analogous process occurs at the end of the exchange specification step. One result of that is to identify the population of programs necessary to implement the population of exchanges.

Again it is likely that different exchanges will have need of similar functions in processing. A stage of reviewing the range of programs thought necessary is recommended to expose these similarities and exploit them by providing common programs.

Common Entries and Responses

It will be recalled that exchanges are composed of four types of element: an entry, programs, files and responses. The existence of common files is taken for granted and we have just discussed the possibility of finding common programs. Quite separately from the consideration of common exchanges, it is conceivable that exchanges which are widely different in purpose could be stimulated by similar entries or generate similar responses. This is a development of the thought discussed earlier that entries are given meaning by their context to provoke widely different processing.

The recognition of common entries and responses is important beyond the advantage of saving specification and programming effort. The terminal users will have more confidence in a system which exhibits consistent behaviour and they will be able to learn to use it more easily. If one conversation requires user agreement to be conveyed with 'ok' while another requires 'yes' the user will not be able to generalize his training. He will have to memorize apparently arbitrary distinctions which would not be necessary with a human respondent.

Similar considerations apply to responses. The display of similar data should normally have the same appearance in any conversation even though it may have been produced by a different sequence of processing. The designer should look for opportunities to make common responses. This will be particularly fruitful in error responses. Even though the errors may relate to different fields a similarity in wording will reduce the learning process and maybe expose opportunities to reduce programming.

Multiple Relationships are Produced

The process of seeking out common exchanges, programs, entries and responses produces multiple relationships between these entities. The opportunity also exists at an earlier stage of fitting common conversations into

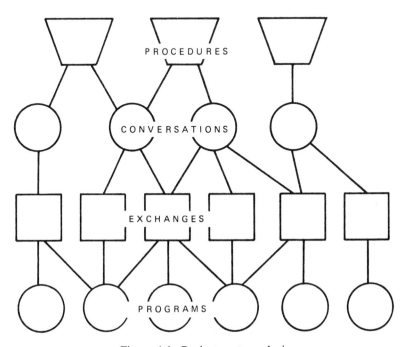

Figure 4.1. Project parts explosion

different procedures. So the final effect, if charted, can resemble a network rather than a simple tree. However the relationship remains hierarchical. The important feature is that the different levels should be seen to be independent to some degree and that there is a many-to-one relationship in both directions. Thus an exchange can be composed of several programs and one of those programs can contribute to several exchanges. Figure 4.1 illustrates the effect intended.

DEFINING BOUNDARIES

Separating Conversations

The principle of 'divide and rule' is being advocated in this chapter so the question of where to divide must be faced. The test for recognizing where one conversation ends and another begins is not an easy one to specify precisely. Analysts will differ in their treatment of a particular project. However the purpose of separation is the provision of suitable units for organizing the early steps in system design. Consequently the test need not be too precise. The precise boundaries of a conversation will not affect implementation provided that the persistence of the CCR is not cut at conversation boundaries. The contents of the CCR are not affected by software—they are entirely controlled by project programs. Disagreement on the exact limits of a conversation is not therefore important.

However some guidelines can be discussed. An extended definition of a conversation might help:

A CONVERSATION is a series of EXCHANGES linked together to record, or assist in the processing of a physical event in the environment which the project serves. Each exchange in a conversation will depend upon others for data and the conversation can be completed as soon as all the data needed to record an event is assembled.

Thus it can be taken that conversations usually correspond to external events or transactions. Conversations should be capable of standing alone in that they can be successfully executed without any prior data being available in the CCR. Short conversations are preferable to make their specification easier to prepare and comprehend. It should be a design objective to minimize interconnection between conversations. This simplifies design and implementation.

The limits of conversations are finally arbitrary in the way that the scope of a project is arbitrary. There will usually be evident subdivisions and provided that these are roughly recognized the exact boundaries are not too important.

Exchange Definition

The definition of limits of exchanges within conversations is the process of splitting up the data contributed by the user into entries. Once the entries are identified in the context of a conversation, the functions of the exchanges are virtually determined. The choice is made during the design of the conversation. Apart from natural divisions in the data itself there are a number of features of the project and its environment which will have an impact. Some of the more important are:

(a) Source of data to be entered—it may be written or spoken and it may come from more than one source.
(b) Sequence of data—it may be fixed or variable.
(c) Terminal type—this may be predetermined and its characteristics may influence design.
(d) Processing—if a conversation provokes considerable processing, the designer may wish to break this up.
(e) Intervening manual activities—the pattern of exchanges can be arranged around the work or can be designed to take advantage of such work by overlapping processing with it.
(f) Intermittent use—the user not using exchanges continuously will want them to be simple to use and understand.

Of these, the questions relating to the manner the data is made available to the users will probably have most effect. The basic questions to be answered are:

(a) Should all the data be presented in one entry?
(b) Should the sequence—of entries or data within the entry—be fixed or variable?

To illustrate, the placing of an order by a customer may be by letter or by telephone. If by letter the data may be in a given sequence dictated by a form or it may be free form. If by telephone, the customer has those choices and he may also give all the information in one utterance or he may provide it piecemeal.

The conversation to permit the order clerk to record the order may have to permit a series of simple single field exchanges, exchanges which can be performed in any sequence or a single exchange containing all the data. The final choice will also have to take into account the user's commercial judgement as to the extent to which the customer can be guided.

These factors and the others listed will not entirely resolve the choice of exchanges for a particular conversation. Indeed some may conflict with others and different designers will resolve the choice differently. The final choice should take into account user preference and cost of implementation.

SUMMARY

Relationship to Other Chapters

This chapter has introduced the framework which this book will use. The concepts of conversation and exchange and their realization in programming by means of the conversation and exchange control records, will be employed from here onwards as pegs to organize methods and documentation for real time systems. These ideas will be married to other principles of documentation to yield a complete and consistent approach to designing real time applications.

The chapters which follow describe this documentation in more detail as the means of resolving the problems raised in Chapter 2. It is the author's contention that these concepts and methods will accommodate all the varieties of real time system described in Chapter 3.

PART II

Application Systems Design

Chapter 5
Stages of System Definition

Continuity with Batch Practice

The general approach to the creation of real time systems is similar to the best practice used for batch systems. Successful systems cannot be installed without a preparatory phase which defines the objective of the system, describes its design and obtains the approval of using and corporate management. Over twenty years of experience with computers has taught that this is the method by which successful projects are installed. This investment in preparation eases the process of installation by planning ahead to meet problems in time to solve them. Attempts to install systems without thorough and well documented attention, first to the purpose, then to the design, have resulted in systems which do not work at all or produce results that cannot be used, or are not cost effective.

Real time applications may differ from batch systems in many ways, but in their need for planning they are not different at all. There now exists sufficient experience to suggest methods for this preparatory phase which will make it more speedy and more sure. It is the function of this section of the book to describe such methods. The remainder of this chapter will describe the general sequence of activities concerned with system definition.

Priorities set by Long Range Systems Planning

This chapter and the book as a whole are concerned in the main with single applications rather than complete corporate information systems. Such applications tend to compete with each other for the resources of the data processing department—staff during development and processing time after installation. A long range systems plan for the company and its EDP function integrates each application with the context of company development while permitting the applications to be managed separately. It is possible to run a data processing department as a housekeeping organization, responding to requests from other departments for single disconnected systems, performed in the sequence that they arise. Such an approach suggests that the data processing function is not directed by top management in the company and is only fortuitously being applied to the company's business needs. A long range systems plan is a device for enlisting top management involvement in setting the objectives of the data processing function so that it responds to company needs rather than those of the strongest departments or its own. Therefore, although the book concentrates on the development of projects, an assumption has been made that these have been selected for adequate reasons. The assertion of top management control over project selection has been treated elsewhere, (Leighton Smith, An Executive Briefing on the Control of Computers. *DPMA*, 1971), for example.

Project Scope Identifies Boundaries

A project comes into existence from the long range systems plan or through some stimulus from a company's operations—stocks are getting too high or sales opportunities are being missed due to lack of data. The first recognizable piece of work associated with the project is a phase of defining project scope. This phase is the means of addressing the project to company operating problems. Objectives are expressed by identifying the benefits in terms of direct gains to the company. The provision of facilities such as 'direct access files' or 'multi-programming' or even 'real time' are not proper objectives for a project. They are simply characteristics of solutions. Genuine objectives should take the form of specifying improved levels of service or reductions of cost, expressed quantitatively if possible to facilitate a subsequent review of the effectiveness of the project in meeting them.

The definition of project scope will thus identify the general area of concern of the project and a first idea of its approach. The particular problem, bottleneck or internal disagreement which triggered the project should be specifically included in the definition of the project. Initial discussions with experienced data processing staff on the application of computers to the problem may well identify the general shape of the system—whether it is to be batch or real time or a mixture. A wide knowledge of the state of the art will be a help at this time.

The other important tasks at this time are to arrange that user and corporate management remain as involved in the solution as they are in the problem and to set the work programme for the next phase of the work. Management involvement will ensure that the system developed is responsive to the actual problem rather than to a misinterpretation of it, that details of the solution are acceptable to the users before heavy investment is undertaken, and that the proper priority is assigned at times when the project is competing for machine time or other resources. Such involvement ensures the commitment of user management to its success. The prior establishment of a work programme makes plain the resources needed for the next phase and sets a budget against which performance can be measured.

Preliminary Systems Design defines the Project

The stage of setting the scope of the project is a relatively minor consumer of the resources ultimately committed to the project. Preliminary Systems

Design, though, is a substantial investment responsible for perhaps 10-15% of the expenditure incurred. It includes several sub-stages:

(a) System design.
(b) Equipment evaluation.
(c) Installation schedule.
(d) Economic evaluation.
(e) Review and approval.

The work done in this stage will establish the general design of the system, specify the economic and other benefits of the chosen design, support the estimates of effort and duration needed to install the system and, depending upon the volume of processing needed for the design, enable the selection of any necessary new equipment to be made. The results of these steps are expressed in a report and reviewed.

These sub-stages are performed in a sequence dictated by the needs of each for information. Systems design is undertaken first to provide the parameters on which the other tasks depend. The economic benefits cannot be stated until the results to be provided are known, the installation work programme cannot be estimated until the work to be carried out by the system is known and the equipment cannot be selected until its work load has been specified. Before proceeding to installation, the design and its budget must be approved by the users, data processing management and corporate management.

The necessity for this work, its extent and its precedence over installation is taken in this book hereafter to be self evident. It was not self evident in the enthusiastic period of the late 1950s and early 1960s, but recent evaluations of the sources of success in computer projects have supported the view that such a planning phase, in that sequence and well documented, is a prerequisite.

Installation is the Largest Stage

The remaining expenditure on a project is taken up with the conversion of the approved and specified design into a running system. There are again several sub-stages:

(a) Detailed system design.
(b) Software evaluation and development.
(c) Conversion preparation.
(d) Programming and debugging.
(e) Physical preparation.
(f) System test.
(g) Conversion.

Of these, programming and debugging are usually and rightly given the most prominence, but the other areas which are performed in parallel—namely, conversion preparation and physical preparation—can make a vital difference to system success. The delivery of correct programs on time will be worthless if the users do not know how to use the system or if the master data is not ready.

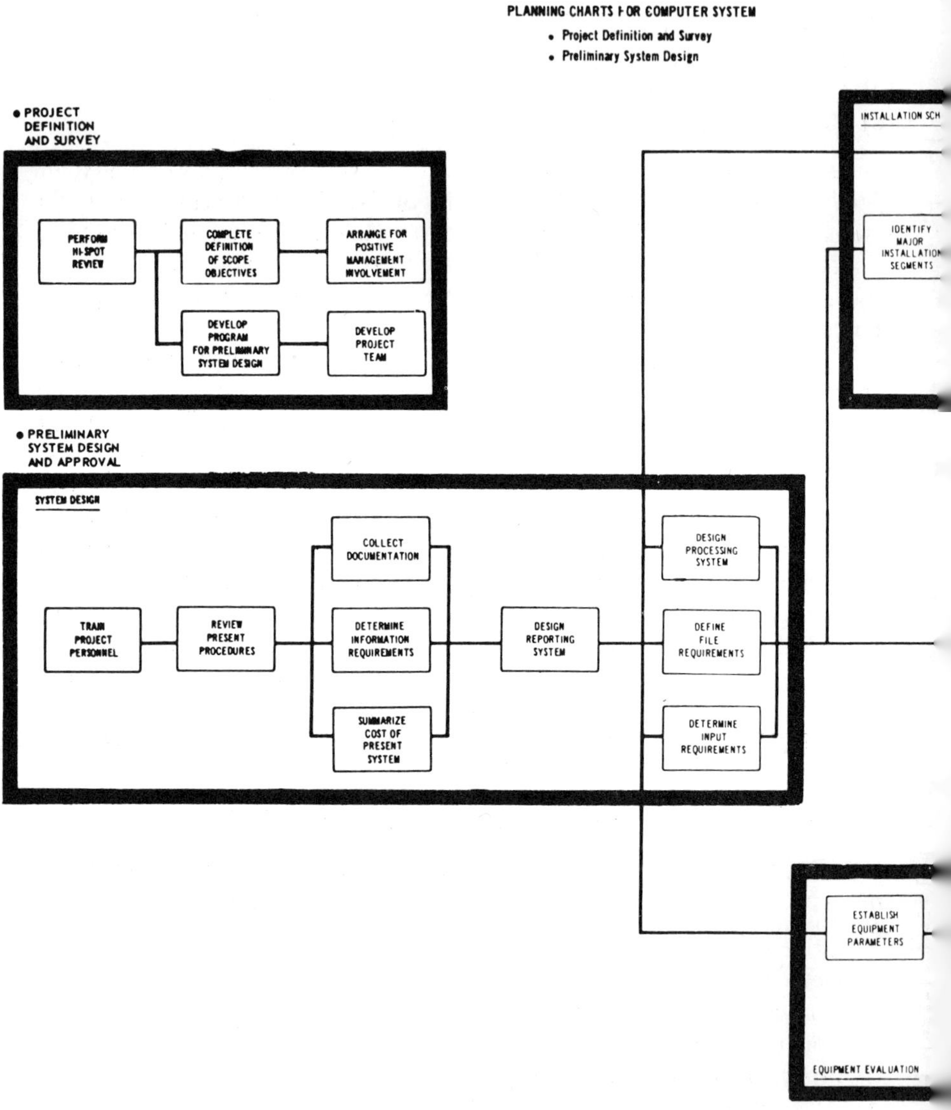

Figure 5.1. Work plan for system design

67

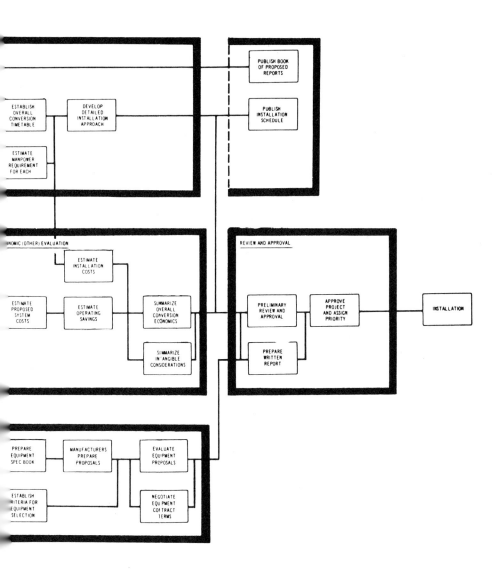

PUBLISH BOOK OF PROPOSED REPORTS

PUBLISH INSTALLATION SCHEDULE

ESTABLISH OVERALL CONVERSION TIMETABLE

DEVELOP DETAILED INSTALLATION APPROACH

ESTIMATE MANPOWER REQUIREMENT FOR EACH

ECONOMIC (OTHER) EVALUATION

ESTIMATE INSTALLATION COSTS

ESTIMATE PROPOSED SYSTEM COSTS

ESTIMATE OPERATING SAVINGS

SUMMARIZE OVERALL CONVERSION ECONOMICS

SUMMARIZE INTANGIBLE CONSIDERATIONS

REVIEW AND APPROVAL

PRELIMINARY REVIEW AND APPROVAL

APPROVE PROJECT AND ASSIGN PRIORITY

PREPARE WRITTEN REPORT

INSTALLATION

PREPARE EQUIPMENT SPEC BOOK

MANUFACTURERS PREPARE PROPOSALS

EVALUATE EQUIPMENT PROPOSALS

ESTABLISH CRITERIA FOR EQUIPMENT SELECTION

NEGOTIATE EQUIPMENT CONTRACT TERMS

Reconciliation Confirms Management Control

The question 'does the system work?' is only partly answered by the system test. After installation the original objectives of the system and the budget for installation must be compared with actual performance. This is the vital demonstration of management concern which will create a data processing department serving the company. If the performance of the project team is not reviewed in this way then their incentive to perform well is missing. There is only limited satisfaction in doing a good job if no one else ever recognizes it. The review of the installation work programme against actual performance enables estimating methods to be refined for the benefit of subsequent projects. The approval of projects, which comes at the end of the Preliminary Systems Design stage, depends upon having reliable estimates of benefit and cost so that the return on investment can be used as a criterion for selecting projects. The validity of judgements then made is only borne out if the actual results bear a reasonable resemblance to estimates.

A complete project therefore comprises four stages: the definition of scope, preliminary system design, installation and reconciliation. Of these, preliminary system design is the most important and installation is the most expensive. It is with these stages that the rest of this book will be concerned.

PRELIMINARY SYSTEMS DESIGN

PSD has Several Areas

The steps undertaken in the Preliminary Systems Design (PSD) stage of a project have already been identified. The sub-headings of this section illustrate them again. The steps are affected to different extents when a project contains real time elements. Before design work for real time projects is described, this section considers the objectives of each of these subsidiary stages of PSD. The sequence of steps is illustrated in Figure 5.1.

Systems Design is the Foundation

The system design identifies and documents all elements of the project. In a batch system these elements are computer runs, reports, input forms, files and programs. In a real time system similar elements exist but the runs are replaced by smaller activities which produce responses rather than reports, and are triggered by entries or events rather than input records. The identification of these elements by the methods described in this part of the book permits a closer understanding of the costs of the development phase and the necessity for computer power. The documentation of the system elements ensures that the system installed is the system approved. The development of the system will usually require the efforts of many different people to permit it to be installed at an early date. Detailed documentation of the design will assist their understanding of the tasks they are assigned and ensure that their results can be integrated. Finally design documentation will assist in explaining the features of design to management and in demonstrating its responsiveness to the problem in hand.

Installation Stage must be Planned

The management of the department wishing to use a system will be interested in the final cutover date. The person managing the project will wish to establish a series of interim dates for the completion of significant steps in the installation phase so that he may have early warning of any lateness and thus the opportunity to take corrective action. He will also wish to set staffing levels for the various types of staff needed during installation. For these reasons, a schedule for the installation stage is required. The system design has identified the system elements whose development is the major user of resources. From these and approximate values for the cost and effort of their development, a schedule can be developed. The schedule for each sub-phase of installation identifies the work steps, states their duration and content and establishes their start and finish dates consistent with available staff.

The installation schedule can be developed reasonably quickly if a methodical approach is adopted. The elements identified in system design must be classified by their degree of difficulty—a three class scheme is sufficient—then an estimate appropriate for the type of element and its classification will give duration and effort. Each organization will develop its own values for these estimates. The activities are then arranged in a logical sequence using barchart or network methods as appropriate, to identify the chain of critical activities which must be completed on time. The other activities can then be scheduled, between limits, to smooth out the demand for different types of staff. The duration and content of the whole project can then be found by accumulation.

The use of standard values for effort and duration is only practical for the repetitive tasks of installation. Many of the steps of conversion planning, site preparation and conversion itself will be more nearly unique and require judgement based on the experience of EDP and of the user departments.

Equipment Selection depends on System Design

This phase assumes most importance when the company has no installed equipment. Then it will be concerned with the identification of both a configuration and a manufacturer. There are several prior steps intended to ensure that the manufacturer and equipment chosen are those suitable for the project. This stage will apply to a lesser extent if equipment is already installed for other projects. Work is still necessary to ensure that time is available and that suitable peripherals are installed. Early real time projects will involve the acquisition of terminal and data transmission equipment even if CPU power is available.

Equipment selection steps are as follows:

(a) Selecting the configuration.
(b) Estimating computer time.
(c) Establishing selection criteria.
(d) Preparing manufacturers' specifications.
(e) Evaluating proposals and selecting supplier.
(f) Negotiating contract terms.

Configuration selection is the process of deciding the general shape of the equipment needed—the amount of main core processing speed, storage device types and sizes, peripheral types, speeds and quantities. Computer time estimates are made assuming the use of this model configuration rather than one from an actual manufacturer. This is an essential stage in the evaluation of different solutions to the system problem since the choice between them will be partly based on their need for equipment.

Supplier Selection should be Objective

Selection criteria are established before inviting manufacturers' proposals in an effort to make the choice of supplier as objective as possible. Specifications to manufacturers contain a detailed statement of the system together with detailed questionnaires on the performance of the equipment and the organization backing it up. The specification prepared in this fashion constrains each of the manufacturers to present his proposal in a similar format. This aids the process of comparison. After choosing the supplier, negotiations are conducted to resolve obscurities in the proposal, to confirm the choice and to establish the commercial contract. The entire process obviously relies heavily on the preceding systems design phase.

When part or all of the application uses real time techniques, equipment selection is affected in detail but not in overall approach. The selection of a configuration involving terminals and communication lines may utilize statistical techniques but is just as dependent on the prior establishment of volumes, frequencies and processing constraints. In real time, the units are no longer documents, cards and reports, but the need for information at a similar level remains. The way it is used is essentially similar. The timing of computer processing is inverted since the purpose is not to calculate how long a given load will take to process but rather how much can be done in a fixed time—for example, the peak minute. These issues have been discussed elsewhere. The exercise of judgement in choosing criteria and applying them to the selection of equipment described in proposals to fulfil a detailed specification, is little different from batch practice.

Economics must be Evaluated

The work of economic evaluation of the project is hardly changed at all by real time features. In short, the savings are established and the investment to reap that return is costed. The rate of return can then be stated as a consideration when deciding whether to proceed with the project. The component parts of the development cost of a real time project will be in different proportions to those of a batch project—system testing for example will be far more extensive—but the methods used are similar in principle. As in batch systems, benefit will be tangible and intangible. Tangible savings will be composed of direct operating savings while intangible savings include other measurable benefits—reduced inventory or greater turnover, for example, and unquantifiable benefits—such as improved management information.

To conduct an economic evaluation, the installation plan and the equipment parameters need to have been prepared although the actual manufacturer need not have been chosen. Any variation between estimated and actual equipment costs of a given configuration will be small and can be considered as a measure of the performance of the equipment selection stage.

If there are alternative system designs or equipment configurations being considered either in whole or in part, economics will play a part in making choices—either on the grounds of a different return, or a different investment.

Management Approval precedes Installation

The end of the PSD phase of a project is the point to decide whether to commit significant funds to the project. The contract with the equipment supplier is prepared and the major part of the development remains to be done. Members of the management of user departments, data processing and headquarters should be involved in the authorization to proceed. A sufficiently detailed statement of the system design is necessary to support equipment, staff and cost estimates and to communicate the sense of how the affected operations will be performed when the system is available. The content of the material will be different because the real time conversations are added to line printer report examples and telecommunications network drawings augment computer room layouts. It is especially important that those approving the content and the cost fully understand the impact that real time processing will have on office methods and even on organization.

Quite obviously then the key step for all the activities of preliminary systems design is systems design itself. Real time utilizes quite different system logic, so it is on the methods and documentation of systems design that this part of the book concentrates.

SCHEME FOR REAL TIME SYSTEMS DESIGN

Real Time Project Entities

A real time project appears to its users as sets of entries and responses arranged into connected sequences, to assist them in their work. The computer expression of the project is a series of programs and files. Systems design in a real time project is the identification of the most convenient set of entries to initiate the work assigned to the computer and then the identification of the necessary files and programs to produce responses in the desired form. This book proposes the new concepts of 'conversation' and 'exchange' as tools to assist the designer in this process.

A conversation with a computer terminal will usually be only part of the work that a user does in connection with the event which stimulates it. An additional entity called a 'procedure' is therefore recognized. This is defined as a user's job performed with computer assistance which is provoked by an external event. Perhaps it is best thought of as equivalent to the batch entity 'transaction'. Examples of such events are easy enough to find—the placing of an order, receipt of a time card, arrival of an airline passenger at an airport, the deposit of a sum of money at a bank, the transfer of shares, and so on.

Not all computer processing in a real time system takes place as a result of terminal entries. Depending on the application, the designer may find it possible to save entries by making some activities occur automatically or as a result of computer operator action. The processing so provoked is a single activity equivalent to that carried out during an exchange. These activities are considered as equivalent for documentation purposes and the definition of an exchange is expanded to include them.

Documents match Entities

Just as in batch systems, the design work is directed towards the preparation of a series of documents organized around batch entities, so it is proposed that a real time design be expressed in a series of documents representing real time entities. During the course of design, sets of these entities are identified—perhaps 5 procedures, 15 conversations, 30 exchanges—and each of these sets is documented. The data needed in design is organized by associating it with whichever entity seems appropriate. So far as there is a choice, the highest entity in the hierarchy is chosen so that duplication is reduced. Each entity can, after all, be composed of more than one of the next lowest. For example, data describing fallback arrangements are most naturally associated with a procedure since the whole procedure will be affected if the computer assistance supplied in its constituent conversations is withdrawn. Similarly, response time is most naturally associated with an exchange as it will depend upon the amount of processing and the size of the response.

Documents Separately Defined

Potentially, different sets of entities have many members. The sets are defined separately from each other and so, within the sets, are its members. When a set member is identified its interfaces with other members are defined to establish the relationships. Then, when the set is completely known, each member can be separately defined behind its interfaces. This method is adopted to ensure thorough investigation and complete exposure of the data necessary to project design without loss of control of the project as a whole. The method will also permit the sharing of work between many analysts. Naturally there will be occasions when design data is found to be common among many members of a set—frequency patterns of all transactions for instance might be tied to the general state of a national economy. Once the separate exploration and design activity has proved the commonality then the permanent documentation can recognize it. The documents describing the members of one set are likely to be bound together in a volume which can have an introductory section or subdivisions. The essential feature is that the commonality is exposed by prior separate development.

Document Plan forms Work Programme

Each of the document sets describes the whole project at one consistent level of detail. Project designers can review the project at each level for consistency and completeness before becoming immersed in the next level of detail. Design progresses one stage at a time thus enabling any omissions found on review to be incorporated with the minimum of disturbance of the design. The members of each set must be completely identified before commencing their detailed documentation since their parent entities may well be adequately served by common members. An Exchange intended to retrieve a master record, for example, could well serve Conversations for inquiry, amendments or cancellation. The diagram in Chapter 4 illustrates this point. The review step for one stage reduces duplication of the members of the next by defining the smallest set of members required in it. A project of 15 conversations might throw up 35 exchanges during conversation design. After review of the conversation specifications the set of exchanges might be reduced to 30 by dropping exact, or combining near, duplicates.

So the different sets of documents are developed in the sequence—members within sets—this fact alone providing a broad plan for systems design. The detail is provided from the requirements of each level for data. Each member of a set will have a specification and the specification of members of each set follows a predetermined pattern. The specifications are divided into sections and each section effectively poses a question which must be answered. The work of each level is thus defined by the investigation necessary to answer the questions. The early documents—procedure specifications—require answers to questions concerning fallback, recovery, conversion and security, thus fulfilling the requirement laid down in Chapter 2 that these matters be considered early in design. The sequence of documents and the contents of each provides a work programme for the design team which, when followed, will produce a complete and robust design.

Document Sections form a Filing Plan

This regimented sequence of work, while standardizing the approach to design, should not constrain originality. Bright ideas will not occur exactly when required by the planned sequence of activities and if not recorded at the time, could be lost. The various sections of the different specifications can be used to perform another function—that of file headings. Before starting a project the structure of documents and document sections is known and can be used as the source of names of files to collect working papers thrown up at any earlier stage. When conducting surveys or interviews, for instance, points will be covered which are not necessarily relevant to the work in hand, but might be relevant to the design of some lower level unit or even some equivalent unit not yet under investigation. Memoranda or handwritten notes can be filed for future reference under the appropriate subsection. The identity of the relevant entity, two or more levels removed, may not be known at the time of originating an item relevant to its design. For that set, general files subdivided by specification section but not by member will be sufficient for the time being. As the members are identified the collected material can be broken up.

For a filing system like this to work, a method of referencing the entities and document sections is necessary. A multi-part reference seems most appropriate to identify:

Project—by some code   e.g. OP for order processing

Member—a serial or mnemonic reference   e.g. A2 for invoice correction conversation

Entity and Section—document reference   e.g. D263 for conversation diagram

Reviews Enforce Quality

Standards for content and layout of specifications discussed will vary in detail from installation to installation. Whatever precise standards are set, the success of the project design does depend upon them being followed. To ensure that standards are followed, all specifications at each level must be reviewed and an allowance made for this process in project work programmes.

Whatever standards are chosen, no data processing manager will be able to define the contents of each document section so precisely that all analysts will produce the same level of results on equivalent projects. Opinions will differ over the most convenient identification of conversations, how much work to do in an exchange, how precisely to define frequency distribution. The analysts on one installation will develop a common understanding of such matters over time if they review each other's work and periodically have their work checked by the chief designer.

Reviews should also involve the users of the system or their management on all matters concerned with the appearance of the project. In batch work, users are frequently asked to sign report designs as acceptable, so for real time systems, users should sign procedure specifications, entry and response layouts. The corporate management should lay down methods like these which have the added virtue of ensuring adequate and early staff consultation.

The documents produced during design should be reviewed for the presence of all sections, the completeness of the data included, the completeness of the cross-referencing between documents and finally, but most difficult, the quality of the design work.

WORK PROGRAMME FOR LOGIC DESIGN

Work to be Done

The work stages of Preliminary Systems Design were identified earlier in Figure 5.1.

The documentation required has been identified as:

(a) Procedure specifications.
(b) Conversation specifications.
(c) Exchange specifications.

To these must be added three more document sets concerned with the PSD stage of design work:

(a) Task descriptions.
(b) File specifications.
(c) Program synopses.

The term 'task' may need definition. The term is used during review of the existing system as a prelude to design. Tasks are equivalent to procedures but relate to the work of the user as it exists prior to the intrusion of the present project. It may be entirely manual or assisted by batch or earlier real time systems. The terms 'file' and 'program' have the same meaning as in batch systems. The six sets of documents together cover the data required to carry the logical design to a sufficient level of detail for management decision on implementation. The subsequent paragraphs of this section place their preparation in sequence and relate it to the PSD stages.

Existing Tasks must be Described

The Task Analysis step is one of straightforward fact gathering to identify the work areas concerned in the project. Task Descriptions are produced for tasks falling within the project scope and identify those parts of each task which could be assisted by computer conversations. The application is first surveyed to identify all the different users of the project, then for each, material describing each of his tasks is gathered by means of surveys, meetings, interviews and observation and is filed by reference to the sections of a Task Description prior to writing up. Task Description material may well be available from formal job descriptions. Such information should be tested by observation since a system designer is concerned with what is done by the users rather than what is believed by their management.

Computer Assistance can be Identified

The first EDP stage of design involves analysis of Task Descriptions to identify the candidate actions for computer assistance. Text books on system design will confirm that this should be done only after a searching review of alternative solutions involving the redesign of tasks or the reorganization of functions. After this, computer assistance can still be provided either by batch methods or real time and the most cost effective solution will frequently be a judicious mixture of the two. Before a company is deeply committed to real time, conversational methods will be more costly than batch so each instance of the method must be carefully evaluated.

The identification of conversation boundaries in extended tasks is somewhat arbitrary—as is the identification of runs in a batch system. While a conversation is an entity clearly related to an external event, the events are interconnected and several conversations may be needed to service one event. Sub-division is finally an arbitrary matter depending on experience. Since conversations set the project design parameters, their identification and specification must be done by experienced analysts. Skill is needed to design a conversation which assigns work to the user and machine in accordance with their different abilities.

Having identified a potential set of worthwhile conversations, the set should be critically reviewed for duplication or overlap to reduce the set of conversations to the minimum necessary for efficient use. Each approved conversation can then be assigned an identity which is added to the affected Task Descriptions for reference. Notes on the structure of the conversation or any thoughts about processing can be filed for future reference. The initial sections of each conversation can be completed to secure the interfaces between the different conversations of the project.

New Procedures will be Needed

The work done by users when the project conversations are available will be different from the work described in Task Descriptions. As a first step to proving the quality of the design, the users' work in the new situation is specified in Procedure Specifications, to demonstrate its acceptability to its users. There will initially be a one-to-one correspondence between the affected tasks and the new procedures. The existence of the project will probably throw up new procedures concerned with project housekeeping, such as the maintenance of master files or system tables which were not previously present. These will be identified and documented as design proceeds.

The Procedure Specifications emphasize heavily the issues of fallback, recovery, security and conversion, to ensure that designers build these aspects into the system from the beginning. These features may well expose the need for conversations additional to those already identified. Their initial sections should again be completed as they are identified.

Data concerning the frequency and distribution of procedure occurrence is collected by observation or by forecasts of later growth. The transaction volume data familiar from batch systems design is very similar and should present no new problems to skilled analysts.

Conversations can now be Designed

Work now proceeds to elaborate the nature of the computer solution. Each conversation is designed by drawing a conversation diagram which identifies the contributions of user and computer to the achievement of the conversation function. The completed diagram will permit the identification of the exchanges in a conversation. During this process some design decisions will be taken concerning computer processing, message content and data use, and notes can be filed according to the sections of later sets of specifications. As more conversations are designed, common exchanges will be recognized.

Terminal Use can be Classified

Before completing conversation design, initial decisions can be made on the types of terminal equipment appropriate to the project. Each conversation specification includes a section identifying the terminal types expected to be used. A variety of types exist and may have been requested:

(a) Display terminals (send and receive or receive only).
(b) Printer terminals (send and receive or receive only).
(c) Badge readers.
(d) Weighing machines.
(e) Microfilm displays (with and without keyboards).
(f) Other special terminals.

The range of terminal types identified during conversation design as desirable must be examined, either to reduce their variety or employ terminal types not requested but already in use in the installation. The range of types is limited with a view to economy and interchangeability.

Exchanges are Selected to Minimize Installation

During conversation design, the exchanges necessary to implement each conversation will be identified. Before those exchanges are designed, the entire set for all conversations is reviewed deliberately to reduce the set to the minimum by cutting out any duplication. Similar exchanges may, with a little modification, be combined, with a consequent saving in programs and hence implementation cost.

As mentioned, some activities in a real time system can be initiated automatically. The set of exchanges should therefore be further reviewed for opportunities to substitute automatic stimuli for user entries. Such activities will still be documented at the exchange level but could save user effort or improve project design. The set of exchanges should now be assigned identities for cross-reference purposes and their initial sections written—purpose, entry content and response content.

The identification of exchanges can be tested by reviewing their interconnection as defined by their parent conversations. The ability of common exchanges to function in their different conversations will ratify the design decisions made in identification.

Computer Elements are Identified in Exchange Specifications

The central task in exchange design is to flowchart the processing to identify its major program elements—such as validating message content, retrieving and updating records and constructing responses. Each task would deserve a separate box on the exchange flowchart. Any references to files should be shown as records are retrieved. As more exchanges are designed and charted, common functions will be recognized in several exchanges. These will be a likely source of subroutines or common programs. The final identification of application programs will depend upon a thorough knowledge of the functions undertaken by the real time software with which the project will run.

Other important sections of an exchange specification concern the content of its entry and its various responses and their response time requirements. There may well be a variety of responses produced by an exchange which may be classified as normal, associated and error. Associated responses are those appearing on terminals other than the one from which the original entry was made.

Exchanges are normally employed in the context of conversations. The context is important because data must be passed from one to the other and the execution of one exchange frequently determines what subsequent exchanges are permitted. Both these aspects of context must be defined.

Transmission Network can be Designed

The exchange specifications complete the identification of the sources of significant load on the data transmission network. The load will dictate the network, the amount of terminal equipment and its installation. The degree of concentration of terminals, the consequent number at a location, the volume of terminal control units and transmission line speed, all depend upon this data. The necessary level of back up in the event of a terminal, control unit or line failure can be determined for the purpose of network design.

The General Arrangement of Data is Designed

The tentative file identities used in exchange design can now be consolidated in file specifications. The general nature of the records and their contents can be identified and information concerning the record volumes, sizes and lives will provide source data for storage device capacity. The access methods to be employed will be determined at this time to confirm access times and the need for additional space for indices, overflow areas or low packing densities. The ability of available software to handle the access methods appropriate to real time will be an important factor in supplier selection.

Computer Element Development forms Installation Schedule

Programs and file records are now identified and rationalized for minimum installation effort. There are also opportunities for rationalizing entries and responses separately from their parent exchanges, since common entry and response formats can be used when the similarity of their contents permits. For example, the entry of a date or a customer name may be made with quite different processing implications in different exchanges. The difference in significance will not alter the similarity of format. The installation stage of formal specification will be reduced if common formats can be employed. This has the added advantage of creating a consistent appearance in the project for the user.

The computer elements to be installed are thus:

(a) Programs.
(b) Files and tables.
(c) Entries.
(d) Responses.

An installation schedule is thus composed of all the activities needed to implement the identified elements. Estimates for duration and effort are added to each using standard estimates for such work as specification, coding and testing. The installation work of conversion and site preparation is not so amenable to standard estimates but a good idea of the content of these areas will be available from the procedure specifications and the network design.

All the material is thus generated for the remaining work of the PSD phase. Economic evaluation and equipment selection tasks will have special problems but the source data has now been exposed.

Figure 5.2 summarizes the relationship between the major PSD phases and the activities discussed in this section.

PSD PHASE AND STEPS	DOCUMENTS USED	DOCUMENTS PRODUCED
Systems design		
Analyse tasks		Task description
Identify conversations	Task description	Conversation index
Design procedures	Conversation index	Procedure specifications
Design conversations	Procedure specifications	Conversation specifications
Identify exchanges	Conversation specifications	Exchange index
Identify terminal types	Conversation specifications	Terminal index
Design exchanges	Conversation specifications	Exchange specifications

(continued on page 80)

PSD PHASE AND STEPS	DOCUMENTS USED	DOCUMENTS PRODUCED
Systems design—cont.		
Accumulate traffic data	Procedure, conversation and exchange specifications	Network design
Design files	Exchange specifications	File descriptions
Installation plan		
Identify programs, files, entries and responses (elements)	Exchange and file specifications	Element indices
Classify elements by complexity	Element indices	Element schedules
Apply estimates	Element schedules	Work estimates
Plan file conversion	File specifications	
Plan site preparation	Procedure specifications and network design	
Plan system testing and conversion	Procedure and conversation specifications	
Prepare planning network and analyse plan		Installation schedule
Equipment and software selection		
Equipment parameters	Network and file specifications	
Evaluate software required	Conversation and exchange specifications	Software features schedule
Choose selection criteria		
Prepare specification book	Conversation and exchange specifications	System specifications for suppliers
Review manufacturers' proposals		
Negotiate contract terms		
Economic evaluation		
Estimate system development costs	Exchange and file specifications	
Estimate installation costs	Equipment schedules	
Estimate operating savings	Procedure specifications	

PSD PHASE AND STEPS	DOCUMENTS USED	DOCUMENTS PRODUCED
Economic evaluation—cont.		
Summarize overall economics		
Summarize intangible benefits		
Management approval		
Preliminary review approval	Conversation and procedure specifications	
Prepare written report	All	Proposal to management
Approve project		

Figure 5.2. Relationship between PSD work and documentation described in this chapter

Chapter 6

Documentation of Outline System

INTRODUCTION

Chapter Structure is Formal

What follows in this and the later chapters is in effect an outline of part of a systems standards manual. It does not specify paper size or how to layout forms but does describe the contents of documents produced by designers and, by implication, the work programme they will follow. The different sections of the chapters each describe the data necessary to specify a member of one of the sets of real time entities introduced earlier. A rapid idea of the contents of each document will be obtained by reading the contents lists of the chapters. The functions of the documents and the definition of the entities has been discussed in Chapters 4 and 5. The uses of each section of a document are indicated in this chapter.

The organization of each document is not the only one that could be developed, nor are the entities the only ones that could be devised. The documentation plan suggested is however intended to expose all the relevant data for the design of a successful real time project.

Sequence of Preparation

The documents will be introduced in the approximate sequence in which they will be developed. Each entity is not however documented in total without pause. The sequence of preparation is described in the previous chapter.

The documents of this chapter all relate to the design phase of a project and will commonly be prepared by systems analysts. Conversations should be identified, and procedures should be specified by experienced and skilful analysts. If desired, these documents can be used as the basis of an intermediate review by management and users of the quality of the design, before committing a larger team to the detailed specification of conversations, exchanges and files.

Design remains independent of exact hardware and software specifications throughout this phase of the work but their general nature will exert more influence on the detailed stages. When describing tasks, analysts are not even committed to a real time solution, whereas when specifying exchanges the designer must have a clear idea of the intended functions of real time software—if not the identity of the package. All of this work is done before selecting hardware and software and provides a sound basis for ensuring that these are determined by the project and not vice versa.

Success Depends upon Completeness

Each of these document standards is applicable to one set of entities. It has been an objective in designing them to permit each member of a set to be designed separately from its fellows. Once the set is complete, the individual documents can be bound together or filed differently. Any duplicated information can then be replaced by references to the sections of a common introduction. This is the only circumstance in which material should be omitted from a document. Otherwise all the sections should be present as a control that all the topics have been considered. The entire documentation set has been designed as a formal means of assembling all the information relevant to project design. So far as exposure and publication of design constraints can ensure that they are observed, this will generate a feasible solution to the project's objectives.

Standards cannot generate creativity however—this still depends on imagination and intelligence. No form of words can convey exactly the same meaning to large numbers of people in a situation as complex as the documentation of a project. Analysts can stick to the text of these definitions and still produce inadequate documentation. The final point that must be made is that the use of these standards does need commitment, enforcement and goodwill—they cannot be rules but they are offered as guidelines to good practice.

TASK DESCRIPTION

Introduction

To illustrate the application of the method advocated, an example of a task description is given—Figure 6.1. The example uses preprinted documentation forms but could as easily be written out on plain paper using the same headings. The data included is drawn from the example in Chapter 1. This document is a record of the current system.

The information recorded would be gathered by the usual analysis techniques of interview and observation. The latter is particularly important since to observe a task is a vital check on the accuracy of the information communicated in an interview. For the sake of brevity, familiarity with usual analyst techniques will be assumed.

The document carries reference numbers to assist in filing and cross-reference. The index number identifies the type of document while the item number identifies the particular occurrence.

A 'task' is not easily delineated but can be thought of as a potential work unit for measuring or scheduling clerical work. Tasks are usually repetitive

		C-151
		Index No.

COMPANY NAME _ABC. COMPANY._

	03
	Item No.

TASK DESCRIPTION WORKSHEET

SYSTEM DEVELOPMENT _CENTRALISED Ordering_

Prepared by: RC TOWNSEND	Reviewed by:	Approved by:
Date: SEPT 10, 1972	Date:	Date:

Name: INVOICE authorisATION

Function:

on Receipt of goods, Manager checks off his own Record of The order placed. Then, or if invoice is separately received he compares goods invoiced against goods received and ordered. if all Three documents match, he passes The approved invoice To Central office for issue of Cheque.

In The case of Part delivery and interim invoices, order is changed to show goods outstanding

Mechanisation benefit:

Follows upon centralisation of order records Supplier will send invoice directly To central office. Store Manager function will end when certified goods Received note is sent To central office

No change to warehouse Manager function in first phase.

References

Manuals: STORE operations Manual - Invoice certification

Procedures:

User/Location	Conditions	Usage
Store Manager -- every store Warehouse Manager	Receipt of invoice	VARIES by store size between 10-100 per day avge 30.

Figure 6.1. Task description documentation form

transactions such as taking an order, dealing with an enquiry or, as this is, approving an invoice.

Identifying Sections

The description will include material which will enable user staff familiar with the work to recognize it. The information should be sufficiently precise that a user can verify that it is complete and accurate.

Task identity can be established in several ways and the subsections shown are recommended:

(a) Item number.
(b) Name.
(c) Function—what work is done during the task;
(d) User—organizational titles of the different groups who perform the task;
(e) Location—organizational or geographic references to any different locations where each user group carries out the task.

Mechanization Benefit

This is the key to the initial identification of which tasks shall be computer assisted and whether by batch or real time methods. The observer should note the sources of benefit and classify them in terms of reduced cost or improved performance. Quantification is rarely possible in the first instance but will need to be done for affected tasks when conversations are chosen. This will justify the choice and provide source material for the project proposal.

References

Initially, the only references will be to existing procedure manuals or to the documentation of earlier computer projects. As this project proceeds, references to the new procedure and conversation specifications can be added.

Conditions

This section identifies the reasons for initiating an occurrence of the task. This information will assist the system designer to identify the factors governing frequency if the task is chosen for computer assistance. The material will also later help in deciding whether to provide for supporting conversations concerned with security or work allocation.

Usage

One of the criteria for selecting opportunities for computer assistance is going to be the number of people affected by the change or the number of occurrences of the task. Computer assistance may be more valuable as the number affected increases. If the task is performed in a number of locations then the distribution of terminals may be affected. These aspects can be recorded as shown.

ABC COMPANY

D-260
Index No.

INVENTORY OF CONVERSATIONS   R. Townsend

CENTRALISED ORDERING SYSTEM   8.1.73

Item Number Index	Name	Used in Procedures	Real Time Class	Outline justification	Terminal Type	Peak Hour Approx. Volume	Peak Hour Timing
D-261-5							
A 1	Invoice Entry	A	Data Collection	Improves keying rate Saves entry of invoice detail	VDU/Full Keyboard	400(Invoice Batches)	Monday 10-11 a.m.
A 2	Invoice Amendment	A	Data Collection	Improves error correction cycle	VDU/Full Keyboard	250 (Invoice Batches)	Daily 9-10 a.m
B 1	Goods Received Note (Full Delivery) Entry	B	Data Collection	Permits entry of variations from order only & puts data per item	VDU/Numeric Keyboard	250(GRN Batches)	Wednesdays 10-11 a.m.
B 2	Goods Received Note (Part Delivery) Entry	B	Data Collection		VDU/Full Keyboard	300(GRN Single)	Wednesdays 10-11 a.m.
C 1	Sign On/Sign Off	C	File Update (Memo)	Housekeeping-to provide forms on screen for data entry		40	Daily 8-9 a.m.
C 2	Recovery	C	Enquiry	Housekeeping-to establish last form entered		Nil	
D 1	Supervisor Assignment	D	File Update (Memo)	Support security of facilities by assigning status and work type	VDU/Full Keyboard	65	Daily 8-9 a.m

Figure 6.2. Inventory of conversations documentation

CONVERSATION IDENTIFICATION

Introduction

Conversations are the first computer entities identified in the project. The set of conversations defines the scope of the computer processing in the real time project and the users' interaction with it. The work performed at this time is either creative—when the analyst can make decisions on the scope—or routine if the scope is self evident. The latter may be the case if the use of real time is well established for the industry or business function.

The documentation proposed is illustrated in Figures 6.2 and 6.3—an inventory of all the conversations and a worksheet for each one. Since the purpose is to review the set of conversations to produce the least set which will achieve the project's purpose, the inventory uses a tabulation format.

Inventory of Conversations

The example shows that there are more sources of conversations than the explicit business functions served by the project. There will be a need for conversations for such purposes as supervising the direct users, controlling the use of terminals, interrogating the system and performing privileged functions in connection with restarting the system after a failure. In a large system needing careful control and rapid recovery, without extensive real time control software these sources of conversations may generate more coding than the business functions. Such facilities are not always evident or publicized in installed systems but the need for such conversations will become evident as the design progresses.

The various parts of Figure 6.2 are described below.

Identity

As each conversation is selected it is assigned a unique item number and name for identification in filing and cross-reference. The procedures in which the conversation appears will be added as the design progresses.

Class

Some sense of the work necessary to design and specify the conversation and its constituent elements can be gained from relating the conversation to one of the classes in Chapter 3. Even in the simplest system, one or two of the supplementary conversations may involve file updating.

Justification

This states the grounds for selecting this part of a task for computer assistance. The criteria used to select conversations are similar to those used for selecting projects—economic, or to support another conversation which is economically justified.

Terminal Type

This is a reference to the type of terminal preferred for the interactive part of the conversation. There may be other terminals involved in responses made to a user other than the one who conducts the conversation. There will be two parts to the terminal, the input and output. A visual display unit (VDU) will be a frequent output medium while a keyboard is a usual input.

Volume

An indication of the volume of the conversations from all sources during a peak hour can be developed from the tasks' volumes. The timing of the peak hour is also useful data at this early stage although it will be superseded by more accurate estimates as the design is developed. At this time the data helps in the review of the scope of the system if this needs to be limited.

Information Worksheet

As each conversation is added to the index a start can be made on the specification by starting a worksheet—Figure 6.3. The main section is entitled Description. Its purpose is to describe the function of the conversation and processing to be achieved. A simple title on the index is unlikely to convey this information. If the conversation is at all complex the expected sequence of exchanges can also be described. The remainder of the form comprises two groups of information—relationship with procedures and secondly the linkage with preceding and following conversations.

Relationship to Procedures

The procedures will not yet be identified but the relationship will be documented later. If the conversation is not mandatory within the procedure, this section can be used to show under what conditions the conversation is used. The 'frequency' section is intended to convey the rate of repetition within one procedure.

Linkage

The conversation may be intended to be used alone in support of a procedure or it may be used in various combinations of other conversations to service several procedures. For example, the amendment of a customer record might involve at minimum a Retrieval conversation followed by an Amend Record conversation. The Retrieval conversation would probably service other procedures such as Cancellation or Customer Enquiry.

		D 261
		INDEX NO.

COMPANY NAME: ABC Company

A1
ITEM NO.

CONVERSATION INFORMATION WORKSHEET

SYSTEM DEVELOPMENT: Centralized Ordering System

PREPARED BY: R. Townsend	REVIEWED BY:	APPROVED:
DATE: 8-2-73	DATE:	DATE:

NAME: Invoice Entry Conversation

DESCRIPTION:

Invoice batches are entered in one message. For each invoice the order and invoice references are entered together with total data only. The entry will only be validated for format. Logical validation against outstanding order and goods received will take place in batch system.

The batch data is output to a log file. If the batch is out of balance it is marked to prevent processing in batch system and an offline error report will be generated. Batch errors and logical errors found in batch validation will be corrected by correction Conversation A-2 at a later date before invoices are due for payment.

REF.	PROCEDURE	CONDITIONS	FREQUENCY
A.	Invoice Entry	Mandatory	one per Invoice Batch

DATA BROUGHT FORWARD	DATA PASSED ON
Operator Identity	Operator Identity
Procedures Authorized	Procedures Authorized
Current Procedure	Current Procedure
	(may be changed at end of conversation)
Operator Performance Statistics to Date	Updated Operator Performance Statistics
Supplier of Last Batch	Supplier of Current Batch

Figure 6.3. Conversation information worksheet

This section describes such linkages by identifying:

(a) data brought forward from earlier conversations
(b) data passed on to subsequent conversations.

The processing environment provides, in the Conversation Control Record (CCR), a means for allowing data to be passed between adjacent conversations and consecutive exchanges within conversations. The section defines the logical content of the Conversation Control Record before and after this conversation, thus establishing the interfaces of the conversation in different situations.

In the illustrative system described in Chapter 1, an Amend Record conversation would update a record already copied into the amending terminal's CCR by the Retrieval conversation.

D-150
Index No.

ABC COMPANY

INVENTORY OF PROCEDURES

CENTRALISED ORDERING SYSTEM

R. Townsend
8.4.73

Item Number Index		Name	Location	Users	Origin
D - 151/2/3					
	A	Invoice Entry Procedure	Central Office	Data Entry Clerks, Data Entry Supervisor	Existing System
	B	Goods Received Note Entry Procedure	Central Office	Data Entry Clerks, Data Entry Supervisor	This System
	C	Clerk Sign On	Central Office	Data Entry Clerks, Data Entry Supervisor	Housekeeping
	D	Supervisor Monitoring		Data Entry Supervisor, Central Office Manager	This System

Figure 6.4. Inventory of procedures

	D 151
	INDEX NO.

COMPANY NAME __ABC Company__

ITEM NO. __A__

PROCEDURE INFORMATION WORKSHEET

SYSTEM DEVELOPMENT __Centralized Ordering__

PREPARED BY R. Townsend	REVIEWED BY M. Bonlam	APPROVED
DATE 8-5-73	DATE 8-10-73	DATE

PROCEDURE NAME __Invoice Entry__

DESCRIPTION:

Enters Invoice totals in batches. Subsequent batch processing matches invoice totals to totals predicted from goods received data and prevailing prices. Invoices which don't match will then have further data entered to identify differences in quantity or price. If totals still don't match invoice extensions must be incorrect. Incorrect data is entered so that invoice may be reconciled to total and payment made. At this time any batch balancing errors are investigated and cleared.

See attached chart for document flow.

CONVERSATIONS

ITEM NO.	NAME
A-1	Invoice Entry
A-2	Invoice Amendment

CONDITIONS

USER/LOCATION	STIMULUS	AUTHORITY
Data Entry Clerk	Receipt of Invoice Batch	Supervisor assigns workload.
Data Entry Supervisor	"	

MANNING

USER/LOCATION	DURATION	HOUR PEAK/FREQUENCY	PEAK MANNING
Data Entry Clerk	2 Parts : —	1000 batches/hour	40
	1. 150 sec/batch		
	2. 10 sec/invoice error	1800 Errors/hour	5
	+ 20 sec/batch error	500 Error batches/hr.	2
	+ 2 sec/batch	(for details see	1
		attached frequency	48
		chart)	

Figure 6.5. Procedure information worksheet

Company Name __A B C Company__

Flow Chart Paper ☐ System Chart-Application __Centralised Ordering__

☐ Program Logic-Run Name __Invoice Entry__ No. _____

Routine Name __Procedure__ No. _____

A ITEM NO.

D-151/1 INDEX NO.

Prepared by R. Townsend.	Reviewed by	Approved by
Date 8.5.73	Date 8.25.73	Date

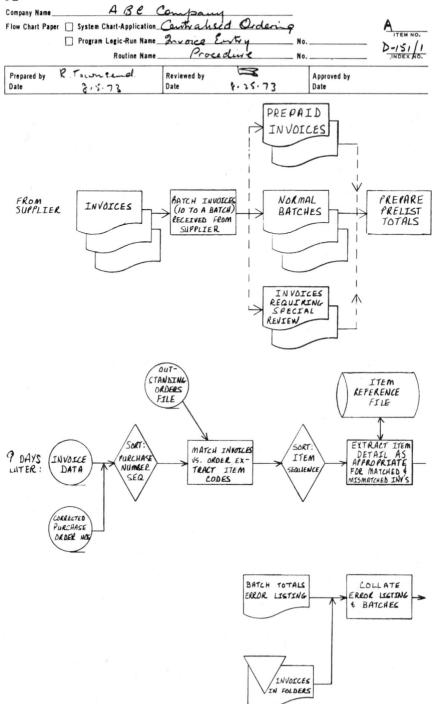

Figure 6.6. Invoice data entry

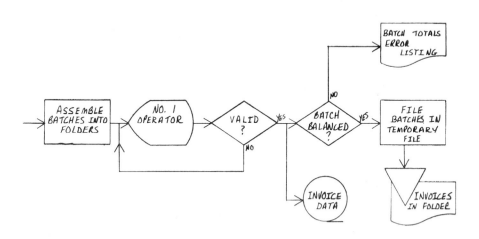

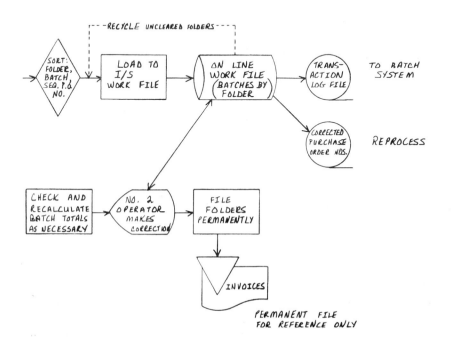

PERMANENT FILE
FOR REFERENCE ONLY

PROCEDURE SPECIFICATION

Identification

The procedures included in the project are assigned item numbers in much the same way as in conversations. An index is drawn up as illustrated in Figure 6.4. The procedure specification contents are illustrated in the series of Figures 6.5 to 6.9.

Description

The description section of Figure 6.5 is a statement to identify the procedure. If there is a close relationship with a current task then this section will refer to the relevant task specification. If the procedure is new and concerned with supporting the project, then a full description of the reason for the procedure will be necessary. If the procedure has functions similar to those of a current task, but the project has caused significant changes or combinations with other tasks, then the effect caused by the project should be described. The conversation(s) employed while performing the procedure should be identified at this point. If several conversations are used, a diagram showing the sequence and any conditions which modify it, may be helpful. An example is shown in Figure 6.6.

Conditions

This section is similar to the corresponding section of the task description. It presents the logical conditions in which the procedure will be used. It is necessary when the project has caused significant changes to work methods.

This material confirms that the project requirements have been understood and records any new security constraints to be implemented in exchange design.

Manning

Manning involves a tabulation of the data needed to determine the number of staff necessary to carry out the procedure at each location. If the frequency pattern is at all complex then this information is best conveyed by a frequency diagram as shown in Figure 6.7. The diagram should identify the major cycles and the peaks in each to identify the need for management attention to smoothing, to ensure that the highest peak remaining is identified. It is this which will determine the peak manning level.

For each user type at each location, the demand for staff for the procedure can be determined at the period being considered either by graphical or analytical means. The necessity for queueing theory will depend on the nature of the stimulus of the procedure—telephone calls will justify it, for example. Any reduction in staff numbers made possible by sharing procedures between different user groups at the same location should be noted. The total

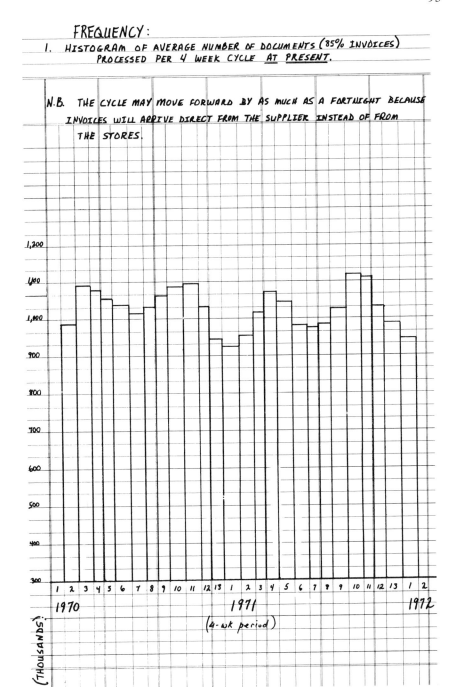

FREQUENCY:

1. HISTOGRAM OF AVERAGE NUMBER OF DOCUMENTS (85% INVOICES) PROCESSED PER 4 WEEK CYCLE AT PRESENT.

N.B. THE CYCLE MAY MOVE FORWARD BY AS MUCH AS A FORTNIGHT BECAUSE INVOICES WILL ARRIVE DIRECT FROM THE SUPPLIER INSTEAD OF FROM THE STORES.

Figure 6.7. Frequency diagram

96

<table>
<tr><td colspan="3"></td><td>D 152</td></tr>
<tr><td colspan="3">COMPANY NAME ABC Company</td><td>INDEX NO.
A</td></tr>
<tr><td colspan="3">PROCEDURE SUPPORT WORKSHEET</td><td>ITEM NO.</td></tr>
<tr><td colspan="4">SYSTEM DEVELOPMENT Centralized Ordering</td></tr>
</table>

PREPARED BY P. Townsend	REVIEWED BY M. Bonham	APPROVED BY
DATE 8 - 10 - 73	DATE 8 - 12 - 73	DATE

NAME Invoice Entry	WORK PAPER REF.

FALLBACK:

There is no business reason why fallback facilities for short interruptions of service need be provided as the procedure relates to the processing of documents not ongoing events. Work delayed can be performed when service is resumed.

For long periods — in excess of fifteen minutes — there would be difficulty in catching up the backlog so alternative facilities must be available. User management has stated that alternative methods of data entry would be too complex and laborious. Consequently, alternatives to each piece of central [G 210/1] site equipment must be available to allow service to be resumed. The system should write duplicate [G 211/4] copies of each file that it updates on separate [I 400/CCR] devices.

At central office spare terminals will be available to stand in for malfunctioning terminals.

RECOVERY:

There is no requirement for special recovery procedures to catch up the backlog after a breakdown. All that is required is a facility to determine the status of the message being processed at the time of failure. This [D261-C2] information can be extracted from the contents of the last filed copy of the CCR.

CONVERSION:

See general working paper E-330 Item 1 for system conversion approach.

TRAINING: As conversion is through progressive buildup of throughput operators can be trained in small groups through the conversion period. Turnover of VDU operators on present system is running at 10% per annum so a continuing [L410/1] training facility will be needed. Training files should [D261/D1] be set up for this purpose and a 'trainee' operator status be recognized.

Figure 6.8. Procedure support worksheet

requirements for a given user at a location can only be determined when all procedures affecting that user have been studied.

This material will be used to determine computer capacity required for conversations and to support the costs or benefits section of the project PSD report. Thereafter it will be used in manpower planning in user departments.

Fallback

In addition to the Information Worksheet and its exhibits other aspects of the procedure are described in Support and Processing Worksheets. Fallback is the first of the topics which will explore the less apparent but maybe more costly aspects of the project. The section states how the procedure will be performed if the computer facilities are not available for any reason. An example is shown in Figure 6.8. There may be variations of method depending on the length of time that the failure persists or the source of the problem. A breakdown in a single terminal is more easily overcome than a breakdown in the central computer. Any project design implications to support fallback which have not been previously discovered must be clearly identified—for example, additional project responses to provide a hard copy of VDU activity. Any difference in manning requirements between 'fallback' and 'normal' operation should be clearly indicated, since those might significantly alter the economics of the project.

Recovery

After a processing service is restored, any special action necessary to regain full project facilities must be designed—if this is not to be automatic. Recovery also includes the means by which a record of activity undertaken during a fallback period is conveyed to the computer system if necessary. This section may uncover the need for new conversations.

The manning requirements for recovery must be clearly defined. Recovery, as well as fallback, may pose an additional workload if special actions have to be taken. It will usually be desirable to resume normal working as soon as possible, leaving any entries to bring the system up to date for slack periods or overtime working. Projects which record demand for a scarce resource such as inventory may, however, have to make special entries to decrement online files to manually established levels to allow for the effect of the missing activity.

The time taken to recover after different periods of downtime should be estimated and recorded.

Conversion

The conversion period of implementation requires early and careful consideration by the designer. Conversion can be accomplished in many ways but however it is done the project users will experience a period of some difficulty since the direct contact between user and computer makes difficulties of equipment installation and errors in project programs, embarrassingly evident. Various strategies can be employed to reduce the stress of this period:

(a) conversations can be installed singly
(b) the project can be made available progressively by location
(c) the different terminal classes can be installed at different times
(d) the project can be made available progressively by user
(e) the project can be employed on less than the complete database.

Any of these strategies might need temporary facilities or raise problems in training or site preparation. An adequate treatment of this topic at this early stage in project design will assist in planning a smooth development and cutover period.

The particular aspects of conversion which should be described include training, interim procedures and manning changes. Training and the use of temporary procedures may both reveal further need for project facilities. During the conversion period, the need for training courses to be run concurrently with the continuation of current procedures can cause a temporary manning peak. The discussion of this aspect can include any information concerning the sources of such staff.

Information Processed

The next worksheet (Figure 6.9) is concerned with identifying the processing effect of the procedure. The first topic considered is that of the data processed. This is described under the subheadings of data sources, transformations performed and disposition of data. Transformations include any calculations that the user must make or decisions he takes based on the data presented. An example not related to the illustration might be the selection of invoices outstanding to match a payment received.

Controls

Controls over the data used are considered by procedure so that all requirements are exposed early and integrated into the design. Controls must be established to ensure that:

(a) all data received is presented to the system
(b) all data presented is valid
(c) errors are detected early
(d) all data accepted is safely maintained and its processing can be traced.

Performance Monitoring

Statistics may be collected in the course of processing to assist in reviewing the performance of users of the system or of the system design. The statistics collected should be a source of improvement in matters like keying accuracy, keying speed, computer utilization. Any new project requirements such as

D 153

INDEX NO

COMPANY NAME *ABC Company*

ITEM NO: *A*

PROCEDURE PROCESSING WORKSHEET

SYSTEM DEVELOPMENT *Centralized Ordering*

PREPARED BY	REVIEWED BY	APPROVED BY	
DATE	DATE	DATE	WORK PAPER REF.
NAME			

Invoice Entry

INFORMATION PROCESSED:

Sources: Invoice Data on Supplier, invoice and order identity and on invoice total amounts is transcribed from suppliers invoices. Data on expected value of the Invoice is extracted from the outstanding orders file updated by goods received data. Price information to value goods ordered or received is on the master Product file. In the event of discrepancies, quantities and prices invoiced and the invoice version of the extension will be transcribed from the invoice.

Transformations: goods received or ordered are priced by extending quantity on file by prevailing price at date of invoice on product file disposition.

Disposition: The approved invoices are passed for payment. Invoices queried are held in suspense.

CONTROLS:

Invoices are batched and batch controls created on VAT (Sales Tax) amount and number of outers. Invoice amount will be controlled by comparison with expected invoice amount. Order numbers will be verified by reference to the orders outstanding for the given supplier (batch system).

Failure of batch controls should generate a listing of the batch for subsequent review and correction during the correction phase. Check for duplicate batch numbers in one folder.

PERFORMANCE MONITORING:

Systems should maintain statistics on ¹⁾invoice totals which fail to match, ²⁾number of line items altered, and ³⁾keying errors by operator.

Figure 6.9. Procedure processing worksheet

100

COMPANY NAME *ABC Company*

INDEX NO.

A / 1

ITEM NO.

VERIFICATION OF *Procedure* WITH USER

SYSTEM DEVELOPMENT *Centralized Ordering*

PREPARED BY: *R. Townsend*	REVIEWED BY: *L Bonham*	APPROVED BY:
DATE: *8-15-73*	DATE: *8-20-73*	DATE:

NAME: *Invoice Entry*

USER GROUP: *Data Entry / Central Office*   REPRESENTATIVE: *Ken Damon*

COMMENTS	DISPOSITION
- the procedure should be convenient to use as now designed.	
- include direct orders (Placed and received by store manager, sent to central office for record purposes only)	Done R.T. 8/19/73
- provision should be allowed for supplier error in invoice extension	Done R.T. 8/19/73
- order number should be entered as its 3 component fields not as one.	Done R.T. 8/19/73
- statistics on mismatch errors may be high but are acceptable	
- the invoices should be entered as soon as received not kept until time to attempt match.	Done R.T. 8/19/73

USER APPROVAL: *K. Damon*   DATE: *8/20/73*

Figure 6.10. Verification of procedure

printed reports, supervisory conversations or operator conversations which are identified as a result of considering this topic should be added to the project documentation so far created.

Verification

Once the procedure has been designed in the respects listed above, many of the important topics peculiar to real time systems will have been revealed. As was shown in Chapter 2, the unique aspects of real time demand special features in computer systems: fallback, recovery, monitoring, conversion and others. By making these topics mandatory in predefined forms, the designer is forced to consider them.

Another unique aspect arising from the direct contact characteristic is the intense involvement of users in processing details. For this reason, a final form is associated with the procedure—a record of acceptance of the design by the user. This can only be completed thoroughly as a result of discussion with the respective users of procedures. Figure 6.10 illustrates a suitable form.

The chapter cannot be considered closed without a repetition of the warning that the use of predefined forms does not of itself guarantee that the analysis is thorough or the design suitable. However, the forms should restrict the likelihood of forgetting to deal with an important system feature.

Chapter 7

System Design

INTRODUCTION

With the verification of the design of procedures the general scope of the system is fixed and the functions which the computer system will perform are chosen.

The work now to be done is the development of the design to the point where files and programs can be identified. The feasibility of the design will then be apparent and enough will be known about the programming task to estimate development effort and running time.

The work proceeds in stages. The first is the specification of the conversations previously identified. The conversation design will identify the component exchanges. The complete set of exchanges can be reviewed for duplication and then each exchange is designed. The end product is the components of each exchange—programs or modules, files, entry and responses.

From this information, coupled with the volume data collected for the procedure design, the hardware aspects of the real time system can be investigated. The traffic in the data transmission network arising from the different locations of terminals can be applied to a map of those locations to determine the most economical means of connecting terminal and computer sites.

CONVERSATION SPECIFICATION

Conversation Diagram

The tool for planning the interaction between user and terminal is the conversation diagram. It is not only used as documentation of the end result but is a working paper used to illustrate concepts to users and redrawn until an acceptable scheme is devised. The designer's objective must be to achieve that division of labour between user and computer which best exploits their different skills, and trades off development effort against user effort.

The logical content of the diagram will be developed by reference to the outline of the conversation function prepared on the Conversation Information Worksheet discussed in Chapter 6. Other sources of information are the various documents of the Procedure specification and verification stage.

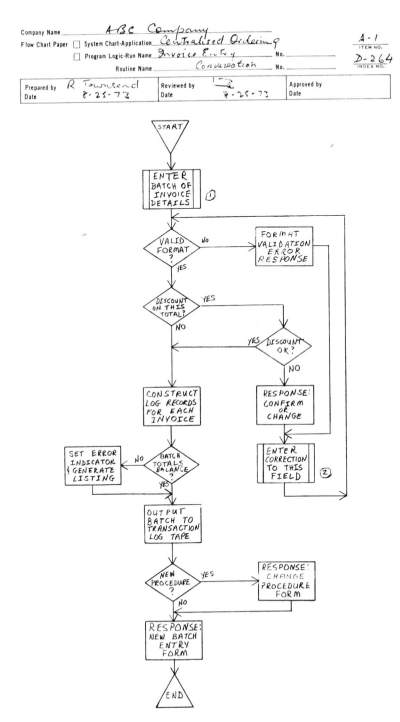

Figure 7.1. Conversation diagram for invoice entry conversation

Figure 7.1 shows the conversation diagram for one of the component conversations of the procedure illustrated in the previous chapter. As can be seen, it presents the components of the conversation in flowchart form. The components are user entries and computer responses. Where alternative entries are possible user decisions are shown. Similarly where computer processing can lead to alternative responses computer decisions will need to be shown. However computer processing is not shown at this level since the function of this diagram is to plan the interaction.

Each entry and its responses will subsequently form a separate exchange—or a potential exchange. There is no need to show minor validation responses and their consequent entries—the designer is identifying logically separate exchanges in the progress of the conversation.

The content of exchanges will be governed by the level of user skill, sources of data to be entered, extent of a user's other duties and the facilities available in the general class of terminal expected to be used. In a particular case, the designer may have a choice between one multi-field exchange or a series of exchanges each of which enters a single field to achieve the same result. The diagram is a design tool for working out a logical arrangement of exchanges.

There are a number of common patterns of conversation which have been identified over a number of years of experience (Martin, James, *Design of Man Computer Dialogues*, Prentice Hall, London, 1973). They can be roughly divided into prompted and unprompted and the prompted divide again into free form and fixed form. Fixed form conversations resemble the manual process of form filling—with the computer providing the form. Free form prompted conversations are like question and answer sessions—the computer asks the questions. If the answers can be presented in the forced choice used in some surveys and tests, the computer offers answers also. The list of answers is often referred to as a menu from which the user chooses items. In an unprompted conversation, the user is passing the computer data in a form which he has previously learnt. This form is paradoxically more appropriate in systems having many conversations since there is little opportunity for the computer to predict what the next conversation at a terminal will be. Unprompted conversations are used in many airline reservation systems for example.

The mechanics of diagramming are best kept simple. The only change to common symbol conventions is the introduction of a means of distinguishing user actions from computer actions. In Figure 7.1 user actions are shown in 'striped' boxes—entries or decisions. Rectangles and diamond shapes have their usual meaning.

Note that the concept of a loop applies in a conversation diagram and the economy of design implied should be deliberately exploited. A short series of actions repeated will mean more economical programming later. The use of loops will also help to keep the diagram simple.

This last should also be a design aim. If the diagram can be kept on a single page it will be easy to understand and explain. If too much paper is used then the conversation should probably be broken down further or else too much processing detail is being shown.

Processing Notes

In the course of developing the conversation diagram, the designer may well wish to note his initial ideas on the processing to be achieved. For example, the method of taking a conversation decision may be complex and so worth recording while the rules are still fresh. There are other issues concerning processing which should be considered at the conversation level. The recording of such material is most appropriate in narrative form so a conversation processing description is proposed.

A possible format, illustrated in Figure 7.2, includes predetermined headings as a guide to the matters to be covered. There are a series of topics which should be considered although not all of them will be relevant for all conversations.

(a) CONTRIBUTIONS TO DATA:
brief notes of any changes expected to be made to the data base as a result of the conversation. Timing considerations should be noted—for example, the need to decrement inventory during early exchanges of an order conversation.

(b) DATA SECURITY:
notes describing the reason for restricting access of other users to data used during the conversation. Material here should be limited to descriptions of reasons for preventing access throughout the conversation. This is different from the use of a 'read for update' facility to prevent access during an exchange which updates records.

(c) ERROR CORRECTION:
notes of particular correction technique planned.

(d) LINKS:
references to facilities of other conversations in this or other projects which may interface with this conversation or which could be employed in performing some of the processing or supplying some of the data used in the conversation.

(e) UNSOLICITED RESPONSES:
references to any activity on terminals in the network, other than the conversing terminal.

(f) SPECIAL STATIONERY:
identifies any hard copy responses which need special stationery, for example, preprinted documents or non-standard perforation distances.

(g) USER ACTIVITY:
notes of the basis on which a user takes decisions, assembles data for entries or uses responses.

Cross Reference	Key	Description
01	1	Invoice Entry
02	2	Invoice Entry Format Correction
		Notes
		Contributions to Data – the data collected will be written to a log file for the batch system. Two record types are written normally – batch header, invoice total item. The invoice total item will be marked if its order number has failed the check digit test.
		Error correction – format errors will be corrected progressively field by field as found. Because of this the entry must be maintained in the CCR between correction exchanges (02). The position reached and data field expected will also be stored there in these cases
		Unsolicited Responses
		Batch Totals Error Listing is printed on a separate device.
		Links – with other project facilities – none – with other occurrences of this conversation The folder, supplier, batch no and batch type can be implied. & Folder and supplier are as last entered until changed. Batch can be always last plus one, batch type is always 'normal' unless stated
		Stationery – special perforation may be required for Batch Totals Error Listing to economise on paper use while keeping one batch per page.
		Processing – check for duplicate order numbers in batch as extra validation Order numbers may be wrongly quoted on invoice so permit invalid check digit after confirmation Invoices with invalid or unmatched orders after batch processing will be held in suspense for correction conversation from listing Batch Totals list can be deliberately requested for balanced batches on special batch type

Figure 7.2. Conversation processing description

(h) PROCESSING:

narrative of the functions to be performed in the conversation. The Procedure Processing Worksheet should be reviewed in case the notes there can now be expanded to match components of the conversation diagram.

Testing Plan

The final document at the conversation level is the result of considering how to test the conversation. This is prepared for two reasons. Firstly, it will force

ABC COMPANY

CENTRALISED ORDERING SYSTEM — Index No. D-263

TESTING PLAN

INVOICE ENTRY CONVERSATION — Item No. A-1

Conditions	1	2	3	4	5	6	7	8	9	10
1. Order Number Invalid (twice)	X	X	X	X	X	X	X	X	X	✓
2. Discount Included?	X	X	X	✓	✓	✓	✓	✓	✓	X
3. Discount Query?				X	X	X	✓	✓	✓	
4. Batch Totals Balance?	✓	✓	X	✓	✓	X	✓	✓	X	✓
5. Special Batch?	X	✓	X	✓		X	✓		X	
Results										
1. Record to Transaction Log	✓	✓	✓	✓	✓	✓	✓	✓	✓	✓
2. Special Batch List Request		✓			✓			✓		
3. Batch Error List Request			✓			✓			✓	
Record to Suspense file (Batch System)									✓	
Response New Batch Entry Form	✓	✓	✓	✓	✓	✓	✓	✓	✓	✓
Conversation Interrupted to Clear Query						✓	✓	✓		

Figure 7.3. Testing plan for invoice entry conversation

the conversation designer into a 'desk check' of his design. This ensures that the conversation will be correctly processed under all permitted conditions identified in the conversation diagram. Secondly, the test cases will provide useful source material for the conversation stage of testing towards the end of installation.

Figure 7.3 shows a test plan for the conversation illustrated earlier. This example has used a decision table format. The 'conditions' of the table can be identified initially from the decisions of the conversation diagram but other conditions still hidden by the lack of detail on that diagram will occur to the designer. For example, unusual data situations such as zero items, maximum and minimum values and settings of indicators might require a different path through the exchanges which constitute the conversation than that indicated by the diagram. The 'cases' of the table will be all the possible combinations of the conditions listed. The 'outcomes' should be those desired by the designer and those implied by the design. A deliberate check that these are identical with each other will verify the completeness of the design.

Verification of Design

The process of consulting with the users over design issues which will be visible to them, is continued with conversation design. The users may well have useful comments on the sequence of exchanges or the viability of asking staff to take the role planned for them. At the very least, positive acceptance of the planned design is a good check on the designer's understanding of the problem.

This step is not being fully exploited unless a full presentation of the conversation is made with participation by the user in the discussion. A record of the meeting, comments offered, and action taken, should be made (see the example in Figure 7.4). The meeting may of course cover more than one conversation but a separate record for each will concentrate attention. A final indication of user satisfaction with the result will provide some assurance that the step has been thoroughly carried out.

MESSAGE PLANNING

Although it is not yet appropriate to plan the entries and responses needed for a conversation in great detail, this is a good time to write down the data which will be used or displayed and to prepare samples for discussion with the people who will have to use them. Samples of the type shown in Chapter 1 can be supported by message worksheets such as those illustrated in Figures 7.5 and 7.6.

The form permits some documentation of message lengths and frequencies to aid subsequent telecommunications network planning. Message lengths can be deduced from accumulating field lengths allowing for the identification of optional and variable-length fields. These characteristics can vary depending on the conversation or exchange in which the entry is being used. The same entry format can be used in exchanges having a quite different purpose.

COMPANY NAME _ABC Company_

INDEX NO. _D - 265_

ITEM NO. _A - 1 / 1_

VERIFICATION OF _Conversation_ WITH USER

SYSTEM DEVELOPMENT _Centralized Ordering_

| PREPARED BY: _R. Townsend_ | REVIEWED BY: _L. Bonham_ | APPROVED BY: |
| DATE: _8-26-73_ | DATE: _8-30-73_ | DATE: |

NAME: _Invoice Entry_

USER GROUP: _Data Entry / Central Office_   REPRESENTATIVE: _Ken Damon_

COMMENTS	DISPOSITION
– an entire batch should be entered in one entry	Done R.T. 8/27/73
– the batch total errors should be left for correction in the second conversation	Done R.T. 8/27/73
– what if supplier misquotes order number? System should provide for invoice to proceed for investigation after batch number.	Done R.T. 8/27/73
– permit procedure change request to be entered with each entry	Done R.T. 8/28/73

USER APPROVAL: _K. Damon_   DATE: _8/30/73_

Figure 7.4. Verification of conversation

COMPANY NAME ABC Company

ENTRY INFORMATION WORKSHEET

SYSTEM DEVELOPMENT Centralized Ordering

PREPARED BY: B. Cook	REVIEWED BY: R. Townsend	APPROVED BY:
DATE: 9-15-73	DATE: 9-20-73	DATE:

NAME Invoice Total Data Entry

PURPOSE To enter invoice total information and batch controls in initial invoice entry and batch total correction.

	CONV EXCH	A1/01	A-2/01	A-2/07		
LENGTH (CHARS)	AVGE	429	73	42		
	MAX	709	85	50		
	MIN	56	56	30		

	DATA INCLUDED		APPROX. LENGTH			FREQUENCY			
SEQ	DATA DESCRIPTION	JUSTIFICATION COMMENTS	AV.	MAX.	MIN.	CONV EXCH	AV.	MAX.	MIN.
10	Folder Number	To identify batch of batches	6			A1/01	.1	1	0
15	Supplier Number	To verify supplier	6			A1/01	.1	1	0
		- both only necessary on folder change							
20	Batch Number	Identity of Batch	2				1		
60	Order Number	To match invoice against order GRN							
	- Store	- will be repeated in initial	4						
	- Date	entry, quoted once only in	4						
	- Suffix	batch correction, not at all in totals correction.	3						
70	Invoice Number	To identify invoice to supplier on payment	4			A1/01	7	12	1
						A2/01	1		
80	Invoice Date	To determine time limit for claims and payment (10 & 28 days after invoice date)	4			A1/01	7	12	1
						A2/01	1		
90	Invoice VAT amount	Statutory requirement to record VAT on every payable	3	7	3	A1/01	7	12	1
						A2/01	1		
100	Invoice Value	Amount Payable-Gross	4	7	3	A1/01	7	12	1
						A2/01	1		
120	Discount		4	7	3	A1/01	.2	.4	.05
						A2/01	.05		
130	Invoice Net		4	7	3	A1/01	.2	.4	.05
						A2/02	.05		
140	Outers Count	To assist in assigning claim to supplier or carrier	3	3	1	A1/01	7	12	1
						A2/01	1		
30	Batch Total VAT	Batch Control / Data accuracy	4	7	3	A1/01	1		
						A2/01	1		
40	Batch Total Outers	Batch Control / Data accuracy	3	3	1	A1/01	1		
						A2/07	1		

Figure 7.5. Entry information worksheet

COMPANY NAME *ABC Company*

D-641
_____
INDEX NO.

RO1
_____
ITEM NO.

RESPONSE INFORMATION WORKSHEET

SYSTEM DEVELOPMENT *Centralized Ordering*

PREPARED BY: *B. Cook*	REVIEWED BY: *R. Townsend*	APPROVED BY:
DATE: *9-17-73*	DATE: *9-20-73*	DATE:

NAME *Invoice Totals Data Entry*

PURPOSE *To provide a format for the entry of a batch of invoices, a single invoice, or a set of batch totals.*

LENGTH (CHARS)	CONV EXCH	A-1/01	A-2/01	A-1/02	A-2/03	A-2/07	C-1/12		
	AVGE								
	MAX								
	MIN								

SEQ.	DATA DESCRIPTION	DATA INCLUDED — JUSTIFICATION COMMENTS	APPROX. LENGTH AV.	MAX.	MIN.	CONV EXCH	FREQUENCY AV.	MAX.	MIN.
10	FOLDER NO.] folder [	Folder number is quoted except on change of procedure	17			ALL	1		
20	BATCH NO.]__[		13			ALL	1		
30	SUPPLIER NO.] supplier [	Supplier no. is quoted except on change of procedure	20			ALL	1		
40	BATCH TYPE]_[		13			A-1 01	1		
						A-1 02	1		
						C-1 12	1		
50	Head Line See D642-T02	Heading of columns for entry of invoices	77			ALL	1		
55	Sub Head Line (T05)	Breakdown of Order No.	17			ALL	1		
60	Batch Totals Heading See D642-T03		41			ALL	1		
70	Invoice Total Entry line See D642-T04		80			A2/01	1		
						A2/03	0		
						A2/07	1		
						other	12		
80	Procedure Change Test See D642-T01	opportunity to change duty.	28			A2/03	0		
						A2/07	0		
						other	1		

Figure 7.6. Response information worksheet

Responses may very well contain literals and the convention proposed for this feature is to quote the literal value in upper case. If the literals are common to several messages then they can be considered as standard text and listed in a register. The worksheet then contains a reference to the register entry (see the field with sequence number 50 on Figure 7.6).

Note that the message lengths developed on these forms relate to data content only. An overhead will be necessary for control characters in order to develop complete estimates of data transmitted. However this factor will not be known until the terminal equipment is identified.

Schedules of entries, responses and standard text should be developed to control the assignment of their identities and to hold cross-references. These are simple lists and are not illustrated. The lists will also permit review for opportunities to make similar items identical and so save later effort.

So far as the user is concerned, the tabular presentation of data will not be meaningful. For discussion purposes samples of the messages would be prepared in the form used to illustrate Chapter 1. These can also be filed with the more formal descriptions since they will better convey a sense of the intended appearance to project staff.

EXCHANGE SPECIFICATION

Inventory of Exchanges

As the conversations of the project are planned their component exchanges will be identified. A list of these exchanges will provide a plan for developing the project to the next level of detail. Before actually commencing specification, the list should be reviewed for opportunities to reduce the number of exchanges by combining similar exchanges from different conversations. Figure 7.7 shows part of the list for the system described in Chapter 1. This format can be modified but the cross-reference function 'used in Conversations' is important and should be included on any list.

Automatic Exchanges

The inventory of exchanges includes one example said to be initiated automatically rather than manually. This classification needs a few words of explanation.

So far the discussion has centred on interaction between a user and the computer system. In many systems this mode of operation will be adequate. However, there are some activities for which the initiating event is better triggered by the computer itself.

A modern machine will include a means of representing the passing of time ('clock') and of causing interruptions to processing based on clock values. The interruption can be at an absolute time or after a defined interval. Added to this the computer has always been programmed for counting.

ABC COMPANY

CENTRALISED ORDERING

INVENTORY OF EXCHANGES

D-270
INDEX NO.

ITEM NO.

R. Townsend
8.30.73.

Item Reference	Name	Method of Initiation	Used in Conversations	Frequency per Conversation %
D-271-4/				
01	Invoice Entry	Manual	A - 1	100
			A - 2	5
02	Invoice Entry Format Correction	Manual	A - 1	10
03	Invoice Enquiry	Manual	A - 2	100
04	Invoice First Amendment	Manual	A - 2	65
05	Invoice Second Amendment	Manual	A - 2	15
06	Invoice Order No. Correction	Manual	A - 2	15
07	Invoice Batch Total Correction	Manual	A - 2	20
08	GRN Full Delivery Entry	Manual	B - 1	100
09	GRN Batch Total Correction	Manual	B - 1	25
			B - 2	25
10	GRN Part Delivery Entry	Manual	B - 2	100
11	Recovery/Start of Day	Manual	C - 1	100
			C - 2	100
12	Procedure Initiation	Manual	C - 1	100
13	Supervisor End of Day	Automatic	C - 2	100
14	Abandon Batch Balancing	Manual	A - 2	5
			B - 1	5
			B - 2	5

Figure 7.7. Inventory of exchanges

The computer is undoubtedly more reliable in performing activities such as counting or measuring the passage of time. The use of such attributes in real time systems is not hard to illustrate. In airline systems, for example, certain events can be programmed to occur at times relative to a flight departure.

Reservations at city centre offices should not be allowed within say one hour of departure. Activities triggered on a counter can be illustrated by a performance monitoring function in which a log record holding counters is written away after every 100 exchanges.

A designer faced with a list of potential exchanges should not only review it for potential duplicates, he should look also for opportunities to replace manual actions with automatic events. This can be both a saving in user activity and an improvement to system design by ensuring that a key event takes place.

Automatic events are classified as exchanges—at least for documentation purposes. The full set of exchanges identified in the schedule will therefore potentially include both types.

Exchange Worksheet

Once the approved list is finalized each exchange can be specified in its own right. A specification can be written in narrative form or by use of a series of worksheets as illustrated below.

The first figure (Figure 7.8) is of a worksheet containing the general description of the exchange. The 'purpose' section acts both as an introduction to identify the exchange and a statement of the reason for its existence. The reason must be defined in plain language understandable to the project's users, as it documents a component of the project in which they are deeply interested. Analysts and programmers will also benefit from being reminded of the place the exchange occupies in the logic of its parent conversations. If the exchange is not in the mainstream of a conversation then the conditions which govern its use must be clearly stated. If the results of the exchange are complex, then the section may mention the generation of associated responses, and subordinate activities, to provide an introduction to the remainder of the exchange specification.

The various components of the exchange, namely its initiating entry or automatic event, consequent responses, files and programs or modules, can be identified as the design proceeds. So far as the responses are concerned, they are described in respect of their frequency of occurrence and desired response time. They are subdivided between 'normal' and 'associated'. Normal responses are those returned to the initiating terminal while associated responses are sent to other terminals. An automatic exchange will have no normal responses since it has no initiating terminal. There must always be one normal response for an entry initiated exchange but only one will occur for a particular instance of the exchange. The frequencies of 'normal' responses should therefore add to 100%. Associated response frequencies may sum to more or less than 100% since they may be optional and need not be mutually exclusive.

Error responses may well be the most demanding in their response time requirements since they need to occur before the user's attention is turned to the next normal exchange. They are listed separately with a reference to the correcting exchange since this will be out of the normal sequence.

	D 271
	INDEX NO.

COMPANY NAME _ABC Company_

EXCHANGE INFORMATION WORKSHEET

ITEM NO. _01_

SYSTEM DEVELOPMENT _Centralized Ordering_

PREPARED BY: _B. Cook_	REVIEWED BY: _N. Townsend_	APPROVED BY:
DATE: _9-2-73_	DATE: _9-10-73_	DATE:

NAME: _Invoice Batch Initial Entry_

PURPOSE:

Permits entry of total values of invoice batch. Checks for and reports format errors immediately. Checks for and marks batch errors for subsequent correction.

Batches are written to a transaction file together with batch trailers for subsequent processing in batch system.

Batch errors generate an associated response on a line printer for offline investigation and correction.

The normal response is an empty form for next entry. Exchange design has been chosen for maximum keying speed leaving exceptions for a seperate less frequent exchange at a different time.

ENTRY ITEM _EO1_ PROGRAMS _HAP400 HAP401   HAP350_

RESPONSES

ITEM	TYPE	FREQ.	TIME	RESPONSE TURNROUND TIME JUSTIFICATION
RO1	N	99	5 sec	Batch end after 2-3 mins keying permits medium response
RO2	N	01	100 sec	change of occupation - no rush
RO3	A	10	12 hours	corrected offline on next day
RO4	A	2	12 hours	''

FILES				ERRORS		
ITEM	NAME	USE		ITEM	TIME	CORRECTION
HAF200	Conversation Control	U		RO5	2 sec	Progressive - D271-02
HAF201	Transaction Log File	A				

Figure 7.8. Exchange information worksheet

The programs and files are identified from the exchange diagram discussed below. The file 'use' is a further note on project logic indicating whether the file is read for reference (R), whether records are altered (U), added (A) or deleted (D). Another more extreme possibility is marking the record so that no other conversation can alter it before the current conversation is completed in a later exchange (see Data Security in Processing Notes of a conversation specification).

Exchange Diagram

The main design aid for identifying the exchange components and planning the details of the processing of the project is the exchange diagram. It is similar in structure to a batch system flowchart since it identifies input, file accessing, processing and output. It relates though to a single entry—equivalent to all or part of a batch system transaction. It is as if a system flowchart were drawn for the progress of a single transaction through a batch system—not a bad idea for checking batch system logic but not often done. An example is shown in Figure 7.9 for the initial entry exchange of the conversation discussed earlier. The processing functions are clearly identified and associated together in program modules. The files used and the points at which they are used in the progress of the processing activity are also shown.

The source of the processing functions will be the familiar steps of validation, updating, extraction and editing together with the specific processing functions planned in procedure and conversation specifications. The diagram must clearly show the decisions which will govern the possible alternative normal responses and the conditions which cause associated responses. Validation error responses may be shown if not too varied, otherwise a second level chart can be prepared. If common validation routines are used for all format checks then that level of detail is probably unnecessary.

So far as diagram format is concerned, a few simple guidelines can be identified. Symbols are similar to those used in batch system charts and program flowcharts. Wording in boxes should be simple and in user terms, to aid subsequent review by the user. The chart should be kept to a single page to permit the easy assimilation of the structure of the exchange. The mainline should show the most frequently-used path. Any loops in the processing should be clearly shown particularly if file access is included since loops will have a significant bearing on the computer component of the response time. Long loops imply successive links between program modules with the possible intervention of software and reference to a stored program library.

Processing Notes

This section should identify any important processing considerations which are not evident from the exchange diagram but which are nevertheless important for the implementation of a satisfactory process.

The sub-headings which are used may vary from exchange to exchange. The suggested sub-headings should be regarded as a checklist of points which

117

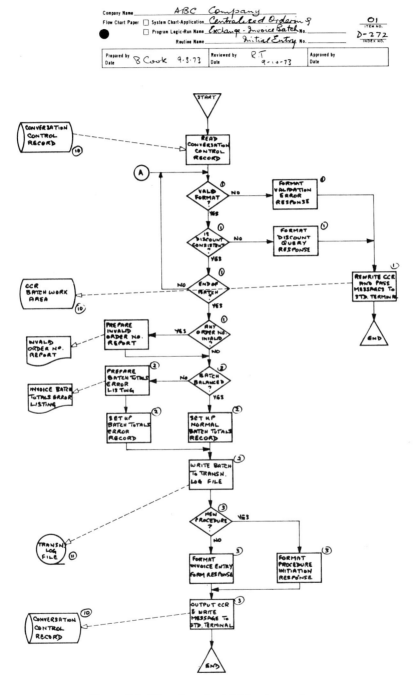

Figure 7.9. Flowchart for initial entry exchange

118

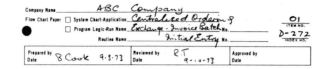

Company Name _____ ABC Company
Flow Chart Paper ☐ System Chart-Application __ Centralized Ordering
● ☐ Program Logic-Run Name __ Exchange - Invoice Batch No.
Routine Name _____ Initial Entry No.

01
ITEM NO.
D-272
INDEX NO.

Prepared by B Cook 9.3.73   Reviewed by R.T. 9-10-73   Approved by
Date   Date   Date

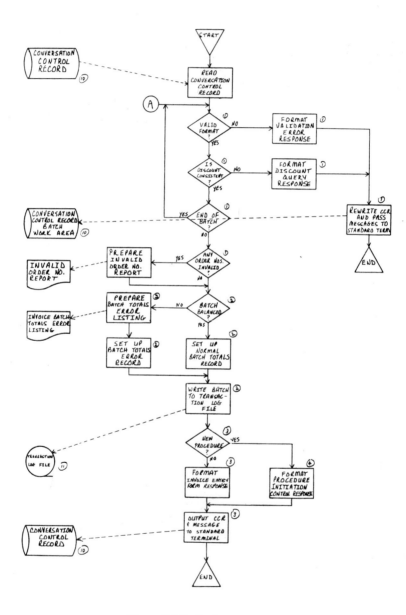

Figure 7.10. Exchange notes

Cross Reference	Key	Description
HAPRT01	1	Format Validation of Invoice Totals Entry
HAPRT02	2	Invoice Batch Balancing and Write Transactions
HAPRT03	3	Build Invoice Totals Form
HAPRT04	4	Build Invoice Change Form
HAF200	10	Conversation Control Record File
HAF201	11	Transaction Log File

Notes

Entry recognition will be by syntax since only two entry types are permitted — the normal entry and the recovery entry. Since that has an action code its omission from the entry will positively identify it as this one.

Entry unpacking must allow for the absence of the identification line if implied fields are all valid.

Special validation — check for duplication of folder number against core table since no folder no. will be used twice in the same 30 day period. Order number will be validated online by check digit. Date is received in form DDMM — will be converted to form YDDD by reference to CCR table. Discount — validated by arithmetic

$$GROSS + VAT - DISCOUNT = NET$$

Calculation — date conversion is calculated on table indexed by month to give year day for month start + month day = year day

should be considered for inclusion in this section. Figure 7.10 shows notes accompanying the illustrated exchange.

SPECIAL ENTRY ANALYSIS

Frequently, entry analysis and validation will be performed by standard software. If any special means of recognition or unpacking are required, which are not provided by the expected software, they should be noted here.

SPECIAL CHECKS

Validations performed during the exchange which are specific to it may merit mention here. For example, airline check-in exchanges may not be permitted at all within 20 minutes of aircraft departure.

CALCULATIONS

Any noteworthy formulae to be applied should be mentioned—for example, use of discount factors in order processing. Another use of the subsection could be to convey complex decisions governing processing. Decision tables will be a useful means of expressing such information.

STATISTICS

User performance statistics.

DATABASE USAGE

This heading describes what processing is used to relate the entry to filed records. The relationship with the database can be classified:

(a) Updates of records during real time processing—what entry data is used and why is the update performed?
(b) Retrievals—for extracting data to add to that in the entry.
(c) Additions to files of transactions or master records.
(d) Deletions.
(e) Retentions of a record for the duration of a conversation.

Testing Plan

The example in Figure 7.11 shows that the function and structure of this section is similar to the similarly named section of the conversation specification. It forces a detailed check of the ability of exchange logic to deal with unforeseen combinations of conditions and provides a test plan for exchange testing. Decision table format should be used again. The conditions will be a mixture of entry format situations and existing values in database records. Particular attention should be paid to maximum and minimum values or other extreme situations, for their effect on the course of processing. The 'outcomes' are the different responses possible from the exchange or variations in the values displayed.

Exchange Linkage

The relationship between the several exchanges of a conversation is a crucial expression of project logic. It has programming connotations which are

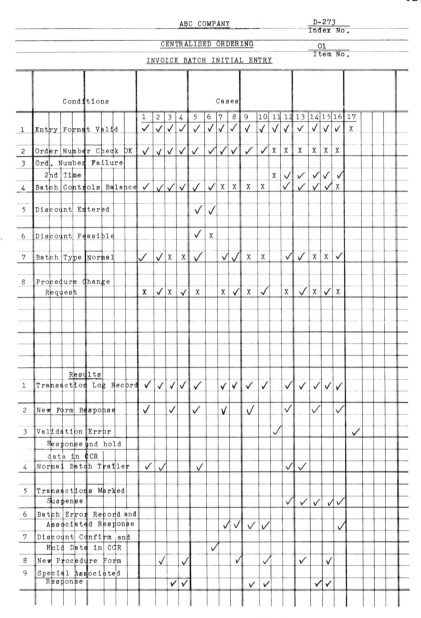

Figure 7.11. Invoice batch initial entry

external to the terms of reference of individual programs and are most naturally documented here. This context is expressed in two ways—in terms of data links with preceding and succeeding exchanges, and in terms of the exchanges permitted to follow this one. The data fields thus identified will be held in the conversation control record.

D – 274
INDEX NO.

01
ITEM NO.

COMPANY NAME *ABC Company*

Exchange **LINK MAP**

SYSTEM DEVELOPMENT *Centralized Ordering*

PREPARED BY: *B. Cook*	REVIEWED BY: *P. Townsend*	APPROVED BY:
DATE: 9-3-73	DATE: 9-10-73	DATE:

NAME *Invoice Batch Initial Entry*

ENTERING THIS *Exchange*

ENTERED FROM THIS *Exchange*

PARAMETERS PASSED	Sign on	Invoice Entry	Invoice Corr?	Recovery	next procedure				next Invoice Entry	Invoice Corr?	next procedure		
Procedure Currently Set	✓	✓	✓	✓	✓				✓	✓			
next Entry = Invoice Batch	✓	✓	✓	✓	✓				✓				
= Field in Error										✓			
= Procedure Change											✓		
Statistics: Chars in today	✓	✓	✓	✓	✓				✓	✓	✓		
records in today	✓	✓	✓	✓	✓				✓	✓	✓		
Validation errors	✓	✓	✓	✓	✓				✓	✓	✓		
Batch Total Errors	✓	✓	✓	✓	✓				✓	✓	✓		
avge Batch Size	✓	✓	✓	✓	✓				✓	✓	✓		
Conversation Type Stats	✓	✓	✓	✓	✓				✓	✓	✓		
Batch Nos this folder		✓	✓	✓					✓	✓			
Current Folder No.		✓	✓	✓					✓	✓			
Current Supplier		✓	✓	✓					✓	✓			
Current Batch		✓							✓				
Last Successful Batch		✓	✓	✓					✓	✓	✓		
Operator Id, Function, Status	✓	✓	✓	✓	✓				✓	✓	✓		
Invoice Data (Invoice No.									✓				
For each Value									✓				
Invoice VAT									✓				
in Batch outers									✓				
Batch Totals									✓				

Figure 7.12. Exchange link map

An example of a linkage plan is shown in Figure 7.12. The exchanges preceding and following this one in the various conversations in which it participates, are identified. The data passed across each interface is identified and listed.

The identification of adjacent exchanges could be subdivided by conversation to aid the construction of permitted next entry tables in the different CCRs.

Verification of Design

The details of the exchange which are approved by the user will include its entry, its possible normal, associated and error responses and the exchange diagram which links them together. At this time the format of the messages is not precisely defined but the finished product should be similar in content and general appearance.

An example of the memorandum following user discussion is shown in Figure 7.13. The nature of the comments made illustrates that the discussion centred on logical points rather than format.

DATABASE SPECIFICATION

Specification is similar to Batch

The concept of treating a file as an independent entity in a system is not unique to real time. Standards for file specifications have been developed before and an installation considering real time techniques is likely to have such standards already. This section of the chapter does propose a specification layout, but an installation's existing standard may need few, if any, modifications.

File specifications as described here contain little precise information on data items. The detailed specification of data is reserved for the installation phase of a project and is therefore deliberately separated from the statement of file requirements. That separation implies that file specifications prepared to the format described below will be quite short. The adoption of a preprinted form to contain the information remaining is quite feasible (see Figures 7.14(a) and (b)). Data files in a real time project are developed quite independently from programs since many programs may share the same file. The information which is included must therefore be full enough to convey meaning unambiguously to its many readers.

Description

This specification, like the others in the series, provides for an identifying statement. In this document, it takes the form of explaining the reasons for collecting data together in this particular file and identifying the objects or events in the real world which are recorded. The major uses of the file might be described in terms of the significant procedures in which it participates.

124

	D-655
	INDEX NO.
COMPANY NAME __ABC Company__	01 / 1
	ITEM NO.

VERIFICATION OF _Exchange_ WITH USER

SYSTEM DEVELOPMENT __Centralized Ordering__

PREPARED BY: B. Cook	REVIEWED BY: R. Townsend	APPROVED BY:
DATE: 9·20·73	DATE: 9·20·73	DATE:

NAME:
Invoice Batch Initial Entry

USER GROUP: _Data Entry / Central Office_   REPRESENTATIVE: _Maureen Sims_

COMMENTS	DISPOSITION
Allow for listing of batches not in error - prepaid invoices - list for store charging	indic set for batch system BC 9/20
Invoice Values can exceed limit allowed. VAT filled will need to increase allo.	formats altered BC 9/20
Invoice items can be priced to half-cents but invoices are always rounded to nearest penny. May cause spurious mismatch.	referred to batch designer
Improve response times on main entry to 3 seconds.	review after detail design
Correct errors by overwriting original field not entering seperately	Done BC 9/20
Check for duplicate batch numbers in folders and duplicate folder numbers	Core table for folders see D310 Current batch list in CCR BC 9/20

USER APPROVAL: M. Sims (mrs.)   DATE: 9.21.73

Figure 7.13. Verification of exchange

Company Name __ABC Company__

MASTER FILE INFORMATION WORKSHEET

D·330 INDEX NO.
H$/M|61 ITEM NO.

Systems Development __Centralised Ordering__

| Prepared by Date | R Townsend 9-7-73 | Reviewed by Date | G.E. White 9-15-73 | Approved Date | GEW |

File Name: Conversation Control File

Purposes: Contain data between exchanges, Hold recovery, statistical and working data. 1 per terminal

Sequence: Random

Medium: Disc

Frequency of Access –
Reference: } every exchange entered
Updating:

Record Types

Key	Record Name	Size	Comments	Estimated Volume
1	CCR	1000	single record type	75
2			– different work area for	
3			each type of conversation	
4			– established on sign on	
5			or change of procedure	
6				
7				
8				
9				

Access Method: Logical terminal number used as relative record number in file. Also accessed sequentially for security copying. Standard Terminal routine will normally retrieve record

Use: Creation – established by network manager "now terminal" exchange
Deletion – initialised on "delete terminal" exchange
Manipulation – data is stored in conversation work area on each entry after validation
Entry is stored in last entry area to permit progressive validation and reentry of invalid fields
Areas are cleared at end of each conversation
Format is changed on procedure change

Reference – record is always updated

Control: Record identity is confirmed on reading by comparing stored terminal number to terminal number of current entry. Number of records on file is held in system control area & updated on creation/deletion

Recovery: Held in duplicate and updated by "duplicate file" routine. File also dumped daily to tape. Second copy read on read error. If both copies in error file is restored from tape copy. If that fails, file is recreated by restoring all terminals

Figure 7.14(a). Master file information worksheet

126

Data Included

Key	Data Name	Number of Characters	Comments
100	Record type	2	
110	Terminal No	2	
120	Terminal status	1	Data Entry / Supervisor / Network Control / Analysis
130	Operator id	2	
140	Operator status	1	Training / Operational and one of :- Clerk / Supervisor / Controller / Analyst / Engineer
	Statistics area		
200	Total chars entered today	6	Common statistics
210	Total format errors	4	
220	Number entries	4	
230	Number conversns.	4	
	Conversation Ctl		
300	Current Conversn.	2	
310	Count of permitted next entries (PNE)	2	
320	Reference no/PNE	2-20	Variable depending on PNE Count
330	Displacement of start of unvalidated data within last entry area	3	
	Screen references Start of message		
340	line	2	
345	character	2	
	End of message		
350	line	2	
355	character	2	
	Error field start		
360	line	2	
365	character	2	
	Filler	35	
	Specific work area	900	See attached continuation sheets — 1 per conversation type

Figure 7.14(b). Master file information worksheet (reverse side)

Contents

The different fields expected in the records of the file should be named and described (see Figure 7.14(b)). This will provide a brief narrative for programmers or casual readers who do not need the later detail. If the relationship of data within records or records within the file is complex, a diagram of the relative position and size of fields might aid comprehension.

Access Method

The manner in which data is withdrawn or added to the file will dictate the general class of hardware appropriate for storage. Most master files on a real time system will be accessed on demand, but some transaction files may be built serially—for example, in a simple data capture system or the logging files used in recovery of an online updating system. There are a number of characteristics to be covered but they can be conveyed succinctly:

(a) Access—serial or demand;
(b) Key data—which logical data items will be used in deriving record addresses?
(c) Derivation—what method of derivation will be used: indexing, calculation, chaining or direct addressing; and what are the details of the addressing algorithm?
(d) Alternatives—will records be accessed by other methods than the primary derivation specified? An example is frequently found in customer files which are primarily accessed by an account number but are occasionally found by name or street via an index.

Record Use

There are a number of sub-sections which will assist the organization of this data:

(a) creation—identify the circumstances under which a record is created and added to the file;
(b) deletion—a similar statement of how a record is made inaccessible to application programs;
(c) manipulation—why are the record values changed?
(d) reference—when the record is read without updating.

Each of these sub-sections should refer to the exchanges which include these activities.

File Dimensions

The determination of equipment requirements will need data defining the demand for storage devices to hold data. That information will be accumulated for each file under a heading such as this. The use of a number of sub-sections will quickly summarize the information needed, such as:

(a) size of record—of each type if more than one;
(b) number of records—of each type;
(c) index item size—if applicable;
(d) record life.

Each of these parameters could be variable and different users of this data will need maximum, minimum and normal values. 'Normal' will usually be stated as the arithmetic mean value, but the modal, or most frequently experienced, value for record size and life might be useful if significantly different. The exhibit shows less information since it is separately summarized on a File Inventory list in the installation from which the example was drawn.

Control

Note here any obvious candidates for data fields on which control totals could be built. Even if the file is accessed at random and never processed serially still there will be control data associated with the file to ensure that processing is accurate. A count of the number of records should be maintained unless the file is not updated. If the file is changed in any way then control totals of the type found in an end-of-file record in a batch system should be maintained. Periodically the file should be balanced against those totals.

Recovery

Procedure specifications considered the problem of loss of computer assistance generally. This section relates to the action to be taken to rebuild a file found to be inaccessible. The usual technique for an enquiry file is to hold a back up version which can be reloaded but the techniques for updated files will need more thought. The problems of recovery and restart generally, have been discussed in the previous chapter but file recovery techniques are many and will need to be tailored for each file. Consideration of this topic may well expose the need for further special coding to be added to the project and even for new control exchanges.

PROGRAM IDENTIFICATION

Interfaces are Designed

The program is the final project subdivision needed in preliminary design. The complete set of programs is yet another definition of the project but at a lower level of detail than exchanges or conversations. The specification of programs is separated into two parts—identification and definition. The two steps are separated here for the same reasons that they were separated in the specification of conversations and exchanges. The identification phase permits a critical review of the complete set of programs to avoid duplication or identify opportunities for amalgamation of similar programs before investing the effort needed for full specification. Furthermore, once the required set of programs is identified, the interfaces for each can be designed before the logic of any is specified in detail. The different programs in an exchange can then be reviewed for compatibility. This is particularly important if the program set has been significantly reduced in review. The review of compatibility can be achieved by 'executing' exchanges on the desk to prove that the parameters provided by a calling program match those required by the program called.

The interfaces of a program are defined in three sections—purpose, parameters and links.

Purpose

The specifications of the different exchanges which use a program will identify the functions which each wishes it to perform. A plain language statement of a program's purpose can therefore be readily derived from the text used in the relevant exchange diagrams or processing notes. A program specification will frequently be the first item of project documentation to be read by the programmer assigned to coding it. At the risk of repetition there will be benefit in making plain the place of a program in the project by identifying the exchanges and their entries or events which use it. This will help link the programmer's general knowledge of the project with this program.

If the sequence in which the program's tasks are performed is important, this can either be described or charted. Top logic charts—or block diagrams—are a familiar feature of program definition.

Parameters

There are two parts to a parameter specification—the formal and contextual. Formal parameters are those explicitly included in the statement made by a calling program, while contextual parameters are other data items held in work areas which are relevant to the processing of the program being specified.

Formal parameters are of the type usually associated with service routine calls or macro statements. In a comprehensive software environment each program may have a formal call line by which it is requested from the program management software. This has the form:

```
(command)   (program name)   WITH   (parameters)
[TO GIVE   (parameters)]
```

of which the first set of parameters are input for the called program while the second are returned by it, if a return is expected. The parameters can be identified by their sequence or by specific names. In the latter case their sequence is not important and optional parameters may be omitted without the need of clumsy punctuation. The mechanism is not important but the principle of a common syntax for all program calls is.

130

COMPANY NAME _ABC Company_

Program **WORKSHEET**

SYSTEM DEVELOPMENT _Centralised Ordering_

		INDEX NO.	D-211
		ITEM NO.	HAPRTO2

PREPARED BY	REVIEWED BY	APPROVED BY
DATE	DATE	DATE

NAME _Invoice Batch Balance and Log_

Purpose:

Following validation of invoice batch entry this program compares batch totals entered to those accumulated during validation for:-

Number of lines

VAT amount

Value

Outers

If batch totals differ an 'invalid batch' response is prepared quoting batch identity name of error field and the entered and calculated values. The response is directed to the supervisors printer. Whether the batch is valid or not, a batch record is prepared showing 'error status' and it and the batch of invoices are written to the transaction log file for processing in the batch system. The individual records are created from the batch work area in the CCR.

The file control totals, maintained in core, will be updated

Parameters:

This is in the mainline of exchange processing so all necessary parameters will be in the CCR or ECR. The interface will therefore be :-
CALL NO RETURN HAPRTO2

Figure 7.15. Program worksheet

The format recommended for the formal parameters section is to quote the required call line, then describe each parameter by a statement of its purpose in the program.

For subroutines and service programs the formal parameters will be the only means of data transfer required since they are fully parameterized to free them from dependence on any context. For 'mainline' programs however much important data will be held in common work areas such as the conversation and exchange control records (CCR and ECR) and in retrieved copies of filed records associated with them. A full statement of parameters is therefore completed by listing the relevant contents of those sources and describing their significance to the interface.

Links

A program in this environment will usually be part of a string concerned with servicing an activity. Some programs will occur in more than one string. The purpose of this section is to place the program in its various contexts by recording the links which it has with others. Programmers, coding on each side of an interface, must share a common understanding since errors due to a mismatch of interfaces can be particularly difficult to find. Some of the links will be made when the program is the object of calls, others when it does the calling. The section is therefore subdivided into 'called by' and 'calling'.

In the 'called by' section each program initiating a link is named. If its reason for calling is in any way different from the program's purpose—perhaps only a part of the function is required—then a supplementary description would be useful. The specification of the initiating program will be checked for conformity with this description when the interfacing of all programs is reviewed.

In the 'calling' section, the application programs which are initiated by the one being specified are named and any necessary explanatory notes on the reason can be given. Such notes need not be very full since the body of the specification will later make these issues clear. Any important notes on the processing consequences of assembling parameters can be filed for later inclusion in the specification.

Document Format

The link map form illustrated earlier in describing exchange linkage (see Figure 7.12) is a suitable document to show the contextual parameters associated with the appropriate interfaces. The identification of the complete set of programs can be achieved by a simple list and the purpose of the program can be written on plain paper as shown in Figure 7.15. The list of programs will identify within which exchanges each program is used and, if optional, under what conditions.

Chapter 8
Application of Design Data

INTRODUCTION

The completion of logical design in the preliminary design phase is the point at which the implications of the design can be reviewed. The implications are here taken to include physical design of the communications network and the estimation of central site equipment requirements, as well as effort and cost plans.

The logical and physical design data can finally be combined to support the estimation of the effort, cost and duration of development. This in turn is one component in a statement of the economics of the system which provides the final source of material for a system report and its presentation to management for approval.

This is a brief chapter since these matters are treated elsewhere and to repeat that material at length would be presumptuous and unnecessary. The chapter is included to show how the necessary basic data can be drawn from the design documentation which it is the main purpose of the book to introduce.

NETWORK DESIGN

Functions

At this point in the design of a batch system, the designer has to quantify equipment requirements. To do this, he uses input transaction volumes, report and output document volumes, file sizes and access methods and processing requirements. With this information and a knowledge of the state of computer and peripheral technology, he can plan a central site configuration, select data handling media and develop processing time estimates for comparison with permitted cycles of data submission and report preparation.

Similar work must be done for the central site components of a real time system but, in addition, the designer must plan the telecommunications network. The further steps include making a choice of terminal type and planning the transmission paths which link terminals with computer. He must make choices between clustered and individually controlled terminals, decide whether to concentrate the data transmission needs of several adjacent sites to take advantage of higher capacity links, whether to place some processing power between the terminal and the central site and if so where, what line speeds and transmission modes to use.

Data Required

The decisions which are listed above will depend upon the two classes of data identified: project requirements and technology available.

The design data related to this particular project includes its data volumes, terminal locations and preferred terminal types. The second class, the technology data common to all projects at a given point in time, includes terminals available, line speeds, line rentals, communications control devices and prices. The design documents produced to this point contain the source material for providing the first class of data.

Data Assembly

Procedure specifications contain the basic volume information on frequency and distribution of procedures or business tasks. The conversation and exchange specifications subsequently show the incidence of each within its parent. The analysis of exchange specifications will give rates of access to files and frequency of execution of programs. The message worksheets give message lengths which, combined with incidence in exchanges, gives transmission load components.

The Peak Hour

The key difference between using this data for network design and the analogous data for batch computer configuration lies in one of the five basic differences identified in Chapter 2, namely demand. The time dimension is much more dominant.

In batch systems the capacity of a peripheral device is dictated by the total volume of activity divided by the time available for its execution—an averaging method. If 120,000 cards must be read in an hour and card readers with a passing rate of 1,000 cards per minute are available, then two will be required—ignoring additional backup capacity. However, in a real time system with random demand, if 120,000 messages, of 60 characters each, are expected in a peak hour of processing, and transmission lines are available capable of accepting 1,000 characters per second, or 1,000 messages per minute, then the required capacity will be nearer five than two lines. The extra lines are needed to ensure that sufficient capacity is available for momentary fluctuations in demand around the average. (Fuller discussion of the statistical analysis of queueing systems, of which this is an example, will be found in Sasieni and Ackoff, *Fundamentals of Operations Research*, John Wiley, 1968.)

There are thus two analyses required of the raw data logged during the design process. For each component of the system, the demand must be estimated in a peak period. With this information and a measure of its

ABC COMPANY

CENTRALISED ORDERING	D-281 Index No.
REAL TIME PEAK HOUR FREQUENCY ANALYSIS	pl. of 3

Procedures		Conversations			Exchanges	
Item	Frequency	Item	Incidence in Procedure	Frequency	Item	Incidence in Conversations
	a		b	a x b		c
A	1000 batches	A - 1	1/batch	1000	01	0.99
					02	0.01
		A - 2	1/batch	1000	01	0.05
					03	1.0
					04	0.65
					05	0.15
					06	0.15
					07	0.20
					14	0.05
B	900 batches	B - 1	1/batch		08	1.0
					09	0.25

Figure 8.1. Program execution frequency analysis

Frequency				Item				Programs Incidence in Exchange			Frequency							
a	x	b	x c					p			a	x	b	x	c	x	p	
990				HAPRT01				1.0			990							
				HAPRT02				1.0			990							
				HAPRT03				1.0			990							
				HAPRT04				0			0							
10				HAPRT03				1.0			10							
50				HAPRT01				1.0			50							
				HAPRT02				1.0			50							
				HAPRT03				1.0			50							
				HAPRT04				0			0							
1000				HAPRT03				0.2			200							
650				HAPRT06				0.25			150							
				HAPRT07				1.0			650							
150				HAPRT06				0.05			8							
				HAPRT07				1.0			150							
150				HAPRT05				1.0			150							
200				HAPRT01				1.0			200							
				HAPRT03				0.05			10							
50				HAPRT13				1.0			50							
900				HAPRT04				0			0							
				HAPRT10				1.0			900							
				HAPRT12				1.0			900							
				HAPRT14				0.75			675							
225				HAPRT02				1.0			225							
				HAPRT04				0			0							
				HARPT12				1.0			225							
				HAPRT14				0.50			113							
				HAPRT15				0.50			113							

136

variability, the capacity requirement must then be estimated using the statistical tools of queueing theory. The peak period is one during which average demand can be thought of as only subject to purely random fluctuation. For most commercial systems an hour will normally be short enough to qualify.

Peak Hour Analysis

Figure 8.1 shows an example of a schedule developed to estimate program execution frequency. The data is extracted from the specifications prepared earlier. The eventual incidence of activity at the lowest level is derived by multiplication.

The schedule format can equally well be employed in estimating file accesses and data transmission volumes.

Computer Power

The peak hour concept applies in determining the demand on the central processing unit. It is rare that real time systems will be the source of the dominant load so they rarely determine the CPU capacity required. However, to estimate utilization of CPU time due to the real time systems, the peak hour frequency analysis is used. It will rapidly show which are the dominant programs. The designer must estimate for the dominant programs, the number of instructions likely to be executed in application code and the calls on software to execute standard functions such as file accesses, program calls, task switching, core allocation, terminal polling etc.

The application code estimates demand experience. The processing paths can be roughly estimated in standard units of arithmetic, editing and general processing modules, each one of which can be approximately timed. Further details of this method applied to batch processing can be found in Blackman, M., A Specification for Computer Selection. Data Processing, **15**, 6, 1973. The number of times each is executed is available from the peak hour analysis.

The timing of the software component of processing requires familiarity with the specific software to be used and the assistance of the manufacturer whose equipment is being evaluated. The logical requirements identified above are common but the computer effort involved in each will be specific to the software. If computer choice is part of the design task then the load caused by this component will need to be estimated as part of the evaluation.

The end result of this effort, so sketchily described, is an estimate of the CPU utilization in a peak hour. The size of CPU will need to be such that, in the absence of any other load, no more than 60% CPU utilization is experienced (based again on a rough approximation to queueing theory).

Number of Terminals

Slightly different considerations apply to determining the number of terminals required. In the first place, terminal requirements must be determined separately for each site since load cannot usually be shared between sites to even out variations in demand. Secondly, there are two different modes of operation depending on the source of load.

Load on a terminal may arise at random, for example, in systems whose data source is telephone calls or personal visitors. Then the random element requires similar analysis to the other random elements in the system to ensure sufficient capacity for peaks.

However real time systems do sometimes experience smoothed load, as would occur in data capture systems with written source documents. They can be batched and presented to the terminal in a steady stream. The number of terminals can then be determined by average terminal use—number of procedures in peak hour times duration of a procedure in minutes, divided by 60. With suitable allowance for back up and training terminals, the number is easily found.

Number of Lines and their Connection

The analysis of line loadings must start at the terminal sites. Just as terminals cannot be shared between sites and each must be self sufficient, so for lines. The transmission load at a site can be deduced from a peak hour frequency analysis similar to Figure 8.1 where the lowest levels are entry and response characters. If an approximate allowance for random fluctuation is made so that utilization is less than 40%, the necessary line speed or line numbers can be found at the site.

At the computer, the loading is the aggregate of the loads on all sites—with one proviso. If the sites experience different peak hours due to differences in function or changes in time zone across the network, then the computer peak will be lower. The superimposition of rough frequency diagrams for the different classes of site will reveal the aggregate peak.

Between terminal and computer sites data transmission paths must be planned. A variety of line speeds are available and their varying capacities can be used by concentrating the loads from different sites onto a 'trunk' line to obtain benefit from the relatively cheaper capacity. The load at each junction will be aggregated in a minor version of the method outlined for deducing the demand at the central site. The objective is to achieve the cheapest network having the necessary capacity at all points.

Further Reading

The foregoing discussion of some of the considerations in network design has been deliberately brief and superficial because the subject is treated at length elsewhere, Martin, J., *Telecommunications and the Computer*, Prentice Hall, London, 1969. There are also software aids from manufacturers. The purpose of covering the matter at all was simply to indicate that the necessary design data is available from the documentation of the logic of the application.

Response Time

A byproduct of the volume statistics developed for network design, is the opportunity to develop estimates of the response time for certain key exchanges. The previous record of response time on the exchange worksheet (see Figure 7.8) was a requirement rather than a prediction. The data is available after network design decisions to check the feasibility of achieving the time required.

There are a number of major components of response time:

(a) transmission time of entry and subsequent response
(b) time for backing storage access to filed records or file resident programs
(c) software processing time
(d) application processing time.

Transmission time will be dictated by message length and the slowest speed component of the transmission path (probably the line terminating at the terminal). File access time will be derived from the number of accesses multiplied by a suitable average access time depending on the file device. Processing time components are derived from the estimates used in determining computer power.

To the sum of these components a factor should be added in consideration of the approximate nature of the data and the other unknown elements such as queueing time within the CPU waiting for resources. If the software overhead is known then a 10% addition should be sufficient. If not an allowance of 20% or more will be more realistic.

If the estimated response time exceeds the requirement then further design work will be needed to reduce it. There are several possibilities both physical and logical. The prime physical source of saving is to use higher line speeds if the extra expense can be justified. Transmission time is typically over half the total response time so provides scope for large reductions.

Changes to the logic of the system can be many and varied. For example, the response to an entry can be sent earlier in the exchange if all necessary data is assembled. Some processing can be carried out as an autonomous activity uncoupled from the work needed to build the response. If these options are not open, the arrangement of data in files can be reviewed in an attempt to retrieve data with less file accesses. As an alternative, the response time constraint might be relaxed by altering the user's duties.

CONTROL OF MODIFICATIONS

The possibility of modifying the logical design to meet physical constraints is a suitable point to consider the issue of making design changes. The need for modification may well arise again if development effort or running costs are found to be excessive. Modifications of a less far reaching nature are positively sought earlier in the design when the verification of the design of procedures, conversations and exchanges is sought from users. At that time though, the scope of changes will usually be limited to the immediate project unit since parent components are already approved. Finally, changes can occur at any time if the scope of the project is changed in some way.

The modification itself should be documented so that a record of the reason for the change exists. Modifications should be numbered and dated for easy reference and to control the implementation of the change. The author and others concerned in making the change should be identified to ensure that the change is not overlooked. The body of any modification form has three parts—reason, action and cost. Cost estimates are necessary for changes initiated by the user or management to substantiate budget changes. The cost of a change cometimes acts as a spur to finding better solutions to the original problem.

The action to be taken to implement a change fully will depend on when in the design process it arises. At any time however, the planning of action is assisted by being able to trace the links of project components. The design documents so far introduced all carry upwards (where used) and downwards (using) references. The procedure specification identifies its component conversations and both are linked by the index of conversations. Similarly exchanges are cross referred to conversations and in turn identify their component entry, responses, programs and files.

Thus the information necessary to support modification is available. If the modified documents themselves refer to modification forms, the chain is complete.

DESIGN APPROVAL

Installation Planning

The different work segments and tasks of the Installation phase are illustrated in Chapter 9. The act of installation planning at this time uses those tasks as a framework upon which to build a work programme for the specific project. The work content of many of the tasks will be particular to the project and will be dictated by its design. Program specification and coding effort will depend upon how many programs there are and what level of complexity they have. The schedules developed during design, of entities whose detailed implementation is yet to come, will provide data for estimating. The schedules cover programs, files, entries and responses. Procedure specifications will indicate the effort needed to prepare training material and procedure manuals. Details of locations and the outlines of conversion plans will support estimates of the effort for other conversion preparation.

The later stages of installation are concerned with testing. As will become clear in Part III of this book, the concepts of exchange and conversation have validity during the assembly of the programmed system as well as the breakdown of the design. Knowledge of the numbers and complexity of each exchange and conversation therefore contributes to the estimation of testing effort.

From the estimates of effort in the various tasks, an aggregate demand for effort of various skills including those in the user departments can be created. The application of that effort over time, using the resources available, will give an approximate answer to the question of the duration of the project.

System Economics

There are two main components to the economic evaluation—cost and benefit. Cost divides between development and running cost. Development cost is an investment to be recouped by the margin between running cost and benefit.

Development costs can be evaluated from the total effort needed for installation together with the cost of machine time devoted to testing. Running costs will be mainly those arising from the hire or depreciation of equipment and the salaries of the staff—computer operators and users—who run the system. The benefits of the system may arise from staff savings or opportunities created by better information—the possible sources were more fully discussed in Chapter 3. The actual sources of benefit in a specific project are outlined in its conversation inventory.

The information contained in procedure specifications will help to identify running costs associated with user manning, since that topic was specifically addressed at that time.

The running costs of equipment will finally depend on what equipment is chosen but the order of magnitude can be deduced from the results of equipment planning discussed earlier in this chapter, which in turn rests on the information developed in the conversation and exchange specifications.

System Report

The final act of user involvement in the design process comes with the review of the design for approval of the installation phase. This should be a formal act after the involvement of users throughout the design process. It does provide the opportunity to bring together all the components of the design and link them with introductory text.

The system report presented to management will have a number of formal sections:

(a) the scope and objectives of the system
(b) the final outputs of the system and their relation to the objectives
(c) outline system logic
(d) equipment plans
(e) installation schedule
(f) economics.

All sections will be supported by detailed appendices. The sections correspond with the major tasks of the preliminary design work program.

The material is similar in all respects to a corresponding batch system report so little more need be said about its format with one exception.

The presentation of system logic in a batch system report would normally be supported by examples of reports and source documents. While the latter have their place in some real time systems, the main source of illustration of the real time section will be sample conversations prepared in a rather similar way to that shown in Chapter 1.

Depending on the importance of the project and the size of the group involved in project approval, a presentation of the system may be appropriate. Once again conversation samples will be appropriate material. The presentation could be made more real by preparing terminal displays so that the audience can obtain a better sense of the interaction between user and machine. An effective technique is to use a sequential device to hold preformatted screen images and a simple program to present them in turn. Obviously this technique needs terminals which will not be available for an initial system. Facilities can be found at a bureau.

Whether in report or presentation, the conversation and exchange concepts provide a method of organizing the material to the very last stage of design. In the next part of the book we explore their relevance to installation.

PART III

Application Systems Installation

Chapter 9
Detailed Logic Definition

INTRODUCTION

Part III of the book is concerned with the major phase of a project, as measured in its consumption of resources, that of installing the programs and data on a computer. Within this phase, the tasks of programming and checking the logical elements of the system take place. There is much work which is common in detail with the equivalent phase of a batch system and is thus not included in the book. Instead, the unique aspects of real time systems are reviewed and the relationship of installation work to the concepts of conversation and exchange analysis is explored.

This chapter first establishes the framework of the rest by identifying all the segments of the phase. Its main purpose is to complete the description of the definition of application logic by setting out the remainder of a program specification. In order to bridge the gap between application logic and the computer it also describes common functions which are provided by software—either supplied or created within the installation. The logic remaining to be specified in such an environment is truly application logic. Finally the documentary interface between application programs and the service routines which form part of the software environment is described.

INSTALLATION PHASE

Some Steps are Common

Installation is the third of the four major stages of implementing a project, following the definition of scope and preliminary systems design. Like preliminary systems design, it contains many different areas of work which are illustrated in diagrammatic form in Figure 9.1. There are eight areas, and sub-areas within each. Each sub-area can be divided again—'code program' for example must be applied to each program—and installation is undoubtedly the major consumer of development resources. Before considering documentation in detail let us discuss the effect of real time on each of these areas and the steps within them.

An established data processing organization will not need to perform some of the preparatory steps in developing every application. It will usually have its

146

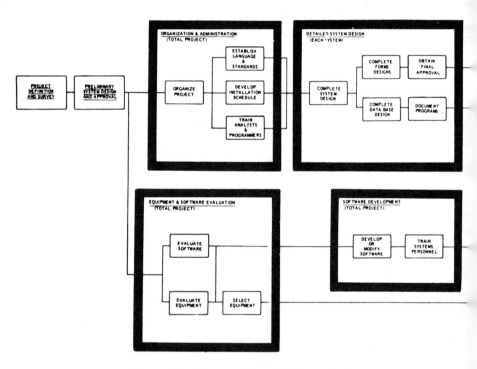

Figure 9.1. Diagram of installation work phase

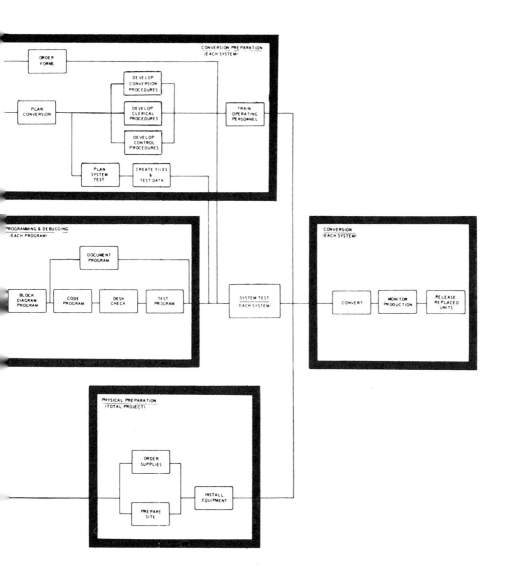

policy on programming languages and standards already set and have trained its programmers and analysts. These steps are shown on the chart because they will need reconsideration when the first real time project is undertaken. To take training as an example, the concepts in this book will be unfamiliar and if its methods are adopted, the analysts and programmers will need to practise them. The programming languages used will have to be supported by compilers which match the new software base—if the computer environment is to support multi-threading, then the compilers used will have to generate re-entrant code. The organization of projects is concerned with the project planning and progress reporting functions which will not be affected by real time, except if the increased number of activities causes a switch to network methods. The project installation schedule is based on that developed at the latter end of the PSD stage, extended to record personnel assignments and expressed in a manner suitable for comparison with results.

Once the project has been approved for installation, equipment selection for the user locations must be finalized. If central site equipment is also needed negotiations for that are completed. Telecommunication facilities must be ordered from the telephone company if terminals are to be remote from the central site.

Systems Design is to be Completed

The work of systems design so far described has identified the computer elements which will need to be coded to implement the system. These elements include data records, entries, responses and processing programs. Detailed systems design is concerned with specifying these elements for coding. The exchange and file specifications are the reference material for this work, supported by the other specifications—procedure, conversation and network —for background.

The results of detailed systems design present an opportunity to update the cost estimates developed during PSD and to review the viability of the project again. The updated estimates for effort and duration of work will be required if progress reporting against a budget, step by step, is to be realistic.

Programming and Debugging

Programming consists of expressing system logic in a suitable programming language for identification and validation of entries, processing, and response generation. The close specification of programs, which forms part of the strategy of avoiding errors, makes the work of programming relatively straightforward.

It is followed by desk checking, which consists of reviewing the program-mer's interpretation of his program's interfaces with others and then running test cases by hand to verify that program action appears to match specification. Clerical errors and inefficiencies of coding should be noted, if found, but their location is not the first objective. The former are better found by the compiler program and the latter are more likely to be corrected by the programmer as he develops experience. Desk checking is an activity which should be shared around the programming team and is a useful training device for the inexperienced programmer if he performs the task methodically.

Debugging can be divided into three stages—program testing, function testing and system testing. These stages are more closely examined in later chapters. For the moment, we can observe that they are the process of reassembling the project once design has broken it down into its separate parts. Special software will be needed to manage test runs of parts of the incomplete project—to create or record core conditions or permit the substitution of peripherals for terminals. The conduct of all tests is governed by careful planning based on explicit test specifications.

Control of Modifications is Essential

The close working relationship between users and the system makes real time projects particularly prone to modification during development. While detailed design is proceeding, various other groups connected with the project are documenting its implications by preparing procedure manuals, training courses and operating instructions. The consequences of early design decisions are being spelt out to the people who will press terminal buttons. If early design has been inadequate, a severe strain can be put on installation resources by a stream of minor and sometimes major modifications. The methods advocated by this book will start the process of control over modifications through the rigour of the early design process and its documentation. The design commitments already made will be adequately documented by the working paper files if the analysis work required to complete PSD documentation has been properly done. The user staff and management will have been involved in the design process at all stages since the information needed has been obtained from them and they are required to assent to all the documents with which they are concerned.

Physical and Conversion Preparation

Some of the work of these steps has been mentioned—procedure manual and training course preparation—and many of the others can be seen from Figure 9.1. The work of preparation will have started long before, when writing procedure specifications and deciding conversion strategies. In particular, any reorganization and redeployment plans will have been prepared by user or corporate management. Staff negotiations and briefing meetings will have preceded the investigation of user activities for preliminary systems design work. If no contact with user staff has yet been made then the failure of the project is virtually assured. Real time projects are so dependent upon the goodwill of user staff and affect their work in so many ways, that early and honest consultation is even more important than it is for batch systems. Matters which will have to be agreed will include salary adjustments for terminal users, hours of work, employment of temporary staff during training or conversion, resettlement or redundancy arrangements for displaced staff, selection of staff to operate terminals, protection of working conditions in respect of glare, noise, heat or dust, the design of the work place to incorporate terminals, the layout of the office to accommodate new methods of working and probably other issues related to the particular organization or to the project. Any financial adjustments which should be made are particularly a matter for early discussion if the grounds for the project are economic. Trades union or staff association representatives should be consulted at the initial planning stages to permit them time to arrange a sensible negotiating timetable which will not delay an agreed project.

The general conversion strategy of whether to phase, and on what basis, will have been settled in the procedure specification stage. Details of the timing of wiring, hardware installation and testing will be determined by the engineering group and must have the consent of equipment manufacturers—and the telephone authorities, if remote sites are included. If conversion is to proceed site by site, one or more trained conversion teams should be set up to accomplish installation, connection, hardware and logic testing. These teams may conduct training if the sites are widely separated. Such teams will need a standard work programme for each site and a rota of site conversions.

Staff training can be a major exercise in a real time project if large numbers of staff are affected. 'Large' means more than 25 as a rough guide. Procedure manuals must be prepared and from them training courses. The courses need slides, preprinted material, terminal examples and examination sequences. The release of staff from their normal duties has to be arranged without detriment to the normal work of their departments. If the number of staff dictates the repetition of courses, a roster must be planned. Thought will be needed for the problem of revision for members of early courses. A firm with marked activity seasons may have to train in one activity trough for a conversion in the next. The actual training process will be most effective if it includes practice with the terminal equipment. Such practice can be delivered with the aid of a simulated system or the real system with a training data base. In either case, exercises must be designed but, with a simulator of the programmed learning type, the system responses must be planned as well. A simulated system is less satisfactory since the variety of system behaviour is virtually impossible to counterfeit. It does permit early training to proceed in parallel with development if this overlap is made necessary by a long training period. Simulation in this sense does require elaborate preparation and needs imaginative and careful trainers.

Control and clerical procedures have an important role in real time projects. Control procedures are particularly necessary if the transient nature of display screens is coupled with the ephemeral source of telephone calls. Clerical procedures concerned with the fallback period of system operation must be designed in detail within the guidelines already set down during procedure design. The subject of the control of data does not change in importance and techniques familiar from batch systems are applicable. The computer system may well include conversations or unsolicited responses to assist the function.

Computer operators in a pure real time system become one arm in a system management group—since the tasks of input and output management, file loading and run to run control virtually disappear during the 'real time day'. Their work becomes more difficult since they have little of a routine nature. Instead they must respond quickly and with initiative to emergencies, under the direction of the system manager. Their objective is the rapid restoration of a processing service in the event of breakdown. To assist the system manager, strict procedures must be designed for recording faults—in terms of evidence, diagnosis and corrective action—the operators must be given extensive training in the details of the systems they are monitoring and regular briefing meetings must be held to keep them up to date. The system manager will need reference documents and specially written documentation setting out procedures for manipulating system facilities and data—how to shut off a conversation type, how to disable a terminal, how to repair a corrupt master record, for example. In addition, there will be some routine work such as starting up and shutting down a network, adding new terminals, altering security locks, changing log tapes, running system integrity checks. The use of terminals in no way diminishes the importance of system operation though the emphasis of their work changes from active participation to monitoring.

System Testing, Conversion and Reconciliation

System testing comprises a number of phases. Each conversation or automatic event in the system will have been tested separately in the course of debugging. System testing is concerned with the whole project running together. It will be performed to prove the final links—those between conversations—to prove that the system will work with realistic transaction mixes and frequencies and finally that the physical network is performing correctly. All but the last objective can be done without terminal equipment—if it does not have to be installed for some other reason. Even then, much testing is more satisfactorily done if terminals are not used since tests can be preplanned and can be exactly repeated to check corrections. System tests include exercises of fallback procedures and of recovery and operation. Any supporting batch system will be included in the test.

Conversion of master data files will be necessary unless all online files are built up by running the system. The chosen conversion strategy will dictate the exact form of the conversion of data. If phasing is achieved by converting the database in stages—for example all the customers in a geographic area—then the procedures for detecting violations and the method of notifying users of the conversion of each stage must be designed. If conversations are being made available in stages then equivalent arrangements are needed.

None of the benefits of the project will be achieved without action by user management following a successful cutover. Their final task will be the monitoring of this process, first by observation of the performance of the system then by an audit of the necessary actions of user management to deliver the benefits of the project. This phase will follow a period during which the project achieves its 'steady state'—inventories take time to run down, staff wastage will not happen immediately and users will need a learning period. During the initial period, the development costs of the project can be summarized and compared to budget, discrepancies can be investigated and any changes needed in estimating planning or reporting techniques can be documented. The documentation of the project can be reviewed and working papers no longer needed for reference can be destroyed.

Conversion means that operating staff assume formal responsibility for the running system. Complete and properly indexed system documentation must be handed over to the maintenance staff, and updating procedures must come into effect. Either the maintenance team will be set up or an existing team will add the new project to its duties.

Chapter deals with Detailed Logic Design

Of the eight steps shown in Figure 9.1 as being part of installation and reconciliation, this chapter will now concentrate on completing logic design. Its main purpose will be to define the documents identified with the project's programs. The technique recommended employs the same concept of a set of entities, separately documented to a predetermined format, which was introduced for the preliminary design stage. Programs and data are documented separately since, unlike batch, no data file can ever be the exclusive concern of one program. The second part of detailed design, that of finally specifying data formats, is covered in Chapter 10.

SOFTWARE ENVIRONMENT

Common Functions

The work of documenting program logic in a real time system would be overwhelming if all the coding which is executed in handling a message from input to output had to be specially designed. However, much of the work to be done is independent of the specific application and can be made common in the way that a batch operating system is common. In fact, the programming work in a real time system is frequently a significantly smaller proportion of the project than is usual in batch. To substantiate this, the program functions which can be common to real time projects will be identified and discussed. Some of those less commonly supplied by manufacturers will be discussed in a little more detail to promote their adoption as software functions in any installation using the design methods of this book. Adoption should be justified and software development on this scale will depend on the scope of the first project and the installation's plans for future development. Questions relevant to software plans are:

(a) how many entries, responses?
(b) how complex are the messages?
(c) is the traffic volume high?
(d) how many terminals, terminal types and locations?
(e) will the installation allow terminal type changes?
(f) are the applications conversational or simply single exchanges?

The more complex the environment, the more beneficial will extensive software be in easing the introduction of real time techniques.

The software possibilities can be separated into two classes—operating software and development software. Operating software is employed at execution time and thus reduces the amount of programming needed for an application. Development software is used to make the tasks of programming and testing easier. This discussion is concerned entirely with operating software—some development software is discussed in Chapter 11.

The common functions of operating software for a real time system can be briefly identified:

(a) telecommunications hardware interface
(b) message reception and despatch
(c) task scheduling
(d) program library management
(e) core management
(f) data management
(g) error processing
(h) system monitoring
(j) communications network modification
(k) shutdown, recovery and restart
(l) entry analysis and response synthesis
(m) logical terminal interface.

TELECOMMUNICATIONS HARDWARE INTERFACE

Telecommunications hardware interface is concerned with the control of the hardware peculiarities of the telecommunications and terminal equipment attached to a specific system. It is an input/output program like those for the peripherals of the central processing unit. It handles the despatch and receipt of single messages for identified terminals, including the buffer management necessary for overcoming the speed and code mismatch between the normal transmission line and the CPU. This software is always provided by a manufacturer.

MESSAGE RECEPTION AND DESPATCH

Message reception and despatch imposes order on the random arrival of incoming messages and arranges the despatch of responses according to the freedom of terminals to receive them. It receives incoming messages from the hardware interface and forms them into a queue. It extracts responses from an output queue and passes them to the hardware interface for despatch to their specified destination. The method of receiving entries may be by 'polling' the terminals to look for entries ready for action or by waiting till the terminal contends for service. Once again, this software will be included by the manufacturer in his real time software.

TASK SCHEDULING

Task scheduling is the application of priority rules to organize the processing of concurrent exchanges. The function is rather similar to the multi-programming function of batch operating systems in that it provides the means for one exchange to use the CPU while another is waiting for an I/O function to complete. This feature is only necessary in systems having a sufficiently high volume to justify multi-threading. However, an installation starting out on low volume real time would be wise to include it as an investment for future systems. Without its discipline, early systems will almost certainly need redevelopment to fit into a multi-threading environment. The mechanics of multi-threading include the use of an exchange control record (ECR) and it will be a function of the task scheduler to create or allocate an ECR for the duration of an exchange. This software is also provided by all major computer manufacturers.

PROGRAM LIBRARY MANAGEMENT

Program library management is the process of achieving transfers of control to a unit of program. The basic function is that of detecting the necessity for retrieving, and if necessary retrieving, the called unit from a library into core and passing control to its first instruction. Even this includes the location of free storage space and the resolution of program addresses to suit the available location. The more specifically real time task is the management of re-entrance to frequently used programs which are kept in core. The steps then needed include the recognition that a called unit is resident and re-entrant, the posting of the new use and the subsequent recognition of the termination of that use. The basic software for loading and relocating programs is provided by most manufacturers but the management of re-entrance needed development within some installations as late as 1973.

CORE MANAGEMENT

Core management is the allocation of storage space to different exchanges for the purposes of holding programs or data records or workspace. Since the mix of exchanges is constantly changing, varying sized segments of core are being requested and released at random. The core management program keeps track of free space, matches requests to space available, records its allocation and release. In complex systems, adjacent areas of free space may be combined whenever possible to permit the service of requests for larger areas. Although this function is always provided by a manufacturer for any system which claims to be multi-threading, the method provided may not be the most efficient so that further development may be justified.

DATA MANAGEMENT

Data Management in a real time system can be simply the same software as is used in handling direct access files in a batch system. An installation has scope for devising its own software for address generation algorithms, duplicate file processing (as part of recovery and restart), free file space management for temporary filed work records, security against overlapping updates and data privacy checks. An installation may wish to extend its data management software as far as the extraction of logical data groupings from different physical groupings, including the expansion of compacted data.

ERROR PROCESSING

Error processing is a suitable topic for software in a real time system. The errors concerned are not data validation errors but program or hardware faults. The common routines will be used to log the fault, take dumps and alert operators. This is not a function normally provided by manufacturers' software.

SYSTEM MONITORING

System monitoring concerns the collection of statistics on the behaviour of the real time system. Statistics can relate to the performance of users in speed, errors, use of facilities, or to the performance of the system in terms of transmission errors, message queue lengths, rate of exchange service, use of core storage or other resources. The statistics can be reported offline or be available for online enquiry, they can be collected continuously or sampled. They are used to verify or change design decisions such as program residence, storage space allocation, etc., or in the special case of transmission statistics, to predict failures in lines or terminals. Little software under this heading is included in teleprocessing packages.

COMMUNICATIONS NETWORK MODIFICATION

Communications network modification supports the system manager by providing him with the ability to make changes to the representation of the network in the computer system. Changes normally needed include the ability to disable and activate terminals and lines, to use network test facilities, to alter the polling sequence or change the frequency of polling terminals. To perform these actions, the software changes control tables which are part of the message reception and despatch software design, and so changes the appearance of the network within the computer without physically altering connections in the network.

Shutdown, recovery and restart. The ability to restart a real time computer system after a failure without loss of data can be a most important facility. The file duplication feature is a restart provision which has already been mentioned. That is used to protect the system against the loss of key data such as the conversation control record (CCR) file. Other problems arise from the possible loss of other parts of the system such as the central processor, terminals or lines. The loss of the central processor can cause difficulties in a data capture system if an exchange is partly processed. In a system which updates multiple files, a failure when part of the data base is updated can be catastrophic. At the very least, the software monitors the progress of the exchange so that an interrupted exchange can be completed or cancelled without loss of control. At best the restart facility will restore the system to full running without the need for repetition of any exchanges by operators or terminal users. (As for example, the SAISIE software developed by Arthur Andersen & Co. as an extension to IBM's CICS package.) Protection against communications facilities failure will include such features as the automatic diversion of messages from a failed terminal or line to an alternate, or the storage of messages pending the restoration of service. The shutdown facility can be thought of as a means for the system manager to prevent uncontrolled loss of service by intervention ahead of a failure. Shutdown and restart facilities are complementary to each other. A further feature frequently included under this heading is the ability for a computer operator to a user supervisor to 'broadcast'—that is enter messages which are repeated to nominated terminals.

The remaining functions are both more unusual and rarely provided by the manufacturer. Why go further? Some of the reasons are mentioned in the discussions of the specific facilities which follow.

Entry Analysis

The processing of an entry before it can be used to achieve its purpose in the system, is the subject of the entry analysis function. There are five possible stages to this analysis:

(a) unpacking—the separation of the string of characters received into a series of separate fields
(b) recognition—the identification of the structure and purpose of the entry and, in passing, its constituent fields
(c) approval—the process of deciding whether a recognized entry is permitted in the circumstances prevailing in the system
(d) validation—reviewing the contents of the fields alone or in combination
(e) conversion—changing the character form in which the message arrived to any form more suited to its processing, for example binary, packed decimal.

The stages overlap to some extent so that their sequence can have important effects on performance. In order to unpack an entry, there must be some plan of its structure available. However to select which plan to use, the identity of the entry must be known. We cannot detect identity until the entry is unpacked, though. To resolve this problem, some choice must be made. The objective is to restrict the amount of unpacking to be done before recognition is achieved. The amount can be restricted by reducing the number of characters of the message to be matched against identifying patterns or to reduce the number of patterns by examining only those which are authorized. Thus unpacking, recognition and approval overlap.

UNPACKING

Unpacking is the act of separating the message into fields. Fields can be distinguished from each other in a number of ways—by the character set used (numeric for example), by having a fixed length or by starting or finishing with a special character. Any unpacking software must deal with a number of common conditions:

(a) variable length
(b) variable occurrence including total absence
(c) variable sequence
(d) occurrence conditional on the presence of another field
(e) occurrence conditional on the value of another field
(f) presence of adjacent fields of similar data type.

As well as separating the fields, the unpack software may discard separators or redundant characters, such as spaces. To be able to carry out these tasks, software programs would need parameters defining the characteristics of each field. There would be a set of parameters for each different entry type. The topic of defining message formats is discussed further in Chapter 10.

RECOGNITION

Recognition could be defined as successful unpacking since to arrange a character string into fields means a match with one of several possible unpacking patterns. However the recognition process may require some investigation of the value of the unpacked fields. Recognizing things in general can be done in two ways—by comparing with a description or reading a label. Entry recognition can be classified in the same way. Either the entry can carry a label in the form of a string of characters of a given value, or it can be matched to a description of its format (or syntax). The IBM package CICS uses labels for recognition. In fact a label or action code is a special case of syntax recognition since a syntax definition must allow for quoting literal values. As discussed, the recognition process can be overlapped with approval by restricting the list of entries used in the matching process. So recognition becomes matching against an *allowed* entry definition not just a recognizable one.

APPROVAL

The approval conditions divide into two classes in a system which utilizes the conversation concept. If a user is engaged in a conversation then he will usually be permitted only a few entry types consistent with the type of conversation and the place within it that he has reached. If he is about to start a conversation, he has open to him the first entries of any of the conversations which he is allowed to use. The recognition process will depend on two different lists of permitted patterns—permitted next entries in the current conversation and permitted first entries of the conversation types available to his status. A system using a Conversation Control Record (CCR) can be programmed to maintain a permitted Next Entry Table (NET) in the CCR of each ongoing conversation. The First Entry Table (FET) can be kept as a core resident list within the real time partition. Both these techniques require some knowledge of the processing being done. They are rarely supported by vendor software but can be developed in house if the discipline of a standard CCR is adopted for the installation. The dynamic variation of the NET to reflect the position reached in the conversation is the responsibility of user programs. If the NET is used, the recognition and approval process can be controlled by syntax definitions without the use of literal action codes, since the number of recognition patterns at any time is small.

VALIDATION

Validation has an affinity with approval since a disapproved entry could be said to be invalid. A new problem arises, that of mistakes in identification. Almost certainly the recognition process will stop once a match has been made. However, if, for example, the user has made a mistake in quoting an action code—RSV instead of RVS—and both are permitted, the wrong validation rules will be applied. The resulting error message may be quite misleading. The same problem is applicable at the field level. It is particularly likely to occur in an entry with optional fields in a free form (not made by form filling). The existence of this problem is the reason why validation software is usually restricted to the simpler cases of checking:

(a) valid character types, e.g. alpha or numeric
(b) value table
(c) reference file
(d) range checking.

CONVERSION

Conversion is the fifth stage of entry analysis and is rather simpler to achieve. The original message is by now unpacked, recognized, approved and validated. There is very little opportunity for misinterpretation of parameters. The functions offered might be the conversion of numeric characters to an equivalent binary value or to packed decimal digits, the encoding of a value list field or the classification of values within small ranges.

When the entry has been through these five stages, control over its further processing may be passed to the first true application program. Its identity will have been established as a by-product of the recognition process.

The availability of software which performed all five functions would reduce application programs to their business purposes of update, data retrieval and extraction, whichever was the scope of the project. However, unless it is offered free by the equipment manufacturer or at a reasonable price by a software supplier, there is a cost of providing it in house. To be extensive and general enough, while remaining cheap in core and processing time, the software will have to be sophisticated. That means expense in development which may outweigh the savings in reduced application coding. If the installation has a number of real time projects scheduled, there may still be an advantage.

Entry analysis software has three components at run time, the analysis program, the compiled parameters describing the syntax of the possible messages and the compiled parameters describing the unpacked data elements passed to the application. The two classes of run time software and development software, previously identified, therefore have further relevance despite the fact that entry analysis is performed at run time.

The opportunities for *run time* software in order of increasing implementation cost are:

(a) data field conversion
(b) data field validation
(c) data group validation
(d) data group unpacking and approval
(e) entry recognition and approval with action codes, or entry recognition and approval by syntax definition.

Development software functions and alternatives, also in increasing cost sequence are:

(a) compiler for generating conversion software parameters of programs from tabular message definitions and field definitions
(b) compiler for generating validation software parameters or programs
(c) compiler for generating recognition and unpacking software parameters using either:
    (i) tabular definitions of message content
    (ii) free form notation definitions of message format (discussed in the next chapter)
(d) test message generator capable of constructing test messages conforming to the format definitions used in 'c'.

Response Synthesis

With the advantage of the foregoing discussion of the process of converting entries into fixed form data for filing, the complementary process of making responses out of field data should take less space to discuss. There are again a number of stages:

(a) assembly—collecting the data elements needed in the response from their sources
(b) editing—or conversion of elements from filed form to message form adding editing symbols
(c) formatting—the arrangement of the elements in a layout
(d) dispatching—sending the message with suitable control characters to a nominated logical destination.

The last of these is a trivial function which must be controlled by the application, although the conversion of a logical to a physical address recognizable by the communications software can be worth generalizing. This function is usually associated with the network management software mentioned earlier.

ASSEMBLY

Assembly is the function least likely to be embodied in software, although the parameters which could control it almost always exist. They are no more than the record definitions normally part of any commercial program. The response data segment can be defined like any other and the records from which the elements will be drawn will already be defined. The process of selecting could easily be achieved were it not that some aspects of assembly need coding to define. The substitution of one coding process for another is unlikely to show much profit. The aspects needing logic are the definition of conditions and the achievement of loops to extract data from several instances of the same record. As an example, consider the assembly of a response to an entry asking for a list of customers, products or employees, meeting some selection criterion. As long as a high level language is available capable of expressing the logic economically there will be no advantage in providing extracting software. However, if the project demands re-entrant code and the vendor does not supply suitable compilers, a case for such software might exist.

EDITING AND FORMATTING

Editing and formatting software has existed for many years for batch reports. Parameters to describe it are well known. However, vendors vary in the extent to which they support the real time equivalent. One consideration is the variability of terminal characteristics. Intelligent terminals and the more sophisticated 'idiots' like the 3270 can provide many formatting facilities by such simple means as cursor addressing. Such an ability means that the message transmitted can be left in a compact state to save transmission time. Software capable of adapting to a variety of terminal types is not in the vendor's interest. The provision of some of these facilities is discussed below under communications interface.

Data element editing is thus the only stage of any significance which might be a candidate for in-house software development. Frequently, routines will already exist for batch processing and these can be readily adapted for real time work by making them re-entrant.

Communications Interface

We have discussed entry analysis and response synthesis in this section and the topic of line control has also been touched on. The need to discuss the action of message transmission any further exists because none of these functions necessarily attains the objective of hardware independence. The project can gain in flexibility if the logical content of messages can be separated from the physical characteristics of the terminals for which they are intended or from which they are received. This property of independence has two advantages. In the event of terminal failure, messages can be switched to a different type of terminal without loss of meaning, though perhaps with loss of performance. Secondly, if terminal *technology improves* in cost or performance, terminals can be changed without reprogramming applications programs. Satisfaction of these objectives is best achieved by concentrating all the hardware dependent coding in one place. It may be covered in the line control software offered by vendors but no vendor is willingly going to make his customers independent of his hardware.

If the application coding is independent of any type of terminal then the direction normally available on such matters as control characters, line lengths, number of lines, etc., will not be available either. Therefore to enforce the property of independence the installation can invent a logical terminal, choose certain properties for it and choose the control characters which will convey application program use of the properties. This can be called the *Standard Terminal* and can be documented with a short programmer's guide. The properties of the Standard Terminal are the interface between the application and the real terminals. Matching the properties of the Standard and real terminals is the responsibility of the Communications Interface program. The complexity of this program is dependent upon the extent to which standard and real properties match, since its function is one of translation. The choice of Standard Terminal properties will be influenced by two pressures—any moves to standardization in the terminal market and second the actual properties of the most likely terminal to be used in the installation. If a variety of types will be used or a variety of models, the interface program will be modular, each model having its own module.

The properties of the Standard Terminal which must be designed are:

(a) cursor addressing—method by which the position of the next message character can be defined by coordinates
(b) line length—number of characters in the standard line and 'newline' control symbol
(c) number of lines
(d) method of defining compacting of repeated characters

(e) relative response positioning—method of defining the position of the first character of the response by reference to the last character of the entry, e.g. 'next character on same line' or 'next line after input'

(f) inclusion of standard text in the message—method to be used if this has not been done under response synthesis. May extend to the generation of complete forms—either blank for entries or for reports, to be completed by other data supplied in the response

(g) broadcasting—method of marking responses to show addresses of more than one terminal

(h) alternate addressing—switching message from one physical terminal to another if the first is not in use

(j) scroll control—the separation of a complete logical message into pages chosen to fit the size of display space available, the production of pages on request and the maintenance of titles and headlines through page changes.

The types of terminal which may be interfaced to the Standard Terminal can be as diverse as displays, character printers, line printers, card punches and readers or even backing storage devices. This latter is particularly valuable since system testing through tape files of messages can be achieved without special software.

The Standard Terminal has duties on the input side of processing as well as output. In particular if entries are made by form filling, the received message will show cursor movement from field to field which must be used to identify the fields in entry analysis. The conversion to a common convention for all terminal types (that used for responses) will simplify application programming.

It is apparent that the design of a communications interface program can be elaborate but the property of hardware independence has been found to be valuable in batch systems. The drawback is the overhead of having yet another program index through the message, character by character, to add to or change its content.

The provision of this software will clearly fall to the installation, since it is, by definition, independent of vendors. Software like this has application to all real time projects in house and the definition of its interface should be part of the standards manual for the installation. The decision on whether to include it and, if so, what facilities it should have, will depend on the long range plans for real time projects and management policy on hardware independence. If the Information Processing Manager standardizes on 3270 terminals, then that is the standard terminal and its programmer's guide is the only one needed. But how would he look if he had decided to standardize on the 2260?

The three functions of entry analysis, response synthesis and logical terminal interface are connected by virtue of their common handling of messages, either incoming or outgoing. If the logical terminal interface idea is used, one or both of the other functions can be combined with it to reduce the number of times that the characters in the messages are handled. In the application used as the source of examples in this book, the concept of a Standard Terminal was used to separate the application programs from the actual characteristics of the terminals used. The output side of the standard terminal was combined with response editing, based on tables which defined the editing characteristics of each response.

PROGRAMMING SPECIFICATION

Interfaces

The final act of system logic design in the preliminary phase was the establishment of programs and their interfaces in order to confirm the programming design of the application. The interface between two programs consists of a formal part—the CALL line and its parameters—and the contextual part. The contextual interface is carried in several places. The most significant is the Exchange Control Record (ECR). This will usually include a work area for passing data between the successive program units in a processing activity. Otherwise data in the interface may be carried in the message area or in retrieved file records attached to the ECR. The Conversation Control Record (CCR) can be included as a file record, holding data passed between exchanges. These components of the interface will be defined in detail in the program specification. Their exact form will depend upon the documentation requirements of the chosen, or designed, software for the tasks of program management and task scheduling.

In the paragraphs which follow, indications of the content of program specifications will be given but illustrations will be omitted. Provided that the topics discussed below are covered, an installation's own standards for program or subprogram specification will be suitable. At the level of program subdivision assumed there will be little difference between a batch segment, section, module, routine or subprogram and a real time program unit. If the similarity is stressed rather than the difference then units of code might be interchangeable and even managed on the same library by the same program management software.

Extent of Logic Definition

If the software base discussed earlier were fully implemented, the functions of entry analysis and response building programs would disappear, to be replaced by tabular definitions of the syntax of the messages being handled. Even without that software, programs having those functions can be defined in a fairly routine manner in which syntax tables or other forms of message definition still feature prominently. A processing program's logic does not permit so standard an approach so that its logic definition will consist of flowcharts, text, decision tables and any other devices which will convey the specifier's intention unambiguously.

Flowcharts

Two levels of flowcharting are recommended—block diagram and flowchart. The block diagram is analogous to the general assembly drawing of an engineering product which shows how components fit together but does not give much information about each. The block diagram is an aid to adopting a modular approach to the construction of the program by identifying the mainline of the program and separating the various functions into logically separate routines. The diagram should make plain any decisions which govern the use of the separate blocks or their sequence. No two people will agree exactly on the level of detail to be shown on a block diagram, but the structure of the program will be more obvious if the diagram can be kept on one page. The individual boxes should describe a unit of processing which will be recognizable to a user in terms that he could understand. Each box on the chart should represent an independent unit of logic which could be separately programmed if the need arose. This will help to make the program easily testable and modifiable. Each box should have a single entry point and only more than one exit if it represents a decision process. The concept of modularity is a logical one and does not stop at the boundaries of physically separate programs. It can be applied down to pairs of instructions.

The source for the block diagram could very well be found in the diagrams of the exchanges to which the program contributes. These must in any case be consulted in case they are incompatible with each other. Each will only show those functions of the program of interest to the exchange, but combined, they will cover all its functions.

The need for additional flowcharting will vary with the complexity of the work and the skill of the programmer. The latter is as yet unknown, so some average level of skill must be assumed. The flowchart is a picture of the processing sequence, used because the representation of complex alternative paths is not easily conveyed by linear text.

The text within flowchart boxes will necessarily be limited to short terse statements. The specifier should, however, attempt to convey the 'why' of the function rather than 'how'. The coding and its accompanying commentary will usually show 'how' the function is expressed very adequately, so the flowchart should be one more way of communicating with the user and other non-programmers. A statement saying 'is tax payable' is more informative than 'is indicator X set'.

System Logic

The processing sequence shown in the flowchart will usually need to be supported by accompanying text—if only because flowchart boxes are not intended to hold much explanation. Processing should be specified in the manner of a high level computer language—short sentences with a small vocabulary using symbolic data names to match record or work area definitions. Decision tables should be used wherever multiple dependencies of conditions govern the choice of several courses of action.

Error situations should be identified within the processing stream. The processing consequent upon an error may be described at that point if it is simple, or left to a later subsection. The separate treatment of errors will encourage modularity and will be the more usual form. When the processing of an error includes the despatch of a brief standard response or status message, it should be identified by a message number. This will be used as a parameter to a service routine which will extract the message from a library. The wording of the message should only be given as an illustration and not treated as definitive.

If processing is at all complex, the specifier may wish to illustrate some, or all of it, with an example of its application to one or more illustrative cases.

Work Areas

A program operating in this environment has a private work area and also has access to the common activity work area in the ECR. A data record specification should be created for the ECR work area for each exchange since the same one will be used by all the programs executed during the activity. A copy of this should probably be bound into the program specification for completeness and the original should then show a reference, so that if its format is altered, new copies can be directed to all using programs.

The program work area will not need to be separately specified—being of no concern to any other document. A formal specification should be prepared though, in the data record format, at least to assign names to the work data items so that the text of the logic section can make unambiguous reference to them. This is a part of the specification which will be altered during coding as the need for other temporary storage becomes plain.

Testing

Consistently, the series of document descriptions in the book has recommended the identification of test cases at the same time as logic has been specified. This document is uniform in that respect. Test conditions should be explored as part of the process of specifying—whether the programs are processing, entry definition or response construction. The manner of identifying test cases will vary with the program type but the need is as strong for each.

In a processing program, the first step will be to identify the logical modules—the 'smaller-than-program' size pieces of logic which can be treated as if they were subroutines to the mainline of the program charted in the top logic diagram. The decision table format, listing all the separate conditions and outcomes and then combining the conditions in various ways to make cases, is first of all applied in each module. When each module has its set of cases defined then an overall table can be added to deal with the combination of modules. In this way the number of test cases is reduced to much less than if the whole program is treated as one unit. A program with eight two-way conditions might need as many as 2^8 or 256 cases, while those same conditions, separated into two modules of four conditions each, need two times 2^4 cases or 33 in all, allowing for one more to test their interface. Obviously, real programs would not show as great a saving as that since many combinations will be made impossible by the structure, but the illustration does reveal the source of savings.

While conditions in a processing program are revealed by its flowcharts, entry definition and response construction programs exhibit their logic in their tables. Their conditions consist of the presence or absence of optional fields, maximum and minimum field sizes or values, maximum or minimum repetitions and deliberate error conditions. A list of conditions must be built up by painstaking examination of the definition of each field. The outcomes in entry definition are properly recognized entries and a group of unpacked, validated and converted fields, or else error responses. This step is laborious if done properly but, if message analysis is reliable the confidence which users will have in the system is greatly increased. The process of entry definition is discussed in the next chapter.

Test cases for response construction programs will consist of properly edited displays. Most field editing will be by service routine so will not be the subject of many cases. Most cases will be concerned with interfield positioning and relationships. If the response is complex, its definition by table may be supported by a flowchart, in which case the considerations applicable to processing programs will apply.

Statistics

There are three measures suggested in this section which should be developed as early as possible with approximate values and subsequently refined for the record. These are frequency of use, execution time and program size.

FREQUENCY OF USE

Frequency of use is a determinant of storage location if this is under the control of the project designer. In a sophisticated software environment residence is controlled by the program management software but this may not be a feature of all environments. The source of information is in the peak hour frequency table discussed and illustrated in Part II. A grading of frequency will probably be sufficient to group programs into three to five categories. The response time performance required of a program's parent exchanges will also have a bearing.

EXECUTION TIME

Execution time will be variable, having a distribution dictated by the presence of optional paths. Execution time will be composed of data transfers, calls to other routines and time to execute code. An estimate can be developed by listing these with their standard times and a statement—perhaps in decision table form again—of their frequency of occurrence in various combinations. The times for each component can be combined to arrive at a total figure for each combination. Where channel transfers are concerned the size of the element being transferred must be estimated. Record identities should be given so that size changes can be accounted for as the project develops. Each service routine and other program call should be identified since their execution times will vary. The execution time of exchanges will be a factor—with transmission time—of their response performance. The calculated execution time may increase when the system is busy and activities have to wait for service, but the information will still be extremely valuable in confirming configuration parameters and—after installation—in tuning the system. In an environment without automatic control of residence, the designer may trade off residence of programs and tables to change the performance of one exchange as against another.

PROGRAM SIZE

Program size is needed to develop estimates of the size of the program library. This will also be done early and approximately and can be refined later. If core organization uses pages or some other physical grouping of fixed unit size, then this statistic may be expressed in that unit rather than instructions or words. The size of program will be governed by the efficiency of the compiler applied.

References

In various places in the specification and in the interfaces defined earlier, references to other documents have been included. The interfaces section identified other programs for example. A separate list of all references included in the specification will help in servicing changes. Also the section can be built up early—before some of the text sections are written. The documents to which reference is likely are exchanges, files, data records, service routine and project program specifications.

SERVICE ROUTINES USER SPECIFICATIONS

Specification Defines Interface

The information needed by a programmer writing a service routine will be provided in the form already described for a processing program. The project programmers who wish to employ service routines will not want to keep that amount of documentation about each routine. A separate document is therefore useful to contain an extract of the routine writer's documentation. This can be referred to as 'user' documentation. The information contained within it resembles those sections of the program specification which define interfaces between application programs—its function is after all identical. The 'user' specifications for all service routines will probably be conveniently bound into one volume, arranged in some suitable sequence for reference. The

168

routines fall into groups—such as response editing and data access—so might well be arranged by routine identity within group.

The documentation provided for each routine will be organized under section headings:

(a) description
(b) parameters
(c) errors
(d) statistics
(e) references.

Description is Limited

The descriptive material has the purpose of identifying the service that the routine offers. It is important that this be clear and unambiguous but equally important that the program specification for the routine is not reproduced. The function of the section is to describe briefly what the routine does. This is supplemented by an outline of the processing as a way of conveying the purpose by different means.

Parameter Description is Main Section

The mechanism for using service routines is to transfer control by the standard method available in the program management software which will require a statement of the parameters supplied for the routine and those returned by it. The form of transfer statement required by the software should be explicitly quoted so that no misunderstanding exists. If parameter transfer needs user program statements in addition to the transfer then all the code lines required should be specified and illustrated.

The function of each parameter should be described, particularly referring to its data type (e.g. numeric) and its use in the service routine, if this could be unclear.

The section will normally be divided under headings of 'input' and 'output'. If the purpose of a routine is to change an input parameter and return a new value, this parameter will be specified in both the input and output lists.

Error Conditions may Exclude Return

The errors detected by a service routine can be classified into two types—those which are notified to the calling program for its action and those which prevent return of control. The membership of an error in one or other sub-section may depend upon whether the activity being processed originated from a terminal or an automatic event. For example, a routine to retrieve a filed record which detected that the requested record was subject to a concurrent update, would report the fact to a terminal-initiated activity so that the terminal was not locked for too long. An automatic activity on the other hand could wait without any disturbance, although this may be undesirable.

The errors are therefore classified into three groups:

(a) errors always giving return of control
(b) errors always resulting in activity termination
(c) errors resulting in termination if the activity is terminal initiated.

In each category, each error should be described and associated with any status value or message identification, whether to calling program, terminal user or computer console, and the action taken by the service routine should be stated.

Statistics Refers to Project Monitoring

The section headed 'statistics' in the user document, differs from that with the same title in the program specification. In the context of user documentation, it refers to processing within the routine, particularly directed to monitoring the project or the system as a whole. Here the documentation should quote any system or project counters updated by the routine.

References give more Detail

A service routine cannot be considered to be part of any one project. Its references cannot therefore include a 'used in' section since the complete set of references will never be known. The only ones which can be given are to those documents which give more detail about the routine. The routine's own program specification should be named together with those for any routines embedded in this one. There may also be some more general statements of installation policy or practice which support the existence of the service routine. The choices made for the system in the management of data files or core, are examples where supporting documentation is likely. These are policies which are typically implemented by service routines.

Chapter 10
Detailed Data Definition

CLASSES OF DATA

The topic of data definition has been much illuminated in recent years by the move towards data bases in both real time and batch work. The independence of data structures from the programs which access data is well established. For real time systems, the use of online files and the physical and logical impossibility of each exchange, or even conversation, having its own private files, has always favoured the separate definition of data files.

In this chapter, data is described in two ways—according to its logical form and according to its structure. There are three forms recognized—input (or source), filed and output (or edited) form. Input data exists as entries, filed data as records and output data as responses. Each of these forms has structure in that each is composed of fields or data elements and the fields are grouped in various ways to make larger and larger units until the entry, record or response is achieved. To represent the data definition economically the characteristics associated with fields are described in a field definition. The definitions of higher level structures need then concern only the relationship between fields and not their separate characteristics.

The chapter will first complete the discussion of file definition started in preliminary design, then consider the problems of definition of each data form at different levels.

FILE DEFINITION

Contents and Identification

The fact of a file's existence in a project was established in preliminary design from the needs for data to service exchanges. In Chapter 7, the documentation needed for the purposes of preliminary design was set out. The subsequent investigation of project cost and duration will have finalized the file structure so that each file can now be finally specified. A file is a higher level of data grouping than the records to be defined later. The content of a file definition is therefore carefully chosen so as not to overlap and repeat information to be held in the record definition. The record is separately documented, so the key characteristics of a file are how and why records are grouped into files. The

Company Name	ABC Company		INDEX NO.
	FILE DESCRIPTION		I-400
Systems Development	Centralised Ordering		HK/M/61 FILE NO.

Prepared by	N Cook	Reviewed by	P McGregor	Approved	PMG
Date	10-2-73	Date	10-5-73	Date	

FILE TITLE___Conversation Control File___ REV. NO.___0___

DESCRIPTION Inter exchange data storage, performance statistics and recovery data. One record per terminal. Set up when a terminal is added to network. Initialised when terminal is inactive. Deleted on terminal disconnection. Updated on each entry

SEQUENCE (Major Field to Minor Field):___ TOTAL BYTES/CHARACTERS___

FIELD NAME		BYTES/ CHARACTERS	FORM	FIELD LOCATION
TERMNO	Terminal reference	2	Binary	

BLOCKING FACTOR___Single record block___ MAXIMUM RECORD LENGTH___1000___

TYPE ☐ CARD ☐ TAPE ☒ DISK ORGANIZATIONS: a. Random b. Serial

COMPUTER PROGRAM USAGE

PROGRAM NUMBER	I	O	PROGRAM NUMBER	I	O
HK251	☒	☐	HE25	☒	☐
HK252	☐	☒		☐	☐
HE20	☒	☒		☐	☐

RETENTION PERIOD___Permanent___

RECORDS INCLUDED

RECORD NO.	TITLE	RECORD LENGTH	APPROX. VOLUME
HKM61	CER - includes one of :-	1000 (fixed)	70 - growing 5%
HKM611	Supervisor Conv. Control Segment)		per annum
HKM612	Invoice entry " "		
HKM613	Invoice Correction " "		
HKM614	GRN entry " "		
HKM615	Order entry " "		

ACCESS METHOD: Entry terminal number specifies logical record number in file. Standard Direct Access (SDA) software is used to calculate address from file control table.
     Same access method is used by program HE20 to dump file sequentially.
     On writing HKF165 copies record to duplicate file before returning control to application

CONTROL: Routine HKF205 reads all positions on file each hour to prove active record count against Control Area counter. HK251 (standard terminal-entry) compares retrieved record terminal number against entry terminal number

RECOVERY: On read error from SDA routine duplicate file read routine HKF170 computes duplicate record number and reads second record. On second read error, console message requests file restore. Routine HKF165 reads loaded tape file and rewrites both copies.

VERSIONS: Copy file HK/M/90 has same file structure
     Back up tape file HK/R/25 comprises same records

Figure 10.1. File description

specification here described can be built by expanding or rewriting the earlier file worksheet.

The file must first be identified, so that other documents can refer to it, and described so that the reason that records are grouped in one way rather than another is made clear. The identifying and descriptive sections will be a reference, a name and a description. The reference will be in accordance with the installation's standards for labelling files and the name will be a short plain language title descriptive of its logical content and structure (see Figure 10.1).

There will be great benefit in expanding on the name in a description of the file since the key characteristics to be included in the specification can be justified. Also the description of a project through its impact on a data base provides a further dimension to documentation which will assist newcomers to the project to appreciate its function. The description of a file could usefully make reference to the sources of data included in the file and the circumstances under which data is added, deleted, updated or just read. The conversations performing these functions should be named to permit the reader to make connections with other parts of the functional description.

Multiple Records

Although not always necessary, a file can contain more than one record type. A batch system transaction file is an obvious example when it contains source records to add, delete and update a master file. The file definition should specify its relationship to these lower level data collections by stating which record types are included. The section will refer to records and so maintain the policy of cross reference followed elsewhere in the documentation. The records included may be repeated and optional so that the means of distinguishing each record type should be defined at this point.

File Structure

Once the records are identified, their relative position and other structural details can be set down. The first characteristic to establish must be file sequence—by record type within some logical sequence related to the file name usually. Whether or not the file is accessed sequentially there will usually be some structure enabling the file to be built and accessed according to key data values.

Other structural characteristics which need to be recorded will include the physical details of blocking factors and storage medium. In a real time system, the blocking of randomly accessed records can increase rather than reduce processing time. However, not all files are accessed at random so blocking status should still be specified. There are sometimes choices in the direct access devices available and tape can be an appropriate medium at times. The specification of file medium is therefore also relevant.

Finally, the size of the file at least in terms of number of records of each type will need to be documented. The size of individual records will be defined in record specifications and may be subject to change as design progresses. However to avoid inconvenient cross referencing the total record size should be repeated and maintained in the file specification. The size and number of records may both be variable and so maximum, minimum and average values should be maintained. The file may also be subject to growth or decay over time so the rate of change will be useful for planning storage space.

Access Method

The method of access to data within a file involves two stages—identifying the data required and then searching the file. Identifying data will have been discussed in describing the file sequence but this section should explicitly name all fields associated with access to data. The method of transforming identifying fields into a record address on the storage device should then be described. The method may be serial or direct, indexed or calculated. The access coding may be supplied by the manufacturer as standard or may be a special routine devised in the installation. Each of these characteristics should be recorded and elaborated as necessary.

Access methods usually handle the stage in data retrieval of locating a record. If there are repeated sets of data within the record, e.g. detail lines in an order, then there may well be a preferred or even standard method for accessing those. This may be recorded here in the file specification or in the later record specification.

Control and Recovery

In the preliminary design worksheet related to the files, the topics of control and data recovery were introduced. The designer should now be in a position to clearly identify the coding which will support these functions for each file. The program units should be named and the chosen method for control and recovery described.

Multiple Versions

To complete the cross referencing discussion one further topic needs mention. In batch systems several versions of what is logically one collection of data must be recognized. For example, a master file may exist in old and updated versions which are respectively read and written by one program and so must be distinguished. Transaction files may progress from source form through valid unsorted and sorted versions. The data description of one file may thus apply to others.

In real time systems this phenomenon is not so frequent. Files are accessed directly so various sequences are not necessary, master files are updated in place so father and son versions are not required. However there can be instances, as, for example, when the before and after versions of an updated record are included on a log file or when a real time file is kept in a back up version. The condition can therefore exist.

If it does, then the file documentation should link the various versions together to avoid duplication and inconsistency. Each file identity will need to be established for programming purposes, so a file specification should be created. However, one should be treated as the standard definition and the others linked to it.

FILED RECORDS

Data has Further Subdivisions

The entities now to be defined are composed of data fields and groupings of them. If the characteristics of every field in a record are defined in the record specification then that definition must be repeated in every record specification in which the field occurs. The repetition is wasteful of effort and is open to the danger of inconsistencies arising between definitions, either initially or as data definition is changed. There will therefore be merit in preparing separate field definitions and this is the practice which will be followed here. The record specification is therefore restricted to describing the fact of the relationship between its components.

For convenience the same format will be used to document collections of data having some logical significance at levels lower than a record. Such a collection will be referred to as a group. Fields can participate in groups and can join with other groups to make further groups. Finally a record is a group which is composed of lower level groups and fields. The use of the three terms record, group and field does not therefore imply only three levels of subdivision. In principle the subdivision can be infinite. Specifications should be prepared for any data grouping and one common format should be adequate for all groups, at whatever level, up to and including records. A format is illustrated in Figures 10.2 and 10.3.

Standard Labels

As with files, the first characteristic to document is the content of the group at the next lowest level. For files, the content is records, for records or groups the content is fields or other groups. The method of identifying content is to quote the standard data label of the component included.

The label used may be a name or it may be a programming label. If the installation has a single programming language the latter is to be preferred to reduce the variety of naming and reference systems. Whichever is used, it should be the means of cross reference to that data item's own specification.

When a group or record participates in more than one higher level grouping then the various uses will themselves need differentiation. At the record level for example, a file updating application may imply an input version and an output version of the record in the program responsible for updating. To refer to the two areas, both having the same layout, the program will need some

Company Name _ABC Company_

RECORD DATA WORKSHEET

Systems Development _Centralised Ordering_

I-500	INDEX NO.
HKM 61	Item NO.

Prepared by	N Cook	Reviewed by	RCT	Approved	
Date	10-5-73	Date	10·15·73	Date	

DESCRIPTION Conversation Control Record   **LENGTH** 1000   **REV. NO.** 0

FILE NOS.	HKM61				HKM90	HKR25			
PROGRAM NO. I/O	HK2S1 I	HK2S2 O	HE2O I/O	HE2S I					

Field Posn.	LABEL	FIELD DESCRIPTION	Number of Pos.	Dec.	Bytes	Occurrence Max.	Min.	Relative Location on
0	CHCNT	Record size – standard field	4		2	1		
1	RETY	Record type – " "	2		2	1		
2	TERMNØ	Terminal reference number of owner terminal	2		2	1		
3	TERMTY	Terminal location type	1		1	1		
4	ØPRID	Identity of operator using terminal	2		2	1		
5	ØPRSTAT	Operator authority status	1		1	1		
	FILLER				10	1		
6	NØCHEN	Daily characters entered count	8		4	1		
7	NØFTER	Daily format errors count	8		4	1		
	FILLER				12	1		
8	PROCCS	Procedure currently set	2		1	1		
9	NECNT	Permitted Next entry Count	1		1	1		
10	PERMNE	Next Entry Code			8	8	1	NECNT
10	TLFGNO	Transaction log file generation	2		2	1		
11	LSTRBC	TLF block of last record written from this terminal	4		2	1		
12	LSTBBC	TLF block of start of last batch written	4		2	1		
	FILLER				4	1		
13	SØMLIN	Start of message-line coord	2		1	1		
14	SØMCHA	" " " -char coord	2		1	1		
15	EØMLIN	End of message – line coord	2		1	1		
16	EØMCHA	char coord	2		1	1		
17	ERRLIN	Error field start - line coord	2		1	1		
18	ERRCHA	char coord	2		1	1		
	FILLER				34	1		
19	HKM611	Invoice Entry segment			900	1		

Figure 10.2. Record data worksheet

176

Company Name	ABC Company					I-550 INDEX NO.

GROUP DATA WORKSHEET

Systems Development _Centralised Ordering_

HDGP15
Item no.

Prepared by	B Mann	Reviewed by	P McG	Approved	
Date	10·30·73	Date	11·2·73	Date	

DESCRIPTION _Standard Order Identity_   LENGTH _9 BYTES_   REV. NO. _0_

Records used on	HKM 15	HKM 29	HKM 45	HKT 01	HKT 13	HKR 15	HF R02			
	HKM 20	HKM 30	HKM 46	HKT 02	HKT 17	HKR 18				
	HKM 22	HKM 41		HKT 10	HKT 18	HKR 24				

Field Posn	LABEL	FIELD DESCRIPTION	Pos.	Dec.	Bytes	Max	Min	on
0	STOR	Store Number	4		2	1		
1	DEP	Department code	2		2	1		
2	HDGP27	Date of order	5		3	1		
3	SER	Order serial number for store/department/date	3		2	1		

Figure 10.3. Group data worksheet

reference to their separate existence so that fields having the same label can be distinguished. A prefix or qualifying clause is usually used. In the documentation of the higher level entity the prefix or qualification should be given. The label or data name quoted for a component of a data grouping will therefore have two parts, its 'own' name and its qualifying prefix in this context. The concept applies equally to record names in a file.

Some compromises will have to be made in programming when referring to a data field which lies many levels down the data structure but in the data specification only two levels are visible at a time, the owner item (the subject of the specification) and its members. In any case the number of levels of grouping rarely exceeds three.

Repeated Fields or Groups

If an item is optional or repeated, then this relationship with the record must be shown. Repeated items can vary in their repetition in different occurrences of a record so the form shows provision for a maximum and minimum value. A minimum value of zero shows that the item concerned is optional. The repetition characteristic can apply both to groups and to single fields.

Data Position

The relationship of the members to each other can be shown in two ways. The members can be written down in their correct relative positions or each can be assigned a relative position number. The latter enables positions to be altered and members to be added without rewriting the entire form, but the former is preferable for conveying a picture of relative position. Both methods are shown in the exhibits since the numbers correspond to the physical position now occupied. Minor adjustments can be made without rewriting but major changes are best documented by rewriting.

Record Size

One other attribute of importance is conveyed on the form. Although it was stated earlier that field characteristics are documented on field definitions, this admonition has been contradicted by showing constituent field and group sizes. This is for convenience of developing record sizes to contribute in turn to the calculation of the space needed to hold each data file. The drawback is that whenever a data item size changes, its owner documents must be altered to suit. This is error prone but must be accepted since in reality there is great convenience in explicitly showing data item sizes.

The total size of the item being specified is developed by taking both member item size and repetition characteristics into account.

Work Areas

The entities which are documented in this way are not restricted to sets of items in filed records. The term 'group' is applied to any collection of items which are treated for some purposes as a unit. This caution is particularly intended to ensure that work areas—Exchange Control Record, Program and Conversation Control Record work areas are documented as carefully as filed records. ECR and CCR data groups will be of interest to more than one application program and should be fully defined. Program work areas will best be defined to the same standard but will be included with the program specification.

MESSAGE DEFINITION

Need for Further Detail

The definition of messages was commenced in the preliminary design to the extent of indicating probable data content and preparing samples. At the stage of detailed design their specification must be completed to provide the necessary information for programming. If the installation has the message manipulation software discussed in the previous chapter, the level of definition of message syntax now to be completed will provide parameters for the software. The exact format to be used will therefore vary between installations but the later exhibits will indicate the detail required.

Message Versions

There are a number of stages through which a message passes between keying and processing. Each stage could be the subject of documentation. An entry starts life at a terminal usually in the form of key depressions. While the entry is being built in terminal storage it is being displayed visually on the terminal, whether on a VDU or a printer. The train of key depressions stored in the terminal will probably occupy less space than the displayed presentation. The entry may be of the form filling type, introduced in Chapter 7, so that the form and field titles are visible on the display but have not been keyed by the operator. The blank spaces on the display, left when moving the cursor, will be represented internally only as control characters.

When the entry is complete, the complexity of the terminal will govern the exact form of the message which will be sent. There are a number of common features:

(a) control characters are sent as entered not as seen in their effect on the display e.g. 'newline' is a single character not a string of spaces to fill the previous line;
(b) erasures and overwrites are rationalized so that the data content of the message is equivalent to that seen;
(c) any previously stored format is not sent;
(d) any fields which might have been entered but were left blank are not sent except perhaps as instances of 'tab' characters;

(e) sequences of repeated characters may be compacted to the form XYZ where X is a control character, Y is the repeated character and Z is the number of times it occurred in the message after resolving corrections. This feature will only be applied to sequences of more than three.

In summary then we have another version of the message, that leaving the terminal.

We will ignore the transformations necessary for its transmission and pick up the message again when it reaches the CPU. Here the standard software function of line control may alter the character code used, to match that of the CPU, and strip off parity and timing control characters. At some point along the route, extra characters will have been added to identify the origin of the message. Line control software will hand the message to message control software which will attach it to an Exchange Control Record and probably store the origin in the ECR. When the message is scheduled for processing, the further transformations to which it is subjected depend upon the availability of entry analysis software. When a true application program gets hold of the message it may be in any shape. The functions of entry analysis software are discussed in Chapter 9.

Transformations of a similar kind are applied in reverse to the messages leaving the application en route to the terminal. There is one additional feature which may be present in the terminal which affects this end. Some terminals have the ability to store blank formats as well as maintain the completed form which represents the last entry. This can be done by maintaining the distinction between protected and unprotected areas of the display. A blank form can therefore be invoked by a simple control character.

Figure 10.4 will illustrate the points in a message's life to which the documentation in this section applies.

Entry Types

Chapter 7 introduced a number of types of conversation, prompted and unprompted. The entries associated also differ. Any real project will need to use mixtures of types so the designer's first task is to match the various situations with the various types.

The major division of entries is also between prompted and unprompted. Unprompted entries are usually free format, that is to say entered, displayed and sent to the computer as a simple character string consisting of one or more data fields punctuated by separator characters or other means of field separation.

Prompted entries may take many forms. They may be free form having had either the sequence of their fields prompted or simply their presence. Prompted free form can be divided again into plain data and menu selection. Plain data is the entry of explicit data values while menu selection is the entry of some temporary identifier meant to indicate the selection from a list of displayed

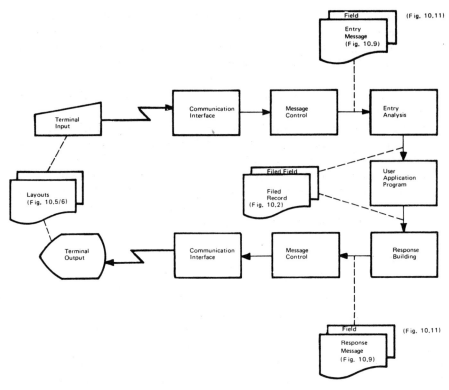

Figure 10.4.

plain values. An example of the difference would be the entry of a customer name:

type   *entry*

plain   JONES
menu   2   —when JONES was included in the second position
                       of a list of names

The alternative to prompted free forms is prompted formatted. Formatted entries are made by literally filling in a form—using the cursor positioning, or 'tab', facility of a terminal to align the cursor with the start of an empty space designed to hold one named field. Figure 10.7 illustrates the type.

There are many advantages and disadvantages of each type. The Figures 10.5 and 10.6 treat the design problem in two ways. Figure 10.5 suggests some criteria for evaluating the suitability of each type while Figure 10.6 suggests entry characteristics which might lead to one type or the other. In practice the relative importance of the criteria will vary and the designer must exercise judgement in the matching of type to exchange. Mixes of types are also not unknown.

Criterion	Prompted		Fixed form	Un-prompted
	Free form			
	Menu	Plain		
Transmission efficiency	poor	good	poor	excellent
Processing to analyse	excellent	good	good	poor
Throughput of entries	excellent	good	good	good
Error rate—format	excellent	poor	good	poor
—feasibility	excellent	poor	poor	poor
—sequence	excellent	excellent	excellent	poor
—presence	excellent	excellent	excellent	poor
Total data per entry possible	poor	excellent	good	poor
Tolerance of variety in entry type	poor	good	poor	excellent

Figure 10.5. Criteria for form design

Entry condition	Cases							
Unpredictable identity	Y	N	N	N	—	—	N	N
Few data fields	Y	N	Y	Y	—	—	N	N
High entry volume	Y	Y	Y	Y	N	N	N	Y
Good analysis software	Y	Y	N	Y	Y	Y	N	—
Variability of content	Y	N	N	N	—	—	Y	Y
Variability of sequence	Y	N	—	Y	N	Y	Y	N
Variable types of data	Y	N	N	Y	Y	N	—	Y
Unorganized sources	Y	N	Y	Y	Y	N	Y	Y
Variety of terminals	Y	N	Y	Y	—	—	Y	N
Expensive transmission	Y	N	N	Y	—	—	N	Y
Experienced staff	Y	N	N	Y	N	Y	—	—
Entry types Unprompted	✓					✓		
Prompted—Free—Menu			✓				✓	
—Plain				✓	✓			
—Fixed		✓						✓

Figure 10.6. Entry conditions related to entry type

Figure 10.6 is presented in the form of a decision table to permit the exploration of different mixes of conditions. It does not substitute for judgement since the graduations of value possible on each characteristic are infinite and the significance in cost will vary from job to job. In any case only a few situations showing a clear preference for one method or the other are considered.

Entry Design

The choices which the designer makes are more extensive than the adoption of one or other of the major classes. The design must serve the usual criteria of economy in user effort or transmission cost, or else in development effort if the first two are unimportant through low volume. Although his freedom of choice may be constrained by the terminal, usually he can make choices at the level of the individual data field as follows:

(a) variable length;
(b) variable occurrence;
(c) different data type from neighbours;
(d) variable position in entry.

Variability of length is exploited, to keep down transmission load. Variability in occurrence is a necessary property if the data item is naturally optional or repeated by a variable amount. Variability of occurrence can be induced if the value of a field is partly predictable. The predicted value can be implied and need only be included in the entry when it varies from the predicted and implied value.

The significance of a data field different in type from its neighbours, is that it can perform as both data and separator so saving keying and transmission. If a field has only a limited range of values it can be assigned codes from the small set of special symbols usually available on keyboards so as to change its data type and permit this technique to be used.

Variability in position can arise when the origins of the data entered vary. A spoken source cannot always be disciplined into giving data in a set sequence. The analysis of an entry with data varying in position requires field identification, and hence entry recognition and unpacking techniques, which must be performed on the entry when received. The functions are those identified in the discussion of entry analysis software in Chapter 9. The entry must be:

(a) unpacked—each field separated
(b) recognized—as to entry type and field type
(c) validated and, finally,
(d) converted—into a filed form.

These functions must be performed either by software or by user program. The ease with which they may be performed is usually inversely related to the need to save transmission cost or user effort. Ingenuity in design should not be perversely exercised if these two criteria are unimportant.

With that proviso our objective is to design the shortest possible entry which can be analysed by human intelligence and hence, by intelligence, expressed in programming.

Implied fields can save the entry of any data whatsoever. There are two possibilities. The default option can always take the *same value*, or the one *most recently* entered. This second technique is most easily achieved with the

Conversation Control Record. Then each operator can be using a different default and it can vary dynamically. For example, a case of a fixed value default might be 'the order date is equal to today's date unless otherwise stated'. An example of a dynamic default is 'the invoice supplier number stays the same until altered'. Default values are generally repeated back in the response to an entry which includes them, for verification.

Another technique to save keying which also involves the CCR, is the use of the Next Entry Table. If only one or two entry types are permitted and they differ in format from each other, then there is no need for identifying action codes. Instead the entries are recognized by comparing them with format definition parameters. This is known as *recognition by syntax*. Its efficiency, in code executed before recognition, can be quite high if the characteristics of each permitted entry which are most different are put first in the entry. This gives the early syntax high discrimination and high information content per character.

Finally the *menu* technique mentioned earlier permits a lot of information to be packed into one character. The technique can be used to select from a limited range of values or an unlimited range presented in groups of permitted values. It is most efficient when every key on the keyboard can be employed, e.g. 64 keys matched against a choice of 64 values. The CCR helps in holding the meanings.

By mixing these techniques in one entry, extremely short messages can be created comprising many different data fields. For example the entry 'J1M1' from an airline passenger check in system refers to 16 different data fields. 'J' is a passenger name initial, 1 is a number of passengers of one weight code, 'M' is the weight code and 1 is the number of bags stowed in the aircraft hold. Also it conveys that there are zero passengers in weight categories, F, C and I, zero pieces of hand baggage, the passenger is travelling in economy class and he has a confirmed ticket (fixed defaults). He is travelling on the BA501 flight of today's date, alighting at Kennedy airport—all dynamic defaults. Also note that by mixing data types there are no separators. Another example of the same entry type is:

$$*TW651/02JANPHILIP3M2F3C2I10/39/5£KINØ$$

Most fields are now present, though not all at their maximum values. The interpretation is:

*	—action code to show change of flight
TW651	—flight number
02JAN	—date of departure
PHILIP	—first letters of passenger name
3M	—three male adults
2F	—two female adults
3C	—three children
2I	—two infants in arms

10	—ten pieces of stowed baggage
39	—weight 39 kilos
5	—five pieces of cabin baggage
£	—first class
KIN	—alighting Kingston Jamaica
Ø	—open dated tickets.

These are both examples of the same entry type, admittedly analysed by extensive user coding.

The example shows some other features. For instance, the month JAN and the destination KIN are both fixed length, if they appear, so they do not need terminating symbols to separate them from following fields of the same data type. The fields KIN and Ø both optional, both of the same data type, cannot be confused because they are different lengths. The sign £ is one of two special symbols chosen to represent the limited values that 'class' could take, when present. It also has a default value. The various passenger number fields could occur in any sequence provided they were in pairs quantity/type and each type did not occur more than once.

Error Entries

Much of the above discussion also relates to error entries but a few more points can be made. Error correction methods can be classified into two types—re-entry and progression. Re-entry, as its name implies, is the repeat of the full entry making corrections where necessary. Progressive correction is the submission of an alteration only to the field in error. It is progressive because multiple errors are reported and corrected singly. It is most easily implemented using the CCR since a record of the entry as so far analysed and corrected must be kept and restored. Progression is particularly useful for long fixed form entries. However, the option to scrap a seriously wrong entry and start over should always be permitted. The Next Entry Table thus always has two entries. This facility is important when the computer has made a mistaken error diagnosis and so failed to provide for the correct progression.

Fixed Length Entries

This is a rare class with keyed entries but some types of terminals are particularly suited to it. The badge reader, for example, can accept data entries which are fixed in content, sequence, occurrence and length of fields. Such entries are not difficult to analyse.

Terminal entries to be used by the general public may also need to be simple and robust so that error occurrence is extremely low. Since the cost of terminal operator's time is then zero, fixed length and sequence entries are supportable and preferable. Little training or skill can be demanded of the user.

Responses

The considerations on type of entry govern the design of those responses which act as prompts to entries. Responses to inquiries for data must be understandable and easy to use. Responses to displays and line printers can be designed according to the same principles as reports. Responses to character printers can be printed on forms or plain paper. The number of characters printed is most important so horizontal spacing is not a good idea. If there is a 'tab' feature then it might be bearable but as good an effect can frequently be gained by 'vertical separation', i.e. changing line.

The positioning of responses conveying error messages can be important. They should not erase the original entry and should leave room for a new entry underneath them if re-entry is the preferred technique. They should quote the field in error, repeat the data in error and suggest the correction to be made. For example, 'SUPPLIER XY123 SHOULD BE NUMERIC' is more helpful than 'INVALID FORMAT'.

In a data capture system using prompted entries, there is no need to signify that an entry is acceptable. The reissue of a clean prompt is enough of a signal and saves line traffic.

Message Layouts

These thoughts may have suggested some clever designs. The documentation must accommodate them. The first requirement is to convey the design to the user for his approval. For this purpose, samples and layout definitions are prepared. Samples can be drawn up pictorially as in Chapter 1, or on printer layout paper. The forms for layout definitions will depend on entry type.

Fixed form entries can be laid out as shown in Figure 10.7 while free form entries can be defined as in Figure 10.8. The difference between them is that the exact space taken up by a free form entry cannot be shown, since in the absence of optional fields all data is left justified. The various notation symbols do not take up real space in the message either, so that the resemblance between the formal layout and real messages is even less marked.

In fact a complete documentation of a fixed form entry would need both types of layout. The fixed attribute is apparent on the display screen but the data entered and transmitted is free form. If the two Figures 10.7 and 10.8 are examined, it will be seen that Figure 10.8 is a definition of the key depressions actually made.

Free Form Entry Definition

The entry defined is a free form version of the first two lines of the entry shown in Figure 10.7. Note that the dissimilarity in data type between Batch Number and Supplier number cannot be used for punctuation since 'Supplier' may include digits. The fixed length of the decimal parts of VAT and Value can however be used as punctuation if necessary although the result would not be very readable.

186

Company Name ABC Company
Flow Chart Paper □ System Chart-Application *Centralised Ordering*
□ Program Logic-Run Name No. _____
Routine Name _____ No. _____

E01/R01
ITEM NO.
I-201
INDEX NO.

Prepared by	Reviewed by Date	Approved by Date

1 FØLDER NØ <nnnnn> BATCH NØ <n[n]> SUPPLIER NØ <xxxxxx> ·BATCH TYPE <c>

4 ØRDER NUMBER   VAT AMNT   VALUE   ØUTERS DISCOUNT NET TØTAL

BATCH TØTAL: <n[n5]•nn > <n[n5]•nn > <n[n5] >

6 STØRE DATE SUFFX INVCE DATE
7 <nnnn><nnnn><nnn> <zzzz><nnnn> <n[n4]•nn > <n[n4]•nn > <n[n4]2><n[n2]•nn > <n[n4] >
8 <nnnn><nnnn><nnn> <zzzz><nnnn> <n[n4]•nn > <n[n4]•nn > <n[n2]><n[n4]•nn > <n[n4] >

21 PRØCEDURE CHANGE <1>

23 ERRØR: LINE [n]n - INVALID q[q20] - q[a20]

Figure 10.7 Fixed form entries

Cross Reference	Key	Description
	①	1 entered when procedure is to change
	②	quotes number of line in error to correspond with number displayed on right of screen
	③	name of field in error on line given
	④	message giving nature of error - left justified
	⑤	all currency amounts are left justified on integer amount but two decimal places for pennies must be entered
	⑥	definition of error response ROS shown in position
	⑦	data line repeated twelve times on form but entry repeat is optional up to twelve

Figure 10.7—continued

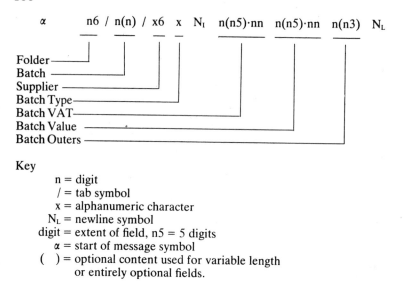

Key

    n = digit
    / = tab symbol
    x = alphanumeric character
    N_L = newline symbol
    digit = extent of field, n5 = 5 digits
    α = start of message symbol
    ( ) = optional content used for variable length
        or entirely optional fields.

Figure 10.8. Free form entries

Message Specification

Following agreement on layouts, the message content needs to be defined to identify field identity. The exact method used will depend upon the type of software. The manner in which the keyed message reaches the CPU depends on the terminal characteristics. The method which has been suggested in the exhibits should suggest what is to be documented, if not exactly how.

There are a number of common design features whose use must be recorded in an economic and standard manner. If conventions for their documentation can be designed, then the implementation of standard software for entry analysis and for response synthesis should be possible if required. The situations suitable for employing the features have already been discussed. The features will occur in any of the types of entry earlier identified. They can be classified into those related to the field alone and those relating to messages or groups of message fields. For this reason the documentation has been split between fields and groups, up to and including whole messages.

(a) FIELD CHARACTERISTICS:
    —field character class e.g. alphabetic
    —fixed length fields e.g. a code number
    —variable length fields e.g. a quantity
    —literal value fields e.g. action codes
    —fields having a restricted set of values e.g. debit/credit
    —fields having a feasible range of values e.g. quantity ordered or invoice value
    —fields matching records in a reference file.

COMPANY NAME _ABC Company_

MESSAGE DATA WORKSHEET

	I-501
	INDEX NO.
	_EO1_
	ITEM LABEL

SYSTEM DEVELOPMENT _Centralized Ordering_   _1_ REVISION NO.

PREPARED BY _B Cook_	RECEIVED BY _RT_	APPROVED BY
DATE _10-1-73_	DATE _10-8-73_	DATE
NAME _Invoice Total Data Entry_		RECORD GENERATED (ENTRY) _HART 01_

USED ON

_D271-01_

_D271-07_

COMPOSITION

LABEL FIELD/GROUP	KEY FOR RECOG.	SEQ.	OCCURRENCE			PUNCTUATION SEPARATORS			COMMENTS (ORIGIN OF DATA IF RESPONSE)
			MAX	MIN	ON	ID	BEFORE	AFTER	
GP04		10	1	0					omitted only in exch 01 when in convrs A2
NEWLINE		20	4	4					
GP05		30	1	0					omitted only in exch 01 when in convrs A1
GP01		40	0	12					omitted only in exch 07
NEWLINE		50	1	1					
"1"		60	1	0					
END MSG		70	1	1					

NOTE 1. that GP01 comprises a 'newline' plus GP02 illustrated in next example
2. need for multiple levels of grouping to convey the correct variety of mixes of 'newline' and 'tab' control symbols.

Figure 10.9. Message data worksheet complete

(b) MESSAGE CHARACTERISTICS:
—optional fields
—repeated fields
—repeated groups of fields
—fields in variable sequence.

There are two methods of documentation of message possible. The first is a tabular technique having different columns to indicate the incidence of different properties in different members. An example is the Record Data Worksheet Figure 10.2. The second method is to define properties by a 'picture' like the PICTURE clause of COBOL where 'metasymbols' are used to convey properties. For example, the property of being optional could be conveyed by enclosing the name of an optional field in brackets:

invoice, value, (discount)

The documentation illustrated uses a mixture of the two methods—a 'picture' technique for fields and free form layouts, and a tabular technique for defining groups and messages.

When the entry analysis process of unpacking, recognition, validation and conversion is complete, the converted message is usually fixed in the length and incidence of individual fields and the data is converted into 'target' form. In this state it is equivalent to a retrieved data record. The documents of filed data definition are therefore employed as complementary to the definitions peculiar to this task.

The message form is similar in intention to Figure 10.3 for filed data. The difference is in the opportunity to specify interfield punctuation. Figures 10.9 and 10.10 show the use of the form in defining a complete message and an embedded group respectively. The complete message definition shows a cross reference to an internal filed form (record generated) and to the parent exchanges (used on). The group definition has a 'used on' reference to a parent grouping.

The columns of the 'composition' table are used to identify crucial characteristics of each member. The column 'Key of Recognition' identifies those fields or groups within a complete message which are necessary for message identification. This is only relevant in situations in which the entry is one of many possible at some point in the interaction between user and system.

'Occurrence On' column indicates an item whose presence depends on the presence of another field. Its sequence number is quoted. 'Punctuation Id' is used to quote any unique symbols placed in front of the item to identify it. 'Punctuation Before' and 'After' columns are used to quote preceding or following symbols used to delimit an item.

FIELD DEFINITION

Three Formats

A data field used in a real time system can have three forms—a source form used in entering data, a filed form used in stored records and an edited form for

I-501
INDEX NO.

COMPANY NAME _ABC Company_

GP02
ITEM LABEL

MESSAGE DATA WORKSHEET

SYSTEM DEVELOPMENT _Centralized Ordering_

1
REVISION NO.

PREPARED BY _B. Cook_	RECEIVED BY _R.T._	APPROVED BY
DATE _10-1-73_	DATE _10-8-73_	DATE
NAME _Invoice Total Line_		RECORD GENERATED (ENTRY)

USED ON _GP01_

COMPOSITION

LABEL FIELD. GROUP	KEY FOR RECOG.	SEQ.	OCCURRENCE MAX	MIN	ON	PUNCTUATION SEPARATORS ID	BEFORE	AFTER	COMMENTS (ORIGIN OF DATA IF RESPONSE)
GP03		10	1	1			TAB		
INVCENO		20	1	1					
INVCEDT		30	1	1					
INYCEVAT		40	1	1					
INVCEVAL		50	1	1			TAB		
INVCEOUT		60	1	1			TAB		
INVCEDIS		70	1	0					VALUE < INVCEVAL
TAB		80	1	1					
INVCENET		90	1	0	70				

NOTE: 1. Distinction between 'tab' used as a seperator between mandatory variable fields, and as mandatory punctuation after optional fields. This is characteristic of fixed form messages and is the price of being able to omit field identifiers.
2. Field INVCENET will be terminated with the mandatory newline character preceding this group in GP01.

Figure 10.10. Message data worksheet—data group within a message

responses. The response form may vary between displayed and printed responses. The field definition must cover all three forms. Definition of all three is best done at the same time for consistency of definition between them.

Physical Attributes

The major characteristics to be defined are those of the physical appearance of the field. The attributes include data type—numeric (n), alphabetic (a), etc; length—the number of positions occupied by the field (minimum and maximum if the field is variable); punctuation—for example position of decimal point in a quantity field. The conventions of a 'Picture' are used to convey these characteristics. Lower case characters represent data type while upper case is used for literal values.

Validation Rules

The physical attributes of the field define part of the validation which would be applied. More complex validation, such as range check, or match to a limited set of values, or match to the values on a reference file, should also be documented.

Editing Rules

The appearance of the field in responses can be described in terms both of the field itself and the associated title. The edited form of the field can also be most economically stated in the form of a 'Picture'.

Examples

The conventions used in defining both the entry and response forms of the field are illustrated in Figure 10.11. As can be seen, the formality of the notation makes the form of real occurrences of the field somewhat obscure until the notation is familiar. For this reason the format can be illustrated. The illustrations should be chosen to show normal, minimum and maximum versions of the field in both entry and response. This exhibit does not include the filed form of the field since the installation from which it was taken used a separate sheet for that purpose.

References

The contexts in which the field appears are quoted to maintain cross referencing. These may be either entries, responses, filed records or the groups used within them. The cross referencing can be extended up to the top physical level for information, although strictly only the next level up is needed. The more levels that are shown, the more work will be needed in maintenance.

Another reference which might be made is to the programs or routines which are responsible for manipulating the field. In particular, the validation of a field

---

I-601
INDEX NO.

COMPANY NAME *ABC Company*

FIELD LABEL: *INVCE VAT*

TERMINAL FIELD DEFINITION

SYSTEM DEVELOPMENT *Centralized Ordering*

REVISION NO.

PREPARED BY *B. Cook*	REVIEWED BY *R.T.*	APPROVED BY
DATE *10-1-73*	DATE *10-8-73*	DATE

FIELD NAME *Invoice VAT amount*

PURPOSE AND DESCRIPTION

VAT amount for total invoice expressed in pounds and pence. Both pence positions must be shown. Currency symbol is right justified when shown.

PICTURE *

ENTRY:	RESPONSE:
$n[n4].nn$	$[\pounds][\,][n]n,][n z]n.nn$

| RANGE: *0.00 to 49999.99* | HEADLINE 1: *INVOICE* |
| REFERENCE FILE: | HEADLINE 2: *VAT* |

EXAMPLES:	EXAMPLES:
3.25	£ 0.75
200.00	£ 200.00
0.75	£ 15,200.00

* SHOW DATA TYPE: A – ALPHA   N – NUM   X – BOTH   C – CODE   OR LITERAL
LENGTH: MINIMUM AND MAXIMUM AND DECIMAL POSITION
PUNCTUATION AND CURRENCY SYMBOL (ESP RESPONSE)

CODES (IF DATA TYPE C)		USED ON (MESSAGES)		
VALUE	DEFINITION			
		GP02		
		GP12		

Figure 10.11. Terminal field definition

might be made the subject of a specific routine, or the extraction of this field from within a record.

MESSAGE HANDLING SOFTWARE

Now that the mechanisms proposed for defining data are clear, their formality will be appreciated. The formality has some training implications in that the notation must be used with some care to define entry and response formats accurately. The formality also has the advantage previously identified that the definitions can be readily coded as parameters for entry analysis or response-building software. The previous chapter set out the functions of these two classes of software and the notation will convey definitions of the data to cover all functions. The exact form of the definitions will vary with the software but the forms illustrated could provide the basis of a compiler for generating entry analysis programs.

Chapter 11
Testing Stages

NATURE OF TESTING

Importance of Testing is Increased for Real Time

Real time applications have a number of characteristics which distinguish them from batch applications. These were discussed earlier in the book. Some of the characteristics imply the necessity for an emphasis on testing which is much greater than that normally given to it on batch developments.

The first and most apparent characteristic was the direct contact between user and system. There are two issues. Firstly, the use of the computer facilities is much more intimately woven into the procedures of the using department. Secondly, failures of the computer are more visible to the users and their management. In the earlier chapter on this subject these ideas were used as an argument for the early consideration of fallback and recovery facilities. The same considerations argue for more attention to testing to avoid the disruption that breakdown must cause. The design and testing methods advocated in this book should prevent the system falling down; fallback facilities should not be needed but are always included as a last resort.

The immediate processing which permits interaction between user and programs is achieved by strings of programs acting to form an activity. The programs may be installation-wide service routines, application sub-routines, or application programs; private to the application under development or drawn from the libraries of existing applications. After the program testing to which each will be subject, additional testing is needed to prove that they work together in the new activity.

Real time processing is initiated by the arrival of messages in a sequence and at a rate which are only partially predictable. At any instant, activities in core are mixed in a virtually random manner. In a moderately complex system, a program may exist in almost any position in core and may co-exist with any mix of other programs. The position of its work areas will vary and the time it needs for execution will vary depending on the volume of business being done by the CPU at the time. Testing must therefore prove that programs are robust and do not interfere with each other. If the application is conversational and if the actions of one user influence the data available to another, then the interaction between users must be proved to occur as required.

For these logical reasons and not because of any special programming difficulty or fragility of equipment, real time systems must be tested more exhaustively than batch.

System Design is a Communication Process

Before identifying the different testing stages, let us consider what testing is. Here is a definition which may put the idea in a rather different light:

Testing is a process of proving the efficiency of a communication system of several stages arranged in series.

System design utilizes many communications steps, at each one of which a transmitter can introduce distortion between the source and the output. An application is conceived and, in a more or less formal manner, is transmitted to a designer. He in turn transmits a design to junior analysts, and so on until eventually machine code is produced for the CPU. Figure 11.1 lists a sequence of communications stages, identifying source, transmitter, receiver and output in each case. The different steps of the design sequence are then matched by a reverse sequence of testing steps.

Sequence	Source	Transmitter	Receiver	Output
1	Real world	Initiator	Development Manager	Project outline
2	User's view of world	User Staff	Business Analysts	Task specifications
3	Task specifications	Business Analysts	Computer Analysts 1	Conversation specifications
4	Conversation specifications	Computer Analysts 1	Computer Analysts 2	Exchange specifications
5	Exchange specifications	Computer Analysts 2	Senior Programmer	Program specifications
6	Program specifications	Senior Programmer	Programmer	Coding
7	Coding	Programmer	Compiler	Machine code

Figure 11.1. Systems design as a communication process

Testing Corrects Distortion

Distortion in a system must be evidence of errors, because no transmitter ever intends a distortion in the interpretation put upon source material. Testing performs the function of a feedback circuit, closing the loop by comparing what was received with what was intended. At each stage in the design process material is re-interpreted by new skills. Each stage introduces more and more detail until the design is expressed in steps simple enough for mechanical execution. What testing does is to ensure that what is executed is what was intended—what is finally received by the computer is what was sent by the people who originally conceived the project.

Real Time Testing has More Stages

A string of programs comprising a run in a batch system is equivalent to an activity servicing an entry or event-initiated exchange in real time. The test of a run is the end of testing in a batch system while in real time many more stages remain to be carried out. In all, there can be as many as six distinct stages before the ultimate test, only possible with a running system, of whether the initiator of the project really knew what he wanted. Each of the stages restricts the scope of its test in order to limit the possible sources of error. At each stage a new property of the programs is being investigated.

Simulation

The development of an application has some affinities with the preparation of a film for the cinema. Programs are the equivalent of film scenes, each made independently, in a sequence which economizes on production costs, according to a plan. Subsequent to filming, scenes are then linked in the sequence that they will be shown. Real time programs must also be linked in the sequence that they will be executed. At the time of being first made and tested, the links may not be possible since the neighbouring elements are not yet made. Discarding the metaphor, the program under test may need a service routine part way through before processing can continue. The function of that routine must be simulated in order to permit program testing to be completed. The simulation of missing parts of the project environment must be carried out by software or by control cards or by elaborate operator intervention. As the sub-assemblies and assemblies of the application are constructed so simulation can be cut back.

The remaining sections of this chapter consider the functions and supporting software of the various testing stages. The following chapter, Chapter 12, discusses testing methods appropriate to the control of the testing stage.

FUNCTIONS OF TESTING STAGES

Program Stage Tests all Detailed Logic

Program testing in a real time project is equivalent to that of a batch system. Whatever sequence is used for programming, the units of coding assigned to programmers must be separately tested before they can be linked together. Unlike batch programs, the real time program will typically have more dependencies on other programs since subroutines and service routines will be deliberately common. The title of 'modular' is likely to be well deserved.

The purpose of this first level of testing is to check that the different paths through the coding do function properly. Every instruction is deliberately exercised at least once—the more central ones much more frequently. Situations which cannot occur in real life are provoked to test obscure error exits. This is the only stage about which it can be said that every instruction has been executed. That might happen by chance in later testing stages but here it is the purpose. Not only must every instruction be exercised, but significant instruction sequences must be tested—such as the execution of loops a minimum and maximum number of times. A methodical review of the coding for all decision points will reveal the full range of conditions which must be created to ensure that every instruction is executed. The decision table produced during program specification can be updated to include all the hidden decisions now revealed in the coding.

This test should find all the errors arising from miscoding. The programmer proves that his program does what he believes that it should do.

Link Tests Build Activities

During program testing any reference to other routines is handled by providing a 'dummy' routine which passes control back to the caller with simulated results.

Errors of interpretation of program specifications should show up when the programs are used in real contexts. Then a programmer's understanding of the specification of his program is tried against that of another programmer with whom he should be in agreement. The question answered is 'does a program do what its users expect?'.

The programs which are linked together will interact in some way and the test cases are chosen to explore the interaction. Perhaps one program will retrieve filed data and process it in order for the next to build a response from the results. Perhaps the form of the response depends upon the results. In unit testing the response program, its programmer will have made assumptions aboput the form and range of values of the intermediate results or even their location in the common ECR work area. The test of the two together will determine whether those assumptions were right.

Link testing, as its name implies, is a test of the congruity of the interfaces of adjacent programs within an activity.

Exchange Tests Check External Appearance

Up to the point where link testing produced a string of programs, the starting conditions in a test were deliberately set up in core prior to starting the test run. When a string of programs appears to be working together, the process of initiation can be changed, to one more nearly resembling the genuine stimulus. When this is a terminal entry, a simulation by punched cards can be used so that all processing—except that concerned with the communications aspect of the system—can be exercised. If the software environment includes a message recognition and analysis service, that will be included. If response editing and addressing services are available, they will be added to the end of the chain. The necessity for this phase will depend upon the inclusion of those services as software rather than application programs, since in the latter case, link tests will have included them.

The tests in this phase will relate to the design of the exchange. The objective will be to prove that entries of a specified form produce expected responses. Test conditions reflecting the context of the exchange—the state of the conversation control record for example—must be created on file before the test entry is sent. Program, file and core management services may be added to the environment for exchange tests. The tests will show that the exchange logic works according to the exchange specification.

Multi-threading

If a system includes multi-threading capability as a requirement, then that property will have been properly achieved if the programs of an exchange can support multiple occurrences simultaneously. The successful execution of several exchanges concurrently is therefore a final test of the logic of each exchange.

The necessary software features to support this phase will be discussed later but the use of simulation is still preferred. The object will be to arrange a series of occurrences of the exchange on a serial device and use the message reception software to set as many as possible in the system's input queue. The live task scheduler feature of the operating software will then ensure that the exchange coding is executed in a multi-threading mode.

Conversation Tests Link Exchanges

Another layer of artificiality can be stripped away when all the exchanges in one conversation are complete. Then, the logic simulated in creating a context for each exchange is available and need be simulated no longer. Test data for a test comprises a sequence of entries to carry the whole conversation through. The various tests are in fact the various sequences shown to be possible by the conversation diagram.

The property now under test is the interpretation of the context of exchanges. Did the designer of exchange B correctly understand the context of filed data which exchange A sets up? The links or interfaces between exchanges are being tested as were those between programs.

Cycle Tests Prove Interaction with Data Files

Generally speaking, a conversation will be concerned with a single business transaction and so with only one record from each accessed file. In a real time system which updates records in however minor a way, the results of a conversation are made available to other application users through the data files. In this sense therefore there are interfaces between conversations which should be tested. The specific objective of each cycle test will be to follow a business situation through the full cycle of conversations, simulating the use of different terminals where this is a requirement. For example, in order processing, a cycle test might create a new customer, place orders and make payments and then delete his record. In the course of doing this, the test controller may need to simulate activity from credit control, order entry, warehouse, cash receipts and customer service users.

At the time of these tests, the entire application program library will be available, supported by substantial files of test data.

Volume Tests Exercise Network

At the end of cycle testing, the logic of the application will have been fully tested. Now other properties of the live situation can be tried with a reasonable certainty that the only errors remaining will be related to the project's ability to run in conditions of high volume. Depending on the complexity of the application and the abilities of the test software, simulation can still be employed by using prepared entries introduced into the test environment from backing storage.

The properties required for successful volume testing relate not so much to the re-entrant ability of the constituent programs as with the ability to handle contention for services and for data. The re-entrant quality of programs has already been tested. Competition for services such as core and channel capacity will be handled by software and should again be reasonably assured. The application property of competition for data is the principal target.

This final test of application logic is not only concerned with ensuring that the same record is not simultaneously updated by two terminals. There will be requirements that certain actions are carried out in a sequence, that actions on one terminal are not interfering with a conversation on another. In airline passenger check-in, for example, clerks at two different terminals may be attempting to check in the same passenger due to a mistaken identity at one of them. Such situations will normally only show themselves under conditions of high volume.

Thus, either by simulation or through real terminals, the entire application network is brought into play concurrently to ensure that the logic is proof against high volume.

Interface with Batch System

It will be a rare real time system which does not have an interface to a batch computer system. The most frequently encountered commercial systems—classified as enquiry and data capture earlier in the book—have no purpose without a batch system to prepare master files and to accept logged transactions. The final system test must be that this interface is successful.

In almost all instances the interface will be through filed data. In theory, therefore, if the definition of data has been properly separated from the specification of programs, then each part of the project need only share common documentation for the opportunity for error to be eliminated. However, practical difficulties of administration may cause problems. The real time and batch system teams may be separated so that modifications to data layout are not always securely implemented in both sites. The programming language used in the two sub-systems may differ since the high level languages preferred for batch systems are not always appropriate for real time. Then the mechanized data definitions, held in source form on libraries available to the program compilers, can get seriously out of step. The necessity for a test stage which links the two sub-systems is therefore real.

The test will be run when both sub-systems are otherwise fully proven. The batch side will have created its own test data, simulating the activity of the real time sub-system up to this point. If the real time sub-system uses files created by the batch system it will equally have simulated those. Now the simulation is dropped. The batch system creates reference files needed for real time, the real time system processes business transactions and logs any data to be captured. This is in turn processed by the batch system and the cycle repeats. Several cycles should be run so that any errors hidden in data capture, which will distort reference files used at a later time, can be brought to light. The test data on subsequent cycles should therefore deliberately access the same records as were created or updated as a result of earlier processing.

Hardware Tests are Left as Late as Possible

Probably in parallel with one of the last two stages, engineers will be making tests of the physical behaviour of the teleprocessing network and its components. The programmers, concerned with the coding which is specific to the physical teleprocessing, will have tested their programs to ensure that the hardware peculiarities have been successfully understood. The interface between the physical and logical parts of the application must be tested before the application can be handed over to the users for trials.

The timing of hardware tests will most probably be dictated by training requirements rather than by program development. The philosophy of testing described here, where one property is the subject of each phase, means that real equipment is not needed until just prior to conversion. However, if a large number of users must be trained, training with real terminals might take such a long elapsed time that some must be conducted concurrently with program development. Then the communications interfaces must be ready sooner and some testing may take place using real terminals somewhat sooner than strictly necessary. The conversion strategy adopted early in project design—discussed in procedure specification—will govern this aspect of testing.

User will make Final Test of Acceptance

The conversion process is the final test. When the users have the complete application available, does it do what they want? Throughout the design process as controlled by the documentation described earlier, the user has been consulted about entry and response formats and logical conditions. In person, or through his management, he will have assented to solutions to queries. Faced with the complete application in its live context, the user may still wish to make adjustment. For this reason, the first stages of conversion or the first location converted should be treated as a pilot installation and regarded as the last stage of testing. In situations where the necessary data is normally recorded in a permanent form, parallel acceptance tests can be run by repeating operations of the older system. This is best done within one or two days, so the events are familiar. The extent to which parallel running is possible or desirable will depend on the nature of the job and the extent to which the previous system generates documentation. From this documentation, users will have to work out appropriate entries and predict responses. If the application is very sensitive to error, this investment may be justified.

Modifications May be Generated at any Level

The testing process is quite protracted. Its purpose is to find errors and it may do so at any level. The later in testing that an error is found then, potentially, the more trouble it will be to correct. The errors found in late stages can arise from fundamental logic errors affecting many different programs. The design scheme recommended should avoid them but when found, the development team must decide how much of the testing cycle they must repeat to prove the corrections. At any point the users, or other groups interested in the application, may also want to make modifications.

Retesting can be extremely dull and the temptation always exists to skip it. Write the correction, compile and then carry on from where the interruption occurred. The decision must finally be a matter of judgement of the gravity of the error. If a response format change is involved then retesting through program, link and exchange can be confidently considered unnecessary. The changed program should of course be tested even in that case, because the discovery of program errors in a system test can be expensive. With logic errors though, the rule must be that tests must be repeated from program level upwards until the effect of the change is no longer evident in an interface. Then that section of the application can be confidently reinserted and testing can continue. Thus if a subroutine is altered but its input and output parameters remain unchanged—in form and in meaning—the correction need only be program tested before continuing. If two different conversations from different departments do not share a common understanding of their interface the erroneous programs and exchanges will need testing through all stages before the error can be confidently pronounced cured.

TESTING OF SOFTWARE ENVIRONMENT

Modularity is Even More Important

The general scope of this book is restricted to application design and this chapter is no exception. The possible scope of a complete software base has been discussed and if this is not available from the manufacturer of a software supplier some may have to be developed in the installation. Its testing will therefore be of interest to the installation management.

The discussion of program and link testing is applicable if installation software is written with the objective of making it as reliable and flexible as standard software. The quality most necessary is independence of the software from any single application. The term 'modularity' should imply this quality.

Interface Defines Test Conditions

The application of modularity is characterized by precise definition of the interfaces between modules—usually by means of formal statements of parameters. If the module is performing a service, it is initiated by a request for the service accompanied by whatever parameters are necessary to achieve the exact effect required. For example in 'allocate core of 200 positions', '200' is the parameter. The evidence of the service having been performed is a similarly formal return interface with other parameters. The existence of these precise interfaces means that, to the software, all the conditions which can ever arise are defined by all the possible combinations of entry parameters, modified by any conditions that the routine seeks in the surrounding environment. In the 'allocate core' example, test cases will be defined by the relation between the given parameter and the amount of unallocated core available, which the service routine will itself determine. So the definition of test cases for software testing can be easier since the use of software is so much more formal.

There will be other stages beyond unit testing if the software is required to be re-entrant or if it, in turn, employs other software. Provided that the concept of modularity is strictly defined, its testing can be precisely defined by its interfaces.

As the services provided get more complex so the interfaces will become complex to match. Services closer to the operating system, such as activity scheduling, or message analysis, will be more difficult either because of environment complexity or parameter complexity. The philosophy remains the same—identify all points at which the program asks for information from the environment in which it operates and the different answers it can get to each question. If the service can be provided under all combinations of conditions then its coding is valid.

Tests Employ Dummy Applications

When testing applications programs, it is sometimes necessary to simulate missing services. Conversely, software testing requires the simulation of applications. Even if application programs are available to drive service tests, their use could prejudice the independence of the software. Dummy applications programs, composed of repeated software calls with monitoring actions interspersed, are easy to write and they ensure that the software is not based towards the needs of the first application.

Traffic must be Simulated

If the software is of the more complex class, such as activity scheduling, then the simulation will be in two parts. There will be a need for a dummy activity program and for simulated traffic. The software in this instance is not so much a closed box as a shell—having a need for a simulated environment inside and out. A particularly good example of this is the communications coding, referred to in Chapter 9 as the logical terminal, standing between the hardware and an application. To test it thoroughly and conveniently, a dummy application (accepting entries and turning out related responses) is needed, fed by simulated terminal traffic. The simulated traffic will have the properties defined by the hardware specification supplied by its manufacturer. In the case of communications programs, a final stage must employ the physical hardware but can still initiate a dummy application.

In summary, the class of software which might be developed on site need not pose insoluble testing problems. Such complex software as compilers and operating systems are not so easily dismissed, but happily these will more often be supplied. If they are not available then very few applications will justify the expense of their development.

SOFTWARE FOR TESTING
Policy of Simulation

The last section considered testing software using 'testing' as a verb. This section considers testing software using 'testing' as an adjective—the use of software aids to simplify the work of preparing and conducting the tests identified earlier.

It will be immediately apparent that, to test a unit of programming buried deep in an exchange, the action of preceding coding must be simulated to set up the conditions expected by the test program when it gains control. An update module will expect the data from a fully validated and formatted entry to have been distributed around the ECR or CCR work area. In general, the opening conditions of an application program will be contained in various core work areas, retrieved records and those still to be retrieved by the program in question. Simulation in those circumstances is a necessity.

The policy of simulation is however advocated for all the test stages except that of final user acceptance. The use of terminals to enter test messages has disadvantages which render simulation preferable at all other times.

Tests should be repeatable so that if an error is found, the potential solution can first be retried in as close to identical circumstances as possible. Tests should be predictable. The policy of planning tests advocated at every stage will be defeated if the planned tests are not carried through exactly as planned. Tests should be economical in time since, if to represent many days' terminal activity actually takes many days, the tests will be difficult to administer and to avoid them will be tempting. Terminals also cost money and to hire or purchase terminals ahead of time has an avoidable cost.

All of these reasons taken together justify a policy of simulating messages rather than using real terminals. So there are two components to the simulation—the simulation of internal activity which for some reason cannot yet be provided and the simulation of the external action of users and terminals.

Simulated Environment

The internal environment of a real time system is composed of many functions which were discussed in Chapter 9. There were the services of core, program and data management, the task scheduling, message reception and despatch and hardware handling functions which protect the application program from the complexities of real time, and the entry analysis and response synthesis processing which reduce the amount of application coding.

These software functions form an environment of many parts, not all of which are needed in the early stages of testing. The task scheduling function relates to multi-threading, while program management is only of relevance when more than one program is being managed. The simulation of the internal environment can therefore exclude temporarily irrelevant software functions. The rest is incorporated in the test software.

Another part of the test software has the function of establishing data conditions to which the test unit can react. There are at least three methods. The first is to write a special test program which will drive the program under test. This driver program sets core values in various areas representing the ECR or CCR, and then passes control to the test program. When the test program needs services or data, its transfers of control are intercepted by the driver program and the required service is simulated. When the test pass is complete the driver program regains control and, after altering data conditions, can reactivate the test program for another test case.

An alternative method of achieving the same end is to prepare special control cards which will perform these same functions. A simple test software routine intercepts the service calls or end of run conditions and reads cards carrying the necessary instructions for proceeding. In the absence of any software, these functions can be performed by patching the test program or by a computer operator reacting to console messages but these approaches are not recommended.

In addition to the stripped down control program and the application simulation, the internal software can be enhanced with facilities for monitoring the progress of the test and capturing its results. The action of intercepting requests for service, by control or application programs, can be the occasion for logging the fact that the request was made, what the request was and also for logging key status information such as the contents of registers or accumulators.

The final software component of the internal simulator is a means for subsequently printing the logged results to provide documentation of the course of the test.

Program Testing

The internal environment is of use when less than a complete activity is being tested. There were two stages identified earlier when this was the case—program and link testing. In the early stages of testing single program units, barely any control software is needed. As tests progress, the software for

206

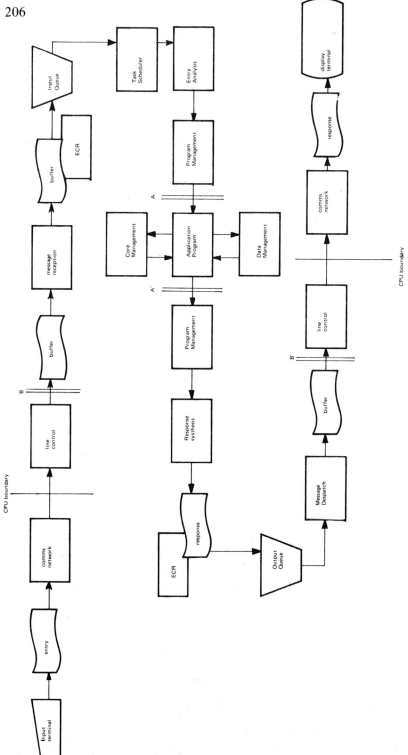

Figure 11.2. Message processing path

handling core management and transfers of control between programs can be brought into play. Then data retrieval from backing storage can be substituted for driver program functions.

Exchange Testing

When all the program units, which are executed between the addition of an entry to the input queue of tasks and the placing of a response on the output queue, have been linked together, the exchange test can start. Now, that sequence of programs is treated as an integrated activity and various examples of the entry can be presented to the activity for processing. For this purpose, a simulation of terminal activity is necessary and virtually all facilities of the control software are used. The Figure 11.2 shows a diagram of the processing path of an exchange. The test software is applied at program test level to simulate everything outside the path A—A'. At exchange test level the test software is applied at points B—B'. In place of line control, a backing storage access program is used to extract simulated entries from a serial device and to direct responses to a line printer. At the point B the simulator program will also direct a copy of the entry to the line printer to precede its response.

Multi-threading

The network simulation program must have extra facilities when driving a multi-threading test. Its purpose is to simulate a network realistically by interleaving messages from apparently different terminals. For logical realism, it must distinguish between many messages from one terminal and one message from each of several terminals. The entry sequence in the first case will still give the effect of single threading, since no further entry should be accepted from a terminal until the preceding entry has sent a response. There are terminals which permit entries to be made before an expected response is received and there are applications which can exploit that feature—but its employment is rare.

To control a test completely therefore, a simulator must include some 'locking' feature to prevent a new entry before a response. If that is included, the simulator will slow down a test unless it can bypass entries from one terminal to allow those from other terminals in the actual serial input stream to overtake. A possible technique is to form separate queues of entries from each terminal for which an entry is already in process. When a response is 'sent', the entry queue from its terminal can be accessed for the next entry. Thus in a test containing entries from terminals A, B and C, in the sequence A, A, C, B, C, A, B, C, the first entry will be passed for processing, the second queued while the third and fourth are processed. The second will be held back until the first has been completed while the fifth will wait for the third, sixth for second, seventh for fourth and eighth for fifth. The implication is that entries 1, 2, and 6 are related, they are in fact successive entries in a conversation. The interactive property of real life entries is of course absent. Entry number two is not a reaction to the actual response from entry one—only to the prediction of it. If a mistake is made, the subsequent entries and responses will increasingly diverge—an effect commonly observed in conversation between people. The test is wasted in that situation. A similar effect is observed if a sequence of entries is made from several terminals but concerning common data. For example, suppose a record was created, transacted upon and deleted. If the opening creation sequence was unsuccessful the subsequent activities on a non-existent record will generate a stream of error messages. Such problems are occasionally worth generating deliberately because they test an application program's ability to cope with errors very severely.

If an installation does not include such software in its complement, a more simple version can be developed which leaves such control to the test organizer. The key characteristic is after all that of being able to achieve multi-threading execution. If this can be done, control of sequence can be exercised in arranging the entries so that two from one 'terminal' are never present in the system together.

This is not as easy as it sounds if the level of concurrency is permitted to vary. Concurrency level is a value defining the number of activities to be concurrently executed. There is some merit in being able to control this, to permit a gradual increase from a concurrency level of one to whatever limit has been determined as a realistic maximum. The simulator program can achieve concurrency in two ways, by 'bursts' or by 'topping up'. The burst method is the simpler and works by feeding a preset number of entries into the input queue, permitting them to complete their processing and then releasing the next burst. 'Topping up' starts in the same way but releases additional entries one by one as each earlier activity is completed. The test simulator is in control of both input and output so can detect when a new entry is free to start. The topping up method is more realistic and more thorough—and is even marginally faster. It does pose problems of entry sequence though, since entries from the same terminal must be widely separated to ensure that they are clear of each other.

Each entry may provoke responses to its origin or to associated terminals. It may also initiate subordinate activities. The simulator must identify each output response by naming its destination, according to the response's terminal address, and its origin, according to the entry's terminal address. The sequence of output is not predictable without an unjustified level of predictive work so the identification function makes subsequent scrutiny much easier. If testing is being done at the same time as live activity on earlier projects, the response sequence becomes quite unpredictable. This feature makes the automatic comparison of actual and predicted responses of little value.

The job control activity in a test falls off as the complexity of the unit being tested increases. Once message testing starts, the programs under test carry out all core work. In exchange testing, conversation control records must still be created to express the context of the exchange. The conversation control record and project records must be examined after a test. When conversation tests are undertaken the conversation control record can be left to look after itself. Finally, when all conversations are available and cycle tests start, the dumping of files for scrutiny after a test can cease. At that point, the files are included in the 'black box' being tested. Ideally, the user is unaware of project file structures—all he sees are responses. The test planner can adopt the same attitude.

Test Data Generation

From the test software used during a test, we can now turn to that used before and after it. The first item considered is a means for generating the filed data used in testing.

The scope of the generator is intended to include not merely the transcription of pre-formatted data from a slow speed medium (cards) to a high speed medium (tape or disc), but also the formatting of the data. One of the by-products of the policy of separate data definition is the creation of a library of machine readable record layouts—a COPY library—whose elements can be included in a program's data definition section during compilation. The practice of referring to data by symbolic names is used to make coding independent of some details of data definition. The same COPY library can be used to make test data definable in symbolic form and equally independent of such matters as a change in field position or size. Test data can then be recompiled in the same way as application coding.

The test data is prepared by stating the type of record required to be generated and the values to be given to significant fields. The test data generator will use those parameters to create a record with the format dictated by the current COPY library entry. The given values are placed in the named fields and initial values are created in unnamed fields. Refinements can be added to permit the creation of several occurrences of a record type with increasing or decreasing values in a field; to generate random values in a field or to select values at random from a predefined set of values.

Test Assembly

The final function we will examine is that of test assembly. At a late stage in program development the programming team will have built up offline libraries of program units and test data. In conducting a link test, or subsequent levels, a programmer will wish to prepare an environment with temporary online libraries for the programs he is using and for the test data files which those programs are expected to access. The Test Assembly software extracts the required members of the offline program and data files and creates the miniature online environment which is required for the test. The test can then be executed.

To summarize, the test software environment has a number of components. They are used at different stages in the progression of testing but all are based upon the philosophy of simulating the live environment as much as possible.

The result is that test preparation is more formal but testing is conducted offline[1] in the same way as the testing of a batch system.

VARIETY IN APPLICATIONS

Many Dimensions of Variety Exist

The ways in which real time systems can vary was discussed in Chapter 3. Several of the dimensions there identified will affect the extent to which the complete scheme of testing need be applied. Real time systems can vary in the complexity of the processing applied to exchanges, in the volume of transactions handled, in the need for conversational transactions and in their requirement for interaction between different users through data files.

Simple Activities Need No Links

Enquiries on an online data file are sometimes satisfied by a display of the filed data without summarization or interpretation of any sort. In an application without software for message analysis or for response editing, such enquiries could well be satisfied with separate single programs. There will therefore be no need for link testing for the programs serving those enquiries. In general, if an activity is composed of one program, link testing does not exist.

Multi-threading is Introduced for Volume

The re-entrant property of programs and the protection against overlapping updates of data records, are necessary only when the volume of messages dealt with by the real time system demands multi-threading. However, even in a single threading environment, the development team must be confident that multi-threading will never be needed before deciding not to test these properties. Unlike the property of processing simplicity, multi-threading may subsequently appear with the development of the installation. If new real time projects are planned which introduce the need for multi-threading, all past and future projects should be capable of execution in the same control environment. The testing of these properties may not be possible when a project is first introduced, due to the absence of the necessary software, but retesting should be scheduled if the environment is upgraded.

Interaction is Not Always Necessary

The use of a conversational approach to transactions implies the need for a conversation testing stage when the interfaces between successive exchanges are proved. Without this feature in an application the stage is unnecessary. Interaction between different users through the data files will only be possible if the files are being updated online is some way. Without such interaction, system tests will be concerned only with proving the procedures at single terminals. The presence of a number of terminals rather than just one will not affect application logic in any way—provided of course that responses appear at the terminal which made the initiating entry.

Variety in the number of different message types frequently relates to the dimension of interaction—little interaction, little variety. If there are few message types, dedicated message recognition and analysis programs are unlikely, thus reducing linkages inside each activity. The need for a software service for this function may be another issue which depends upon plans for further development.

A Profile can be Drawn for System Classes

The dimensions identified are more or less independent of each other and do not necessarily correlate with the reference systems identified in Chapter 3. The need for different stages of testing can be deduced if the properties tested at each stage are recalled. However, Figure 11.3 is offered as a guide to the size of the testing task in each class of application. The words 'yes', 'likely', 'unlikely' and 'no' are used as four points on a continuous scale and neither 'yes' nor 'no' is absolute.

In summary, testing for real time systems is a greater proportion of the installation effort than in batch applications. There is more planning, more software, more stages and more test data. The development of sound methods is as important for testing therefore, as for systems design.

Stage of testing	*Application classes*			
	Inquiry	*Switching*	*Data capture*	*Online updating*
Program	Yes	Yes	Yes	Yes
Application link	Unlikely	Unlikely	Not if input is field by field	Likely
Exchange	Only for complex inquiries with many parameters	Unlikely	Yes— especially for multi-field entries	Likely
Conversation	Only if parameters are built up by conversation	No	Yes—if transaction has many simple entries	Likely
System cycles	No	No	Maybe—if captured data can be interrogated	Likely
Volume tests	···············depends on volume·································			
Pilot tests	Unlikely	Likely	Likely	Likely

Figure 11.3. Need for testing stages

Costs can be High

The many testing stages and the effort put into planning, executing and reviewing tests add up to a significant proportion of the total effort in an application. In total the effort devoted to testing can amount to half the cost of a project—more than the cost of programming and design together.

The different stages identified relate to the design stages. At each stage there is a set of system components to be tested, the number of members of each set reducing as the components represent larger sections of the total application. For each component of each set there are the steps of test specification, data invention, data load, job control preparation, job control proving, test execution, comparison of results to prediction, identification and correction of program, data or job control errors, cross referencing of final results to specification and review by supervisor. Of course, as the larger sections of the system are tested errors will become fewer but the effort is still substantial. To the pure testing effort can be added any other effort needed to develop test software.

It would be possible to quote estimating guidelines, for example three manweeks for a program module, two manweeks for an exchange—but to do so would be misleading. Each installation will vary in the program language, test software, application complexity, quality of staff, to name but a few variables. An idea of the order of magnitude is conveyed by the rule of thumb that total effort on testing is at least as much as the effort for design, specification and programming put together. In support of this guideline the airline check in system referred to earlier took thirty-five man years of effort of which fifteen could be classified as devoted to testing.

Chapter 12
Testing Methods

TEST SPECIFICATION

Identification of Cases is Foundation

No matter how thorough the documentation of testing can be made, testing will be no guarantee of program quality without careful selection of the test cases to be tried. Test case selection has been considered throughout the process of design described in Parts II and III of this book. The method of identifying cases by decision tables used in proving design, is the foundation on which the planning and execution of testing is built. A table is constructed at each test stage in which a program participates, in order to explore the property being tested in that stage.

The test case table comprises lists of all the conditions to be tested and the possible outcomes. The cases are identified by combining the conditions in every way permitted by the logic and predicting the outcome of each combination. This table is the definition of the test plan. Illustrations of conversation and exchange test tables are shown in Figures 7.3 and 7.11.

Specification Ensures Complete Test

Another principle used in the book which is employed in this chapter, is that of prior specification. A specification of the test permits the test plan to be reviewed before any machine time is used or data prepared. It is more easily digested than listings when checking how the program is to be tested.

The specification format remains essentially the same for each testing stage. There is a logical statement of the cases in the decision table format described. This is followed by a statement of the data values used to provoke each test case and the data values in its outcome. The necessary manipulations prior to, and during the test case are also described. This topic is discussed more fully later in this section.

As is usual with specifications, they lose their value if not maintained. Test specifications have the advantage of being prepared late in the life of the application, so are rarely subjected to design modifications. Their own subject matters can be altered though as a result of review or after the discovery of logic errors. Maintenance could involve either the case definition section or the data values for each case.

Test Preparation is Reduced by Common Data Files

Real time systems have a characteristic in common in that many different users wish to interact by means of shared data records. A record is set up by one user, updated by another and inquired upon by a third, each using different exchanges and conversations. There is therefore a significant benefit to be gained from setting up common test data records which between them exhibit all the common conditions of data. The specification of test data then consists of a nomination of a test record and instructions for making adjustments to it create the exact conditions required. The records are not all in an initialized state or else adjustment effort might exceed that for setting up new ones. Rather the life of each record is traced as a series of 'snapshots' which freeze significant points in its life cycle. An order record in a file updating order processing system for example, might have 'snapshots' of its condition after first being posted, when some items are shipped and others in a backlog, after delivery, notification, after goods are returned, after payment and after credit note issue. The test order file might contain examples of single line order, multiple line orders with and without overflow records, for sole traders, branch customers, head offices, customers with the same and different order, delivery, invoice, and payment addresses, overseas customers and inhouse customers.

The order file could be supported by customer and product files and any others included in the system. Test data on this scale can be described as a test 'model'. In fact the scale need not be overwhelming—the object is to avoid perhaps 75–80% of test file preparation work on the part of the individual programmer.

The technique has an incidental advantage of furnishing an independent check on each programmer's interpretation of data structure definitions—files and groups. The maintenance of the test data files can be a problem but the existence of the record definitions in the COPY library can ease this considerably. If a test data generator is available the records can be quickly created. Otherwise the test data can be created by simple programs which assign values to items by name and use the record definitions to place those items in position.

The test data files will only be willingly used by programmers if their contents are widely known. The data generation programs will produce listings which will show item names and values for each record but a summary of the contents in plain language will be more accessible. The main features of each record which justify its inclusion can be briefly stated and the whole issued as a handbook for each programmer.

A mechanical matter which must not be overlooked is, that if several snapshots exist for the same record, its natural key will not be enough to identify a particular snapshot. The order record used earlier in illustration would have a natural key of order number. Every snapshot will carry the same order number so an extra key to distinguish between versions is necessary. This could be called the frame number. The test assembly software outlined in the previous chapter could use the frame number to extract a specific snapshot from the test file. The frame number could be inserted as a standard header field by the test data generator software. The frame number would need to be stripped off the record before running the test since it is unknown to the application.

The test data need not be created entirely at one time. Early programs may need different records or ranges of conditions. Programmers can be encouraged to contribute data to the test file thus sharing the work and getting maximum value from it.

One Submission can Include Several Attempts

The cases identified for testing need not correspond to submissions to the computer. With planning, cases can be grouped to form submissions so that by suitable manipulation of opening conditions by the driver program or its equivalent a new run through the test program can be initiated without programmer intervention. The conditions set up when the first test is run will need to be modified to repair the results of the first test and create conditions which distinguish the next from the first. The functions of program test software were discussed in the previous chapter.

The effect of these facilities on the organisation of testing is to permit cases to be grouped into submissions. Grouping will either be made to minimize the manipulation required between runs or to bring together cases with some logical connection—all the error responses, for example.

PROGRAM TEST SPECIFICATION

Specification has Pre-defined Sections

The purpose of insisting on a predetermined format here, as in all the documents described in this book, remains unchanged. A format provides a guide for the inexperienced programmer to the method to be used in conducting a test and permits the work to be transferred from one programmer to another if necessary. No general format can be given since any forms would need to be adjusted for the circumstance of an installation. In particular, the characteristics of the test software available will influence the method used to achieve the functions described below as 'job control'.

The test specification described in this section is for the smallest unit of coding separately tested. For convenience this is called a program, but an installation might use the term 'segment' or 'module'. This specification will have the following sections. The first is the test case table which acts as an index to the remainder of the document and expresses the test plan in one place. Then for each case identified in the table, the data values chosen to satisfy the case are quoted, followed by the results which those values will generate. For each case the necessary control activities are listed to specify in advance how the test will be run.

The test plan can be reviewed easily by taking each case in the opening table and following it through the program flowchart. When all cases have been examined, every path through the flowchart should have been exercised.

Case is Embodied in the Opening Conditions

The opening conditions section should be subdivided according to the means whereby the conditions are made apparent to the program. The main source will be values created in core to represent work areas or retrieved records apparently passed on from an earlier program. If the program retrieves any data during its processing, the test data retrieved is a condition—whether it be filed data, tables or system constants. For clarity, each of these expressions of the test case data should be shown separately. Filed data should be drawn from the predefined test data files whenever possible to minimize preparation effort.

In program testing there will very rarely be a need to include entries as opening conditions. Even the first application program in a string will receive evidence of an entry as core values since there will be a preceding telecommunications hardware interface program which will translate received bit strings into machine code and perform other housekeeping. The use of 'pure' messages as input to a program test is of interest only to the first program in an activity in any case. The subsequent program units might never need to access a true message at all since its data is most likely to have been split up and stored in ECR or CCR work areas. However, if the programmer can relate more easily to an entry then the 'opening conditions' section of the specification can quote the implied original entry.

The format adopted for this section should be aimed at conveying its information as succinctly and unambiguously as possible. For this reason a simple table layout is recommended, quoting each data value against its application item name. If necessary another column could be added for notes—for example to interpret code values. The explicit definition of items should be limited to those of significance to the processing and those which distinguish one case from another. If a sequence of cases uses the same data record, only its first appearance need be spelt out. Subsequent cases can make reference to the earlier case, noting only the differences in item values.

There is an obvious danger that this section will become unmanageable and very tedious to prepare for a complex program. The existence of the test data files will reduce the preparation since their item values can be implied by simply quoting the record identity. An input section which is still too long might be evidence that a program was too extensive in scope and might be a candidate for segmentation. A large program is not only difficult to test, it is difficult to modify because its many functions become inextricably mixed. Deliberately separate modules do tend to stay separate and can be independently maintained or replaced.

Job Control Functions are Listed

The various methods possible for the job control functions of testing have been briefly discussed. The functions include making changes to test data files, creating work area and other core values according to the opening condition definitions, dealing with trapped control program calls, simulating the actions of missing programs, simulating missing files, taking dumps of core and restoring control to the test program for the next case.

The job control functions should be listed in sequence to act as a specification for the later preparation of a submission. If the test software utilizes cards for these functions then the list can be written directly on punching sheets in the required format. In principle though the section should be composed of simple unambiguous commands at whatever level the available software requires. If the statements are so coded as to be intelligible only to skilled programmers, they should be accompanied by commentary, for example:

> ...... create exchange data area
> ...... retrieve test record 52
> ...... alter customer type to wholesaler
> ...... start test
> ...... dump updated customer record

Results are Predicted in Advance

The final section for a case is a statement of the results of the program's actions, its closing conditions. The evidence of the program's correct execution is its production of predicted results in legal and illegal conditions. Regardless of how efficiently the program works, it is functionally correct if it produces correct results. The quality of its design is not the subject of a test, only the success achieved in carrying out its functions. There is a great temptation to skip this part of the planning—to wait for the results then examine them. However conscientious the examination, obscure errors which distort but do not apparently corrupt will be overlooked. Far more security will be achieved if each significant data item is predicted in advance and then compared with test results. A common argument against this course is that people are poor at being mechanical and they make more mistakes in prediction than they do in programming. It is however precisely this inability which makes the predicted results a partly independent check on the same person's own programming. The programmer knows what he wants the program to do and will not execute the program by hand to predict the results. Rather, he will take short cuts and so expose errors where his coding ability was not up to his predicting ability. Mere clerical errors in the predicted results are readily found in the test but do ensure close examination.

The format used for this section would be similar to that used for expressing input conditions. Results commonly consist of updated file records and changed core values. Even if the program under test naturally initiates responses, they will usually exist as core images before being passed on to software programs for formatting and transmission. If there is test software which will generate a simulated response for subsequent printing, an extra section can be added named 'responses'. Results will be a mixture of final and intermediate effects. If dumps are requested or if a monitoring facility is being used, its results should be predicted also. It is as if the production were being done for mechanical comparison. Every letter and digit on the final listing must be explicable.

Program Testing Applies to Parameter Programs

In a software environment providing the services discussed in Chapter 9, message handling functions are provided by specialized programs, comprising parameters controlling a generalized program. Most notable are the entry analysis and response synthesis programs which are coded by completing tables. These parameter programs must be tested as much as the regular coding. The test specification concept applies just as much to them. The test case table for a message definition is constructed by considering each entry field and each defined attribute and listing these as the conditions.

The cases consist of examples of the satisfaction and violation of each condition combined in representative ways. To explore every possible combination of conditions will frequently be impossible and only rarely necessary. For a complex multifield entry the combinations possible will be virtually infinite. However, all combinations of dependent fields must be tried. It is in the exploration of cases that deficiencies in the choice of parameters may be exposed and better ways to use the software are learnt.

The specialized nature of the message definitions as opposed to programs will show up not in the conditions section of the test case table but in the results section. Their results will always have a similar form, the presentation of an unpacked entry and the nomination of the first application program to receive control.

A response definition presented to response editing software will be tested in a similar fashion. The results will be a formatted version of the response ready to interface with the manufacturer's hardware dependent communications handling program.

LINK TEST SPECIFICATION

Links have Various Patterns

The essential property being proved by a link test is the effect of one program upon another. For convenience the terms 'superior' and 'subordinate' program are used, where the superior program is the one which has the initiative in creating conditions to which the subordinate reacts. This relationship is used to construct a title for the test of the form LINK (superior) WITH (subordinate). The patterns in which programs can be linked are various. Some are illustrated

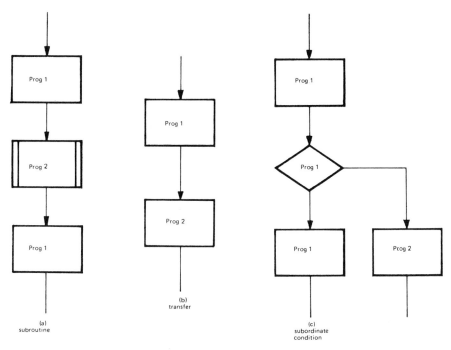

Figure 12.1. Program linking patterns

in Figure 12.1. In each case it is the interface between two programs which is being tested. Test cases are therefore likely to be fewer than those of either of the programs being linked.

The format of a link test specification is similar to that for a program test and so it will not be described in detail. Instead the following paragraphs consider the selection of link tests and the exposure of test cases.

Strings are Built Up

Before proceeding further, let us make plain that the separate test of every possible program pair, every three and so on, is not advocated. The number of link tests can be controlled by carefully assembling the program strings—not in sequence of execution but by using the superior-to-subordinate relationship.

Program strings are rather like simple engineering products. In a manufactured article some parts are 'used on' while others are 'using'. Link tests are economically planned either by starting with a program which does not use any others and then linking to the program which uses it or by starting with a mainline and adding subordinates successively. An established pair can then be regarded as a single unit and the next superior or subordinate can be linked on. Building up or down from one level in this way enables bigger and bigger units to be built up without the necessity for testing every possible combination of two, three or more.

220

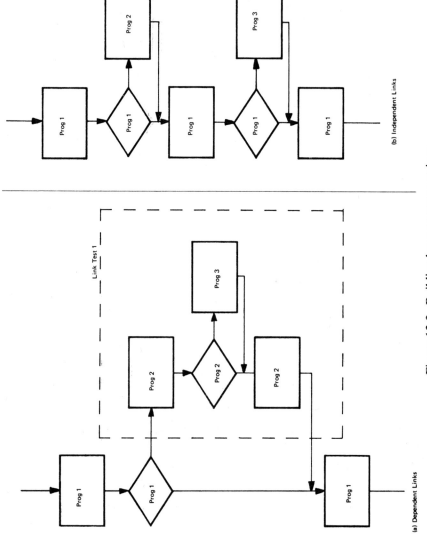

Figure 12.2. Building large program strings

Take the examples in Figure 12.2 and assume the method of building upwards. In case (a), program 3 is not a superior to any other program so it is first linked with program 2. The two together can then be treated as one entity used by program 1 with which a second link test can be made. In case (b) there are two possibilities. If, as the caption indicates, programs 2 and 3 have no effect on each other then both can be linked to program 1 in a single test. If program 2 does however create conditions which govern the execution of program 3, then program 3 should be first linked with program 1 using test control actions to simulate program 2 before testing all three together. The approach may appear to be unnecessarily cautious but its purpose is to contain the sources of error within strict limits.

These examples are obviously idealized and are easy to plan. Connections in real life will be more obscure and the identification of limits to link tests more uncertain. Finally the choice will depend upon the opinion of the test supervisor and the skills of his programmers. As they gain experience they will be more capable of handling bigger units. There may well be an advantage in planning big units initially and only subdividing them if errors are found. A test case table for a large unit with many links will be difficult to manage though. Despite the apparent duplication of effort in testing and retesting the lower levels of program, link tests tend to be easy to plan and to carry out. Many small tests take little longer than a few big ones.

Tests can use Data from Program Test Stage

Much of the apparent labour of link testing is removed if the test data developed for unit tests is utilized. The purpose of the link test is to cause the subordinate program to exhibit all of its actions upon stimuli from the calling program. The interface can therefore be tested by selecting from among the superior program's tests, those cases which cross the interface. In cases when the subordinate program returns control to the superior, the same results as occurred in program tests of the superior should be achieved. Only when control is not returned must new results be predicted. Even then the input need not be rewritten.

In a case like the second test appropriate to Figure 12.1(a), the unit test specification of program 1 can be used unaltered except to remove those test control instructions which simulated program 2. The link test specification is then a simple cross reference to the original supplemented with notes on the change. Generally speaking if program A calls program B, the test cases from B can be used with the appropriate data from A.

Linkage Table Identifies Cases

The test cases for a link test cannot always be taken so easily from a program test specification. More generally some guidance is needed. By bearing the purpose of link test in mind, the programmer can identify the cases readily enough. If the guidelines recommended in Chapter 7 for the formal definition of interfaces have been followed, the cases can be deduced by the linking statements. When one program calls another by a CALL (program) WITH (input parameters) TO GIVE (output parameters), the cases necessary to test that link may be defined by the parameters. The different values each input parameter can take, together with the different values each output parameter can return, constitute the possible population of conditions across the interface. If the subordinate program can end without returning control, then those exits constitute other conditions. Where the output parameters are the result of the subordinate program's interrogation of its environment as well as the input parameters, that environment constitutes different conditions. From the list of independent conditions, combinations can be made up to create a sufficiently varied set of cases to test the link thoroughly.

If a link test adds more than just two units together—for example as in the first interpretation put onto Figure 12.2(b) above—the list of conditions will get much longer. Then each CALL line must be explored to determine the full list of conditions to be tested. The longer the list of conditions the larger the number of combinations which can be made from them. The increase in cases can be much more than doubled if the number of conditions is doubled.

Once the 'black boxes' which are being linked do contain more than one program, the test specifications title page will explicitly identify them for the reader. In the format recommended earlier, LINK (superior) WITH (subordinate), either can be a string of program identities.

TESTS WITH MESSAGES

Simulation is Recommended

Once link tests have built program strings to the boundaries of the application, testing progresses to the use of the interface between the computer and the outside world. The 'black box' now becomes the physical computer.

Message based tests have many phases and can be subdivided as discussed in the last chapter. At any point in this long sequence, tests could be performed using terminals. Their use should be avoided for as long as the test software will allow. By prior preparation of entries on cards the content of tests is more precisely controlled. Despite the most explicit instructions, a terminal operator cannot be guaranteed to press keys in exactly the desired pattern. If a test does reveal an error, then the same test should be repeated after a program correction. Repetition is difficult enough when only one entry is involved, but if the subject is a long sequence or a complex multi-thread conditions anything may happen. Simulation ensures that exactly the same entries are made and their sequence is undisturbed.

If the long sequences of entries needed for later testing stages are transcribed from cards to magnetic tape or disc, another advantage of simulation is realizable. The speed advantage of channel transfer, or even card reading compared to terminal operation, makes possible simulations of many days' activity in an hour or two of elapsed time. Also tests can be run remotely and there is not the need to assemble a large body of people to push keys instead of doing their normal work.

Test Cases are Identified from Tables

Exchange and conversation test cases have already been discussed in connection with the design of conversations and exchanges. If the designers were conscientious and the design documentation up to date, the test tables contained in those specifications will be adequate. Certainly new tables should not be prepared. Rather, testing should be used as the occasion for reviewing them. New error responses may have been discovered and need to be added to the tables. The conversation and exchange diagrams can be reviewed again to test the completeness of the original set of test cases. The purpose of these tables remains as stated earlier—to explore all reactions of an exchange to its entries and all possible patterns of exchanges in a conversation.

Cycle and subsequent tests are more difficult to make comprehensive. No routine method can be suggested which will identify all situations which must be tested. Once a situation is selected for testing, a methodical approach to all its opportunities for variation will identify the cases needed to cover the situation exhaustively. This does not however answer the need to identify the situations in the first place. At this stage, the original qualities of the project as envisaged by its users will provide a guide. The advice of user management and experienced user staff will be invaluable. Their help should also be sought in the work of generating realistic entries and in predicting responses. The testing purpose is now in curing the distortions of the first transmission between the user and the analyst. The preparation of test specifications for these late stages should still be supervised by analysts to ensure the completeness of the test. Perhaps a further warning should be given that test specifications are still as valid for these later stages as they were earlier for program testing.

Terminals are Used to Prove Network

Tests with terminals and application programs together should be undertaken only after the project logic is apparently proved. Then the purpose of testing is to prove that the computer map of the network accords with physical facts—that messages intended for the Chief Accountant do not appear on the Managing Director's terminal. Once the logic is reliable, the detailed content of messages is not material to the success of the test. The only object is to provoke the exercise of the network. Even the logic of the program which handles communications between terminals and the system should by now be tested and reliable.

High volume tests may be used to prove response time performance as a separate test purpose but this will be the only other valid purpose. If this aspect is tested, the test planner must provide a realistic environment in terms of core and file space available or responses might be delayed longer than in real running.

Finally, at some point before acceptance tests, the manual procedures associated with computer operation, fallback and recovery must be tried. These will be most realistically tested if emergencies are created during acceptance tests. Though strictly not related to testing, the project designers should ensure that user management are aware of the importance of regular drills on these aspects of the project before relinquishing responsibility. A schedule for such drills should be incorporated into the procedure manual for user supervision.

ADMINISTRATION OF TESTING

Assignments must Avoid Loss of Interest

The procedure for program development recommended in this book provides for many distinct activities. The steps include program specification, coding, test specification and testing and the corresponding activities for the entities of exchange and conversation. There is a temptation to use these steps as tasks in scheduling work to members of the development team.

It is a temptation which must be avoided to some extent because fragmentation can be harmful. Work scheduling has to be conducted so as to serve many different purposes. Knowledge about each part of the project must be spread around so that the absence of any member does not hold up progress. The timetable for carrying out jobs must be as flexible as possible so that work is evenly spread among the team and so that artificial dependencies are not introduced in the work. The people working on the project will need to be highly motivated since their actions should at all times be for the benefit of the project. Intellectual activity of a design nature is difficult to supervise for quality and this characteristic is therefore dependent upon the goodwill of the people doing the work. The multi-stage communication process identified as the subject of testing is already unavoidably long and further fragmentation will only mean more sources of error.

These purposes can be reconciled to some extent but finally judgements must be made. At this point a guideline can be offered from experience—make assignments so as to maintain responsibility for significant and identifiable pieces of work with individuals. No systematic evidence has been collected to support this view but it is consistent with findings in the management of other human activities. If a person is given responsibility for the development and testing of an identifiable piece of the project, his interest will be greater, he will be happier and the quality of his work will be higher. If scheduling flexibility is made the paramount aim, no person will be able to identify a part of the project as his own and quality becomes an externally imposed property which is not his responsibility.

Reviews Provide Quality Control

The best motivated programmer may still make mistakes or misinterpret specifications or standards. The fault will most frequently be unintentional and the team member as much as the project manager will want a review function to be performed. Good practice means more than the publication of standards—it means training, practice and review. There is however no need to treat a review activity as part of the reward and punishment system by deliberately assigning reviews to superiors. Reviewing can frequently be done by people of similar status to those who originated the work in question.

Because of the frequent sensitivity of real time systems to error, an elaborate review process can be devised. Figure 12.3 illustrates the possibilities. Few applications will justify all these stages but at some point, the test cases must be checked for completeness and the test data must be verified as fulfilling the specified test conditions. For the final review, a person senior in experience should be used to look out for testing possibilities in unusual data conditions. Unusual conditions can frequently demonstrate short-comings in design at any level—for example, an order when all products must be replaced by substitutes, cash payments when a customer does not owe any money, flights when no booked passengers appear but all passengers are transferred from another airline.

Task	Review Process	Reviewer
Specify program	Follow up references to check all functions covered. Check specifications for format according to standards. Check program structure permits clean modularity. Review logic for efficiency and accuracy.	Another specifier
Code program	Desk check coding by trying significant cases against coding. Compare coding to flow chart and specification. Check for adequate commentary according to standards.	Another programmer or analyst
Specify testing	Check test cases for completeness by reviewing against flow chart. Check that test data for each case does satisfy case conditions. Check that results predicted match program specifications. Check test specification for conformity with standards.	Another programmer
Test program	Compare test data input and results achieved with contents of test specification. Review coding for absence of patches and use of current data definitions, program listing for absence of syntax errors. Check documentation of program is complete and clean.	Senior programmer

Figure 12.3. Definition of review stages for program development

Annotation of Results is First Review of Tests

The process of marking a computer listing of test results is a very convenient time to permit the programmer to check himself. Marking consists of separating cases in a submission and within each case, cross-referring to the original test specification. The references written on the test results must identify each component predicted in the original test specification. If a record is updated the altered items are underlined; if a response is built it must be tied to input. If this process is done carefully by the person responsible for testing, he must review his own work automatically. The subsequent review with a senior programmer will then resemble counselling because the programmer will be entirely confident of the testing he has done.

Common Programs must have One Keeper

The design methods in Part II have been developed to maximize the use of common coding and so minimize the development effort. The actions of identifying exchanges in conversations and programs in exchanges have this aim. As a result, the stages of testing, later than program testing, must create many simultaneous opportunities for change to a single program. Equally, an error discovered late in testing may affect several different programs. The management of change therefore needs some attention.

When errors are found there are different entities to be managed—the errors must be corrected completely and the programs must be carefully changed. The change procedure must recognize these two and assign a different person to be responsible for each. As an error is found a memorandum is created to notify the error to anyone affected. This memorandum, or discrepancy notice, must bear the name of a person responsible for its clearance. Errors are given an identity—a serial number—from an error register and a history kept so that uncleared errors can be quickly located. A register is also kept of programs in the project—each entry showing the name of the programmer responsible. That programmer is the only one authorized to make changes to the program. In this way corrections which overlap in time do not lead to the existence of several incompletely corrected versions of the same program nor do the corrections get overlooked. The man looking after a correction is a progress chaser who ensures that corrections do not stay undone for long. The programmer can adopt an orderly approach to identifying and implementing new program versions.

Errors will generally fall into three classes: those which must be done at once, those which can wait for the next emergency and those which can be processed when there is nothing else to do. The discrepancy notice should state within which class an error lies. The responsible programmer can then schedule the correction for the next issue or plan it for a later date. The correction 'officer' can coordinate the activities of several programmers if necessary, to achieve a complete correction by a set date. He can then verify that the error is corrected and record it as complete. The program 'officer' will complete his function by managing recompilations independently.

The management of the correction process thus has two components—recognition of the existence of two sides to an error and the assignment of separate responsibilities.

System Tests Need New Organization

Gradually, as the project progresses from program testing to tests of entry sequences, the organization of the project team will change. The separation of error and program maintenance functions is the first step. In the early stages of link testing, each member of the team might carry out both functions interchangeably. He might be testing one conversation, and therefore acting as its correction officer, while acting as program officer for half a dozen programs. As cycle testing is approached there is less opportunity for this arrangement. At the cycle testing stage there is only one entity being tested—the real time application, and the whole team is concerned. An organization by function is therefore appropriate if the project team is large enough to need splitting.

There are three major functions which can be the basis for grouping team members, though each can be subdivided if this is necessary. There is a test operation function, a program maintenance function and a scheduling function. The operation function consists of preparing entry streams, predicting results and checking output. Program maintenance involves corrections to coding and to documentation. Scheduling is a new function which is rendered necessary by the complexity of the task of determining which tests can be run. Each decision involves considering the errors outstanding and selecting the errors which must be corrected to permit runs of the tests which are waiting. The scheduling function may be one for the project leader or he may need help with it.

The operations function has a maintenance element in its work. The various test cases in its keeping each consist of sequences of entries. Discrepancies between predicted and actual results may well arise from errors in input so there must be provision for correcting entries by content and sequence. If, as is recommended, the entries are stored on tape to speed up tests, their maintenance can become a significant task which also involves the preparation of computer runs.

The operations group will be responsible for detecting discrepancies but the responsibility for diagnosing a cause will rest with whichever group has the senior programmers or analysts. Once identified, discrepancies are cleared by the procedure described earlier. The discrepancy notice is cleared when the operations group is satisfied that no discrepancy remains. A discrepancy should be carefully reviewed so that not only is its direct cause ascertained, but also all its effects are properly explained. If an input error causes unexpected results, are they consistent with what the system should do in the new circumstances of the error? If an input error is found, was it properly detected by the system or is the design deficient?

Error diagnosis must allow, as a last resort, for problems with software. Problems may exist in the software used in executing the processing or it may be in that used to ease the testing task. Software development will be the province of a separate team of people even if it is done within the installation. One or more members of the project will be assigned to liaise between the two.

Testing, then is a significant undertaking in its own right in the course of project development. It generates its own documentation, needs separate procedures and has a bearing on project organization. This reflects its enhanced importance in ensuring the higher quality of finished programming necessary for real time.

PART IV

Conversion and Conclusion

Chapter 13

Conversion and its Documentation

THE APPLICATION USERS

Real Time Introduces New Operators

The work of computer operating takes a different emphasis in real time. This difference can be readily appreciated when a system or equipment error occurs. Through their terminals, users will frequently experience problems before they become apparent to the computer room. This will be particularly true of program errors which can show up by unlikely results before causing any hardware failure or generating console error messages. The minute to minute operating tasks of feeding input and extracting output are transferred from the operator to the user. That part of system development concerned with writing operating instructions and clerical procedures therefore changes its nature—the topics are distributed differently and new topics are introduced.

In making these observations, we are discussing only the real time applications—the instructions on running batch systems remain unchanged. These are still vitally necessary for efficient operation.

Terminal Users Need Instructions

In place of, or in addition to, the clerical procedures and control procedures describing the sources of input and use of output, there now exists a need to describe to the user exactly how he should manipulate the system to carry out his work. That part which, in a batch system, would have dealt with how to generate a punching form or what codes are used or how to judge whether an input field is feasible, will still be required, but in place of procedures for clearing error reports the instruction will describe reactions to responses. The material will be organized differently—around jobs rather than individual forms and reports. The instructions will also tend to be more explicit.

It would be fair to say that user instructions have a more important function in making or breaking a real time system than a batch system. The user must understand instinctively what part he plays in the system to be able to react quickly to system behaviour. The instructions to the user are a further stage in project development. Until this work is done the designer might believe he knows how to make the system work but writing down instructions for other people—unsympathetic people maybe—which will guide them in his absence, will be the proof. This work should be performed in parallel with detailed design so that changes arising from both activities can be implemented before programming starts. Since user instructions are part of the development of the design, they must be tested before the final tests of the system. User training will be their final test.

Computer Operation Includes a New Role

At the computer centre, the operating function changes emphasis from participating to monitoring. So far as an operator is concerned the function served by the system is no longer just mechanized—it is automated. His job is to watch and wait and react to emergencies. Furthermore, a new production function is introduced—the System Manager. The System Manager has the role of contact man if the users experience an error. 'I have not had a response on my set for three minutes' says a voice on the phone, 'What shall I do?' The System Manager has an investigatory role to isolate the problem and if necessary call on specialized services, engineers, operators or programmers, to put it right. This part of his work is consultative and he must have a correspondingly thorough grasp of the design of the hardware, software, and applications. We will consider this new function later in the chapter.

Operating instructions must therefore be organized as a set of diagnostic aids rather than a determined sequence of instructions. There will be operating procedures concerned with particular tasks which are routine but the greater proportion of the System Manager's contribution will be that of the consultant and manager rather than the servant.

Chapter Does Not Specify Standards

Unlike the previous chapters, this one will not suggest formats and section headings. It will instead discuss something of the contents of the manuals required to provide a sense of the topics which ought to be covered in writing such instructions. It is possible to make some simple observations about the physical form to ensure they are not overlooked. The instructions must be loose leaf and clearly segmented to facilitate maintenance. The instructions should be robust—good paper in stout binders—because if they are properly written they will be constantly in use. The text must be well signposted with indices, and with labelled separator cards so that necessary information can be found quickly. Text should be printed on both sides of each page to keep the bulk of the manual down. The text should use short sentences giving instructions. Beyond these routine matters, each manual will be compiled in accordance with formats already in use for the computer room or the user departments. The following sections consider matters which may be covered in each.

TERMINAL USERS DOCUMENTATION

Construction Reflects the Organization

Many real time systems will include procedures which are reserved to certain users—either supervisors or specialists—for security reasons. The Users' Manual will enforce this security if it is constructed by procedure so that each user can be issued with only those parts of it which are of concern to him. Obviously this action alone will not be proof against misuse of project procedures but it is a confirmation that the protection of these reserved facilities is important. The procedure and conversation concepts for dividing the project continue to be relevant in the conversion phase and procedure descriptions are best issued as conversations are converted.

Usually therefore there will not be one version of a Users' Manual but many, and the system for the distribution of updates must recognize this fact. Perhaps the documentation can be regarded as a series of job specifications. It might include a formal description of the job to act as an index to the various procedures contained within it.

Training and Reference Material Needed

Documentation for the users must satisfy two functions—those of reference and training. The material contained within the Users' Manual will serve both purposes but there will, in addition, be training material. Formal training courses are usual to familiarize users with equipment as well as the system. The course will be used for longer than the conversion period to assist in the induction of new staff. The training will act as a guide to the more immediately accessible reference material, which should be issued on the course. The training material will consist of exercises covering the ground of the system in much more detail than will be usual in the reference manual. It will of course be organized differently, in the manner of a case study—making its points from examples. The training will best take the form of following these exercises on the terminals. If the training is assisted by special training programs which detect and check training entries against a predetermined sequence, then the responses from this software to a student may well have to be significantly different from the responses of the live system. The usual change is that they are much fuller—more of a commentary on what the student might be doing wrong. These responses will need separate documentation—at least for the teacher if not for the taught.

Reference Manual Reflects Procedures Identified

The contents of the Users' Reference Manual will consist of introductory material, instructions and appendices. The introductory section should provide the background on the function and justification of the whole system and on the various users—one of whom will be the subject of each version of the manual.

A section identifying the equipment to be used by the recipient of the manual will help. This equipment can be related to a picture of the whole network. If the terminal manufacturer provides a User's Guide which is responsive to the user's need for information this could be bound in.

The main section will consist of descriptions of the procedure which have to be carried out by the user. These should be readily identifiable from the procedure specifications produced early in preliminary systems design. Their cross reference sections will lead the writer through the design documents to whatever level of detail he feels necessary. The preparation of procedure descriptions is the final test of the system design because the system is being examined from a new viewpoint and possibly by a new person. Whereas the design has been considered from the inside—what to do with entries, now it is being viewed from outside—how to make entries to match a situation. The scheme of documentation recommended for systems design and the approach that it implies should have kept the new viewpoint firmly in mind, but now comes the confirmation of its success in doing that.

It may be that the procedures separately described can frequently be combined in predictable sequences to meet common or important situations. In an order entry system, there may well be a lengthy routine to be followed if a head office of a customer group changes its address. Such 'situations' offer a good opportunity to index the detailed material if they are described or tabulated using references to their constituent procedures. An airline example is the situation where an aircraft assigned to a flight is changed. A large number of the individual procedures have to be used together to effect an orderly transfer of passengers, baggage and cargo to a new configuration of seats and cargo holds.

The appendices which complete the manual permit such matters as formal entry specification to be kept out of the text to make it easier to use for quick reference. There is a balance to be achieved between making the original material easy to read and saving the loss of time entailed in turning from one section to another.

Describe Each Procedure in Script Style

The recommendation to short direct sentences can be enforced to some extent by adopting a playscript format for the instruction. In a real time system the 'actors' are the user and the system with a 'supporting cast' composed of those persons with whom the user interacts. The names of the parts played are quoted on the left and script says what they do:

Order Clerk:	enter first three letters of customer's name
System:	display list of matching customers
Order Clerk:	(a) if customer intended is visible, enter line no.
	(b) if not visible and MORE displayed go to next page by PAGE
	(c) if TOO MANY given, enter more letters

(d) if customer not found, press EXTEND SEARCH key

(e) if customer not found after EXTEND SEARCH, pass order to supervisor

The effect resembles the conversation diagrams used in systems design to identify exchanges. In fact, these could very well be reproduced with the script. The wording used should be so explicit that for example, exact keyboard actions are identified rather than ideas. 'Ask for an extension of the search' is not as explicit as 'press EXTEND SEARCH key'.

At the start of a procedure, its stimulus should be clearly identified to tie the procedure to concrete events such as the delivery of a form or the occurrence of a telephone call. If the user must perform any coding (though this is more a job for the system) the code key should be stated, or identified in an appendix. If the user must verify an action of the system such as the expansion of an abbreviation or the display of default values, the instructions must cover the point. The disposition of any printed responses will be specified and so will the maintenance of any control information.

The script will need to cover alternative conditions, when actions might follow a different sequence. This structure can be conveyed by numbering the actions and using 'PERFORM' statements. The error situations which might occur can be classified into common and specific. The common errors are those detected by software or service routines which recur throughout the system. The writer might decide to cover those in an appendix and simply include a general instruction on every page referring the user to that appendix to cover any responses which are not described.

The procedures described must include those concerned with fallback. The earlier procedure specifications will have described fallback in general terms but the procedure for it must now be described in detail. The place of fallback procedures within the manual can vary but should be clearly labelled. Each physical manual is likely to refer to one class of user and can have a separate labelled section. There may be a variety of fallback procedures depending upon the length of time the computer has been out of service. These should be arranged in a sequence based on ascending periods of time—each leading on to the next.

Another mandatory section subject to similar observations is that concerned with recovery after the computer service is restored. The elaboration of recovery procedures will depend upon the necessity to bring the computer system up to date. An inquiry system needs no update activity while a data capture system may need the missed transactions or may allow for them to be entered in a batch mode prior to the next processing run.

Appendices are Required for Formats and Errors

The description of a procedure in the playscript style would be clumsy to use if every entry format were exactly described as it occurred. The same entry may well occur in several places in a procedure or in several procedures. Formal definitions of entry formats are therefore best covered by using appendices. The formal specifications of detailed systems design could be used as set out in Chapter 10. Any formal definition must be liberally illustrated.

An appendix is a good vehicle for listing error messages also. Much of the software will generate error messages applicable to many entries in different procedures. Their repetition in the body of procedure descriptions would add to the bulk of the manual unnecessarily. The skilled user wants a quick reference section for unfamiliar responses. If these are arranged alphabetically, a rare one can be quickly found. Each response should be described by stating its likely reason and prescribing the appropriate action to permit processing to continue. There would be some value in listing the entries which can generate the response in case conditions giving rise to it vary, and so that the user can see whether his entry should have generated it.

An appendix might well be the place for a description of the equipment especially for simple service information such as changing paper on a printer.

The sequence of the manual is arguable. What have been described here as appendices are the most used sections, once the initial learning period is over. There could be a case for making them the only parts of the reference manual, keeping the rest as training material but each organization will have its own preferences based on previous standards for clerical procedures.

System Modification Procedure Affects User Documentation

Both training and reference material will be developed before system installation. Both are therefore at the mercy of modifications arising from the late discovery of errors and omissions. Although the development technique advocated in this book is intended to expose problems at the time appropriate to their solution, some will slip through. In making modifications the designer must cover the user documentation as well as that for the programmers and analysts. This problem can be attacked with a check list. The modification notice should have printed on it a list of all documentation manuals to be checked. The cross references in each system development document leave no gaps in the chain from program module back to original project scope statement. Procedures and conversations will lead into the users' reference and training manuals.

SYSTEM MANAGEMENT MANUAL

Operator Functions Change

In a real time system, the operating function is changed and subdivided. A new function is introduced—that of System Manager. His responsibility is for the total system while the computer operator retains the function of managing the computer room. This division is imposed since the operators retain their participatory role in running batch systems. Only in rare installations will real time be the only method of running. With respect to the real time system, the operators retain their normal functions of loading and unloading the system at the start and end of the real time day, but between these two events the real time system runs virtually unattended. There may be a need for changing log tapes but otherwise the role is that of fireman. Alarms take the form of messages on a console printer or operator's terminal but corrective action should be under the control of the new production controller—the System Manager. The following paragraphs discuss the documentation provided to him. His functions include monitoring the output of the network monitoring software discussed in Chapter 9, and using any network monitoring hardware to monitor the transmission network.

Besides his firefighting duties, the System Manager will have a number of routine activities connected with the efficient running of the system. Typical tasks are, start up and shut down routines, file reorganization, file integrity checks, adding new terminals, altering security locks on data and facilities.

But while some of his work is predictable, much is not so and must be serviced by a manual rather different from batch operating instructions.

Instructions must be Separate from Descriptions

The key feature of the 'firefighting' section of the manual is that it is composed of many different procedures which he can use in diagnosing or curing trouble and that these are convenient to use. It must be a tool kit ready to hand. To help the System Manager use a tool quickly the material on it must be arranged in a standard way with key facts first and background second. The System Manager must know what tools he has in his kit, though an index will save him from remembering their sequence. Each procedure should then be defined by its function, action and system response. Then the specification can elaborate on the use of the procedure, examples and references to other material.

Some problems will be reported by status messages to the operator on the computer console. To help them both find cures for these, a list of such messages can be given with references to suitable diagnostic or corrective procedures.

Some Instructions will be System Wide

Some parts of the firefighting manual will be concerned with situations independent of particular applications. Computer peripheral malfunctions or hardware problems with teleprocessing lines will be the subject of similar corrective action whichever application activity caused the trouble. These sections will form a general manual.

The procedures particular to applications can most conveniently be treated as supplements to this general manual. To help in its use, the System Manager might enforce a system of identifying status messages by code which will show whether the message is concerned with an application problem or a system problem.

Network and System Patching must be Possible

Examples of firefighting procedures needing rapid action are those concerned with preventing a small failure from bringing down the whole system. If one terminal is transmitting bad data or if a single exchange has an error in one of its programs, an unpredicted situation might affect the CPU or put corrupt data on the files. On the other hand, once such an error is found the whole system should not be stopped. The System Manager will want standard routines for repairing a corrupt record, cutting off a terminal or rendering a program, an exchange or a conversation, unusable. These actions will not be affected in principle by the expansion of the system—though the reference lists on which they will depend will reflect changes to the terminal network and the program library. With the ability to switch off machines and facilities must go an ability to switch them back on again. This latter mechanism may also be the means of expanding the system in the first place. Another related tool for the System Manager is a monitor or trace program which, though normally used in testing, can be invoked for a suspect program online.

Actions such as these are much easier to apply if the need for them has been recognized early in systems design since the tables they need can be integral with the design.

With a facility for intervention as powerful as this built into the system, security measures must be included which restrict intervention to authorized users. The initiating actions will be recorded as available only on production of a system management authority code and only if done on a designated terminal. Physical security measures can be employed to restrict access to that terminal. To guard against its failure though, there must be an ability to designate other central site terminals as 'master'.

Corruption of Data

Among the group of 'firefighting' tools which will need to appear in the system management manual are those concerned with patching out data errors. In principle, every data item occurrence should be capable of being corrected by terminal action, but such facilities must be rigorously controlled. The application programs should include reconciliation checks so that details match summary records and records are protected by 'hash' totals. However there will be occasions when hidden program errors cause corruption which, because of the built-in integrity checks, can tie up an application. Then the System Manager must be able to intervene to undo the error.

For the System Manager to be able to do this with some confidence, he will need to be familiar with an application's file structure. The formal definitions of files and data records will be reference documentation but they will be more understandable if they are supplemented by a special introduction describing the flow of data through the files. The progress of a customer order through sales files can be quite complex as it moves from the order file through the despatch and invoice files to payment and history. Given an understanding of the application as seen from its files, the System Manager can call up records or groups for display and amendment using standard service routines which only he can access directly.

Procedures are Needed for Logging Incidents

Such powerful tools demand careful control and the system management manual must lay down procedures for recording all such activity. Like a bomb disposal crew, a System Manager should note each action he makes in diagnosis or cure, for the guidance of those whose task might be to pick up the pieces. The procedures should be supported by forms so that the steps can be easily noted and as easily understood. The log should show the time each step was taken and any identifying facts such as terminal number, record identity and address, action code or verb of facility used and parameters supplied. The interaction with the computer will ideally be recorded automatically on a printer terminal. The print roll extract should be filed with the log.

The log will be a source of statistics for management on the effectiveness of the installations, the performance of its equipment and applications as well as a trace of system manager action. Its proper maintenance will require the definition of handover procedures between shifts and especially between the last shift of one day and the first of the next, if system operation is not continuous.

This section of the manual will be supported by a list of crucial telephone numbers in case the incident gets out of hand. When a real time system is closely integrated with company operations the emergency telephone numbers will range through the data processing hierarchy all the way to the chief executive. The incident procedure will specify grades of incident and lengths of time without service at which the various people are to be called.

Housekeeping Activities are Important

There will be a number of more predictable activities for which the Manager will have prescribed procedures and privileged exchanges. For example if the 'real time day' of the installation is less than 24 hours, the duty Manager at the start of the day will confirm the network status with a start up procedure. The object of this is to ascertain which terminals are both working and manned so that messages are not waiting in the system for the attention of a disabled terminal. The Manager should be able to call upon an exchange which will automatically send a 'good morning' or 'wake up' message to every terminal, worded to remind the user to send an 'on line' reply. Until that is received by the system the terminal is marked as unmanned and any messages for it are routed elsewhere. Terminals which are not working will not respond to the original signal with a signal enabling the message to be sent. Their status will be 'inoperative' rather than 'unmanned'.

At the end of the day an orderly shut down procedure will be employed with each user signing off before he switches off his terminal. The System Manager will be required to log these so that he does not end the 'day' while some users are still trying to work. At this time and at other times during the day when the system must be shut down, the Manager can 'broadcast' messages which will be received by all users or some designated subset. Broadcast facilities are important in a system with a 24 hour day since changes to equipment or to the system will always have to interrupt service. The start up and shut down procedure then is a good example of a routine task of a real time system.

Another indispensable procedure is that for restoring service after an unpredicted breakdown—the restart procedure. There are two parts to restart—that of restoring the system to a state where it can service applications and the subsequent stage, covered in the application design, of restoring the applications. Only the former should concern the System Manager though the two may be confused in a single application installation. The restart arrangements will depend upon the hardware—usually consisting of a mixture of hardware dependent activities and procedures dictated by the operating system as well as the real time software.

Routine activities which can be scheduled—like batch processing work—may also be introduced by applications. Online file updating systems will require periodic checks on the integrity of data, such as checking all overflow references or following chains through network files. Indexed access methods mean that files require reorganizing to correct serious overflow situations. Many systems will enforce periodic efficiency checks by rerunning system tests or simulating fallback situations.

These routine activities can be documented according to the standards used for batch processing work.

System Management Facilities should be Integrated with Applications

This section has described something of the work of running a real time installation. This has been done to show that the operating task has changed and that the System Management manual is a substantial part of system documentation. It has also discussed again some of the production functions which need conversation and exchange support. These should arise naturally from the system functions and not be tacked on as afterthoughts, but this discussion may have exposed some possibilities not otherwise considered until production starts. If the System Manager is thought of as a user of the system and procedure and conversation specifications prepared for him, then system running should be adequately planned in advance.

CONVERSATIONS IN CONVERSION

Conversion Strategies

The real time system units of procedure, conversation and exchange have been mentioned again in this chapter as having relevance to the organization of documentation for system users. This final section relates the concepts to the implementation of the working system.

In an earlier chapter (Chapter 2) the different conversion strategies were mentioned in the discussion of the implications of the direct contact characteristic of real time systems. These can be briefly listed as:

(a) conversion by system facility
(b) conversion by terminal location
(c) conversion by terminal type.

An actual system conversion may employ all of these—a multi-dimensional approach. However it is the first of these which will be discussed here. Bearing in mind that system development and user preparation effort is associated with facilities rather than with locations or terminal types, it is this strategy which will take much of the drama out of the conversion of a real time system.

System Recognition of Conversations

The early discussion of the consequences of the conversation concept in Chapter 4 introduced the idea of the conversion of an application by conversation. In Chapter 9 the discussion of entry recognition software expanded on the function of recognizing and approving entries. Two devices were discussed in this connection—the permitted next entry table (NET) and the first entry table (FET). The NET is a part of the Conversation Control Record which records the status of a conversation by defining which exchanges in the conversation can next be entered. The FET is a list of first entries in the recognized conversations of the project which can be made at any point that a new conversation can be started.

Entry Analysis Control Tables

The necessary function of entry analysis—that of determining which application program modules to execute to service an entry—is therefore the means of managing conversion in an orderly fashion. If a conversation's initial entry does not appear in the first entry table (or its equivalent in proprietary software) then, to the system, the conversation does not exist. This means that the various system elements—programs, message control tables and data files, can be installed safely in the backing storage libraries. When they are all in place and fully tested, conversion is the simple act of extending the FET to include the new conversation's first entry.

The FET may well be used in the enforcement of one of the security provisions—that of restricting access to facilities. The FET will quote the required authority level to use the conversation. If one of the levels—the highest—is that of analyst, the new conversation can be added to the FET first with 'analyst' as the only authorized user. The final stages of system test of a new conversation can thus be permitted on an otherwise live system since its use will only be permitted if the terminal user is an analyst. Added security can be achieved if the execution of a test conversation's first entry is only allowed from terminals located at the computer centre.

Continuous Conversion

With such a method of controlled introduction of conversations the significance of project boundaries and concentrated conversions can be discarded. Instead, each conversation can be considered to be a convertible entity in its own right. The introduction of a project's facilities can therefore be planned in some logical sequence—for example enquiries, then data capture, then file updates. If file updates are the immediate application of previously captured data, the original data capture conversation can be replaced with a file update conversation, when the more complex facility is ready.

The adoption of this technique requires the initial implementation of the software base which includes the entry analysis function. The long range plans of the installation for real time facilities will show whether this software investment is worthwhile.

The FET technique can be complemented by the terminal control table which services the network management function also discussed in Chapter 9. The combination of these two techniques will service both the major conversion strategies together.

Chapter 14

Conclusion

SUMMARY OF CONCEPTS

System Subdivision

In conclusion, a short chapter to draw together the main thread of the book. The concepts introduced will be summarized and set against the requirements developed in the opening chapters.

The chief idea of the book is to provide a structure around which to organize the work of real time application development. The structure was chosen to reflect what seems a natural subdivision of any commercial or administrative real time system. The purpose of subdivision is to help clarify the functions which the computer system must provide and to design programs which will satisfy those functions in an economical manner. The employment of the scheme of subdivision helps to identify a methodical programme of work for a system designer new to real time systems.

The chosen construction is to separate the logic of the project into a hierarchy whose levels are procedures, conversations, exchanges, and programs. The data used in the project is classed into messages and filed records, the messages are split between entries and responses and all are subdivided into data groupings and fields. At every level of subdivision the entire project is reviewed for opportunities of exploiting common features then specified. At each level, certain properties of the project are explored to reveal consequences on design. Each level has a prescribed method of specification to guide the designer into performing the appropriate investigation or considering a specific design problem but not to restrain creativity. The design tools of the conversation and exchange diagrams and testing plans and message definition syntax notation help the development of a robust system.

Computer Realization

The concepts identified for organizing systems work were found to have some relevance to the internal structure of the programs and software environment. The primary feature is the conversation control record. This forms the top level of a hierarchy of work space, including the exchange control record (identified by other writers and featured in available software packages). The conversation control record provides the means of carrying data forward from one exchange to another, so accumulating many data items in simple stages. It also provides a means of controlling the progress of a conversation by defining, at any point in its progress, the set of meaningful or permitted next entries in the next entry table.

The formality of the notation for defining message syntax, whether responses or entries, shows the way to specifying software for entry recognition, validation and conversion and for response assembly, editing and formatting. Both these software facilities can be integrated with a third, that of the logical terminal interface. Taken together with the more usual operating software facilities of program, storage and data management, communications control, message management and task scheduling, the software environment handles the technical problems of real time, leaving the applications designer free to concentrate on serving the business functions required in the application.

Testing Structure

If the method of system subdivision is natural, then the same structure is appropriately applied in reverse to the work of testing and assembling application components. The concepts of program, exchange and conversation are used to organize testing to produce a reliable project.

The major computer unit, the conversation, is proposed as the means of organizing conversion while the procedure is suggested as the basis for organizing reference documentation for the terminal users and System Manager.

SYSTEM CHARACTERISTICS AND TYPES

Real Time Characteristics and Consequences

The method of analyzing real time projects described in this book satisfies their special requirements. In Chapter 2, five characteristics common to real time systems were identified and their consequences on design or installation methods spelt out. The five characteristics were direct contact, immediate processing, concurrent execution, less predictable demand and novel technology. Their consequences were listed in Figure 2.2.

Satisfaction of Requirements

Figure 14.1 repeats the consequences of the five characteristics and identifies references to the methods proposed in the book. The requirements not treated in the book are already covered by commonly available software or reference material. It has been the aim of this book to address itself to a problem not tackled elsewhere—the definition of a methodical approach to revealing problems and applying solutions in real time systems development.

REQUIREMENT	BOOK REFERENCES
Direct Contact	
User-system interface	Chapters 6 and 7 user verification
Security features	Chapter 6 procedure specification
Intolerance of breakdown	Chapters 7 and 12 test plans and specifications
Conversion disruption	Chapters 6 and 13 procedure specification and conversation conversion
Immediate Processing	
Transactions call programs	Chapters 4 and 9 ECR and program specification
File sharing	Chapters 7 and 10 file and other data item
Retrieval of single records	Standard software
Unpredictable combinations of events	Chapters 9 and 11 software environment testing strategy
Concurrent Execution	
Multi-threading	Chapters 4 and 9 ECR and software environment
Overlapping data updates	Chapter 9 software environment
Competition for resources	Chapter 9 software environment
Less Predictable Demand	
Random arrival rates	Chapters 6 and 8 procedure specification and peak hour analysis
Random activity identities	Chapters 4 and 9 entry analysis software utilizing CCR
Complex queueing	Chapter 8 network design
Novel Technology	
Equipment more complex	Chapter 8 network design
Extended choices	No reference
Equipment obsolescence	Chapter 9 Standard Terminal concept and software
Fixed location	Chapter 6 procedure specification

Figure 14.1. Satisfaction of real time project requirements

System Types

Chapter 3 identified the major classes of real time systems as enquiry, message switching, data capture and file updating. For each, there were a series of specific design considerations which needed attention. Also, the characteristics of real time systems just discussed are clearly relevant to all those classes of system. Even in message switching there can be direct contact, immediate processing, concurrent execution, unpredictable demand and novel technology. Every system class can be conversational although the applicability of that word to pure message switching might be rare.

It must be admitted that process control systems were not one of the classes of system for which the approach was developed. The 'users' with whom there is direct contact would not be people but machines or processes, but their relationship with the computer could be aptly described as conversational. The methods would need minor amendments to cover such matters as user verification and message specification syntax but beyond that the techniques appear to be valid.

In fact the techniques have to be applicable to all types since commercial applications, for which the book was written, are most frequently combinations of those system types. Data capture, for example, almost always includes enquiry, if the online validation performed makes use of reference files. A full scale file updating system includes all four types of commercial system.

Conversation Types

In Chapter 10 the discussion on designing entries touched on the various approaches to conversing with a computer system. The distinction was made between prompted and unprompted conversations, and prompted were subdivided between free form and fixed form. Finally, the further subdivision of free form 'menu' was described. Most real systems will utilize all these techniques in appropriate circumstances. The utility of the conversation concept and the CCR in keeping track of prompting and interpretation of user entries is clear. Unprompted entries are usually kept short in order to prevent overburdening the user in remembering entries so that the conversation, or sequence of exchanges, is applicable again.

Applicability of Concepts

An actual system then is likely to show traces of various application classes and utilize each conversation type. The only remaining dimension is that of simplicity. The hierarchical development approach might be thought unnecessary in a system whose exchanges have no connecting sequence. Certainly in that situation the need for the conversation control record to pass data between exchanges does not exist. However, the individual exchanges still have a procedural context and the exchanges still have entry, response, processing and data components. The concept of conversation can be omitted from both development and testing but everything else stands. Even so, it is a common experience for users of simple systems with single exchange functions to wish to develop conversational systems as the basic techniques are mastered.

Finally the test of the methods is, do they work? Throughout the book the concepts have been illustrated from a live application drawn from the familiar function of order processing. That application was a data capture system using form filling conversations. It is a complete contrast to the world of airlines and online file updating in which the methods were developed. Although the illustrations were sometimes simplified to save space their very presence is a demonstration that the methods are applicable. If that demonstration does not convince, why not try them for yourself?

Glossary

INTRODUCTION

The following list defines common terms associated either with real time systems in general or this book in particular. The definitions are intended for use in the context of this book and may not be generally standard. They are however intended to be compatible with normal industry usage. In an attempt to keep the definitions concise, complex concepts are frequently defined using terms which appear elsewhere in the glossary. In such cases the terms defined elsewhere are shown in bold type.

A number of terms are new and are key to the matter of this book but are included in their appropriate alphabetic position. To make their relevance to the book clear, when they appear in the glossary they are in bold capitals. A quick appreciation of the book may be gained from tracing definitions of these terms in the following sequence:

Message, Entry, Response, Exchange, Exchange Control Record, Exchange Tests, Standard Terminal, Conversation, Conversation Control Record, First Entry Table, Next Entry Table, Conversation Tests, Procedure.

ACTION CODE

A series of characters contained within an **ENTRY** which define the type of processing being requested. Not all **ENTRIES** need an explicit code since in certain contexts in a **CONVERSATION** based system, the nature of the **ENTRY** is evident. A good example is an **ENTRY** in answer to a prompt or cue.

ADDRESSING

A method of establishing which **RESPONSE** should next be transmitted from a queue of **RESPONSES** ready for transmission. The need for logic at this time is caused by the practice of sharing a line among many slower speed terminals. This means that the line needed to serve the first **RESPONSE** in the queue may already be busy so that the decision rule 'first-in first-out' must be modified.

Systems are said to give **Addressing** priority over **Polling** if the despatch of **RESPONSES** is attempted before the receipt of **ENTRIES**. This rule is usually applied to keep the processor free of completed **RESPONSES** so allowing less chance of exhausting core storage.

ASSOCIATED RESPONSE

A **RESPONSE** transmitted to a **Terminal** other than the one whose **ENTRY** initiated its creation.

AUTOMATIC EVENT

A means of initiating an **EXCHANGE** alternative to an **ENTRY**. Such an **EXCHANGE** is executed autonomously usually at a low priority and generates unsolicited or **Associated Responses**.

An event may be set to occur by an **ENTRY** initiated **EXCHANGE** so as to allow resultant processing to proceed in parallel with the transmission of a **RESPONSE**. An event may be triggered at a preset time, monitored by the processor, or after a determined interval, or upon some counter reaching a determined value.

The purpose of such a facility is to minimize **ENTRIES** or to minimize dependence on human ability to count or watch clocks accurately.

BACK UP

The advance provision of facilities, logical or physical, to speed the process of **Restart** and **Recovery** following failure. Such facilities might include duplicated files of transactions, periodic dumping of core or backing storage contents, duplicated processors, storage devices, **Terminals** or **Telecommunications** hardware and the switches to effect a changeover.

BAUD

A unit of measure of data transmission speed meaning bits per second. The measure is of the speed at which the bits are produced and received since their actual transmission speed is that of light.

BROADCASTING

The transmission of a series of identical unsolicited **Responses** to some or all **Terminals** connected to a **Real Time** system. Such **MESSAGES** are normally originated from a **Master Terminal** but in some circumstances a system design may extend the facility to all **Terminals.** The facility is particularly useful in sending **MESSAGES** warning of imminent closedown.

CATHODE RAY TUBE (CRT) TERMINAL

A particular example of a **Visual Display Unit** using cathode ray technology to form an image on a CRT screen of characters in an associated buffer store.

CHECKPOINTING

An **Integrity** feature of operating or **Real Time** control software which causes a copy of key core areas to be written to backing storage at intervals. The areas copied or **Check Pointed** usually include information on the position of serial files so that upon **Restart** following a loss of core contents the system can be restored to a consistent state from which activity can recommence.

COLD START

The **Restart** activity appropriate when a serious failure has occurred in a **Real Time** system which has made the contents direct access storage is inaccessible so that no trace of the recent processing can be used. The system must be reloaded and activity **Restarted** as though at the beginning of a day.

CONCENTRATOR

A data communications hardware unit which enables several **Terminals** operating at a slow speed to share one high speed channel whose rated capacity is less than their sum. This is possible because the **Concentrator** allocates its high speed channel on demand and the total instantaneous demand is predictably less than the gross since all terminals are not transmitting instantaneously. In fact **Terminals** used in an interactive fashion may well transmit for only one or two percent of their **Real Time** day.

Such a device is frequently programmable and may be a regular mini computer.

CONTENTION

A method of establishing contact between a **Terminal** and a processor in which the **Terminal** takes the initiative. Each **Terminal** is contending for the processor's attention. The method is appropriate in systems with a low throughput to avoid the waste of processor time in **Polling** in vain.

The **Terminal** sends a control signal to the processor when it has an **ENTRY** ready. This causes a hardware interrupt which the processor services by assigning a buffer and permitting transmission to start. During transmission the processor can continue processing other work until the end of the transmission causes another interrupt.

This process may take place outside the main processor in a front end processor.

CONVERSATION

A sequence of related **EXCHANGES** needed to cause the processing required to support a **User** in the performance of a part or whole **PROCEDURE**. The existence of a **CONVERSATION** is evident in a **CONVERSATION CONTROL RECORD** which could be created upon the receipt of the **ENTRY** of the initial **EXCHANGE** and cancelled after the final **RESPONSE**. For convenience this record is usually associated with a **Logical Terminal** and remains active as long as its **Terminal** is connected to the system.

CONVERSATION CONTROL RECORD (CCR)

A filed record used to hold data temporarily for communication between the related **EXCHANGES** of a **CONVERSATION**. The record is usually identified with either a **Terminal** or a **User** since one or other will normally be continuously occupied on successive **CONVERSATIONS**. The record can be used to reduce the number of keystrokes needed by permitting the prompting of the **User** (analogous to forced choice and other types of form filling). The CCR retains sufficient information about the prompt to permit the decoding of resultant very abbreviated **ENTRIES**. The record will also assist in enforcing security by holding details of **ENTRIES** permitted by a **User** or a **Terminal**. The restrictions may be fixed or dynamic—depending on the progress of the **CONVERSATION**.

CONVERSATION TEST

Tests of the matching of the interfaces between adjacent **EXCHANGES** up to the assembly of a complete **CONVERSATION**.

CURSOR

A hardware feature of a **Visual Display Unit** which indicates the position on the screen at which the next keyed character will appear. It is usually made evident by the display of a special symbol which is overwritten when the next character is keyed—appearing instead in the next unprotected space.

CYCLE TESTS

Tests of logical sequences of **CONVERSATIONS** needed to follow the life of a complete business cycle such as placing an order, receiving the goods, matching the invoice to the order and authorizing payment. A high level or late stage in the system testing of a **Real Time** application.

DATA CAPTURE

A class of **Real Time** systems whose principal purpose is to replace conventional data recording methods such as punched cards with a keyboard technique which involves a direct connection to processing capacity. That capacity can then be used to provide functions not otherwise available such as immediate validation of format and feasibility, the addition of implied data to save keystrokes, the prompting of data entry, the suggestion of possible values for fields.

This class of system can be supported by a dedicated small processor unless the volume of reference material needed in the system is too great or other **CONVERSATIONS** are included in the system which demand more facilities.

DRIVER PROGRAM

A special case of **Test Simulator** for creating an environment in which a program unit can be executed. It has the additional function of regaining control after the execution of the test program so as to present another test case to the program without operator intervention.

DUPLEX

A data transmission line is said to be **Duplex** when it can transmit application data in both directions. A **Full Duplex** line can transmit in both directions simultaneously while a **Half Duplex** line can transmit alternately in each direction.

ENQUIRY

A class of **Real Time** systems (adj), the activity of such a system (v), whose principal purpose is to provide stored information on demand via a **Terminal**. Such a system will provide advantages over conventional listings prepared in advance, of ease of extraction of desired information, speed of turnround, lack of paper handling and selectivity. Its costs derive from the equipment needed including the occupation of direct access file devices throughout the period of the **Real Time** day.

ENTRY

A **MESSAGE** transmitted from a **Terminal** to the central processor of a **Real Time** system.

ENTRY APPROVAL

The process of deciding whether a recognized **ENTRY** is permitted for the **User** or **Logical Terminal** making it.

ENTRY RECOGNITION

The identification of the purpose and structure of an **ENTRY** and hence the selection of the means of **Unpacking** it. A common technique for achieving this function is the prefixing of an **Action Code** to an **ENTRY**. In certain circumstances an **ENTRY** may be recognized by its conformity to a certain syntax pattern—a technique used in compilers to recognize program statements in high level context free languages such as **Algol** 60.

ENVELOPE

Part of a switched **MESSAGE** carrying information as to the origin and destination of its text portion.

EXCHANGE

A fundamental unit of a **Real Time** system's logic which covers the processing provoked by an **ENTRY** or **Automatic Event** and completed by the transmission of one or more **RESPONSES**. The existence of an **EXCHANGE** is made evident by an **EXCHANGE CONTROL RECORD** created when the system becomes aware of its stimulus (**ENTRY** or **Event**) and cancelled when its immediate processing is complete.

EXCHANGE CONTROL RECORD (ECR)

An area of core storage assigned for the duration of an **EXCHANGE** to hold all data private to the **EXCHANGE** such as intermediate results, unpacked fields of an **ENTRY**, core or backing storage locations of data records needed during the processing of the **EXCHANGE**, register contents as at the last interruption of processing. Specific **Real Time** control programs use their own terminology—for example, Task Control Record in CICS, Tab in Driver.

EXCHANGE TEST
Tests of the ability of a system to service every **ENTRY** condition which initiates an **EXCHANGE** type. Analogous to a batch system program string or suite test.

FALLBACK
The provision of alternative systems to enable applications to continue to function, even at a lower level of service, during a failure of the main system. **Fallback** for a **Real Time** system may be a manual system using printed or microfilmed reference material for **Enquiry** and punched cards or paper tape for **Data Capture**. No **Real Time** system design can be considered complete if provision for **Fallback** for varying periods of failure has not been made. **Fallback** and **Integrity** facilities are complementary in the sense that if adequate **Integrity** minimizes the maximum length of failure, **Fallback** facilities will be less extensive.

FILE UPDATE
A class of **Real Time** systems (adj) or the activity of such a system (v) which maintains the true business files of an enterprise concurrently with the occurrence of the **Transactions** being recorded. The changing state of the files of customers, suppliers, employees or products reflects the actual state of the environment in which the business operates. Such a system therefore forms the basis for analysis and summarization of activity necessary for management information or automatic control. The technical problems of such systems stem from the sensitivity of the enterprises which they serve, to their breakdown or malfunction. To their direct cost must therefore be added additional costs of extra equipment to increase their **Integrity**, special routines to expedite their **Restart** and **Recovery** from the consequences of breakdown in any component.

FIRST ENTRY TABLE
A system control table holding a list of the initial **ENTRIES** of all **CONVERSATIONS** currently live in the system. Each initial **ENTRY** may be coded to indicate the requisite security status of **User** or **Logical Terminal** needed for use. The table is accessed by **Entry Recognition** software whenever an **ENTRY** is received from a **User** or **Terminal** whose CCR indicates that he is permitted to start a new **CONVERSATION**. The table can be accessed by the **System Manager** via a **Master Terminal** to disable a faulty **CONVERSATION** or to add a new **CONVERSATION** to the system after acceptance.

FRAGMENTATION
A phenomenon observed in systems using dynamic allocation of core storage which permit variability in the amount allocated. Smaller areas of core tend to become frequent as requests are met by allocation of larger spaces. The number of separate spaces which fail to meet requests increases giving rise to an

increasing list of spaces available and an increasing time to service requests. Curable by reorganizing core. Preventable by allowing only a few fixed sizes of buffer in core requests.

INSTALLATION

The final and major stage of development in a computer application. The major segments of work achieved are detailed design of files, programs, sources and reports; project team organization and training; programming and debugging; system testing; conversion planning including writing user reference material and conducting user training; physical planning and installation of equipment; cutover to new system.

In a **Real Time** system additional work is needed to test the **EXCHANGES** and **CONVERSATIONS**, to install **Terminals** at remote sites and to train **Users** more intensively to suit the interactive environment. Detailed design is extended to include the definition of **MESSAGE** formats.

INTEGRITY

The resistance of a system to breakdown; automatic backup in which the system detects a potential failure and automatically uses alternatives to the failing component. An example would be a duplicated reference file employed so that the copy would be used if input errors were detected on the primary version. Another example would be a permanently connected switch to provide two data paths to a storage device.

KEYBOARD

A data entry **Terminal** using the pulses generated by key depressions on a typewriter or special purpose keyboard, to form binary coded characters for transmission immediately or after the collection in a buffer store of a complete **ENTRY**. Often associated with a data output **Terminal** such as VDU to form a keyboard send and receive (KSR) unit.

LINK TESTS

Tests of the matching of the interfaces between adjacent program units—subroutines, modules—up to the assembly of the entire program sequence needed to service an **EXCHANGE** type.

LOCAL

In the immediate vicinity of a reference point. **Terminals** may be **Local** to a processor implying that **MESSAGES** passing between them pass along direct cable connections. However if the **Terminal** is **Remote** from the processor, the **Terminal** itself may be considered as the reference point in certain contexts so that it becomes possible to talk about a **Local** processor for a **Remote** terminal implying some form of control unit capable of limited processing **Local** to the **Terminal**.

LOGGING

The function of copying all **MESSAGES** received or sent on to a serial file usually with the addition of identifying data such as serial number, time, date, origin or destination. The resulting log can be used in **Restart** or **Recovery** activities or can be a work file for the investigation of security violations or can provide an audit trail of the activity in the **Real Time** system.

LOGICAL TERMINAL

A means of addressing terminals by their logical function rather than their physical address. Translation from logical to physical addresses is achieved by a common routine using a table. The table can be updated during online operation by the **Network Manager** to alter the physical terminal assigned to a logical function. The routine can be incorporated into that used to achieve the concept of a **Standard Terminal**.

MASTER TERMINAL

A **Terminal** designated as reserved for the **System Manager** and thus privileged to initiate **CONVERSATIONS** for **Network Management** not available to **User Terminals**. The identity of the **Master Terminal** may be changed when necessary by entering a special **Network Management Entry**, after **Sign-on** by a user recognized to be a **System Manager**.

MEMO UPDATE

A class of **Real Time** systems (adj) or the activity of such a system (v) whose principal purpose is **Data Capture** but additionally maintains current values in certain key fields of reference files used in validation. For this reason the reference files are temporary working copies of the true master files which are permanently updated in a batch system.

The memo updated files will frequently be used for **Enquiry** purposes in addition to their use in validating captured data.

MESSAGE

A string of characters transmitted between a computer and a **Terminal**.

MESSAGE SWITCHING

A class of **Real Time** systems (adj) or the activity of such a system (v) whose only purpose is to pass **MESSAGES** from one **Terminal** to another. Such systems are functionally similar to the public switched telegraph system but have the advantages of speed, cost reduction, ability to repeat **MESSAGES**, ability to copy **MESSAGES** to several terminals, ability to queue **MESSAGES** for a busy **Terminal**.

MODEM

A data communications hardware unit which links both processor and **Terminals** to a public **Telecommunications** network. Its derivation is from its functions which are to modulate **MESSAGES** entering the public network and to demodulate them as they leave. Modulation is the conversion of a digital signal to an analogue signal and the addition of a carrier wave to enable the signal to share a channel with other signals at different carrier frequencies.

MONITORING

Collecting statistics of the performance of a **Real Time** system in respect of, for example:

(a) concurrency
(b) queue length
(c) core occupancy
(d) file accesses per exchange type
(e) data errors per entry type.

The statistics are used to detect the need for system improvement or assess the effectiveness of an implemented improvement.

MULTIPLEXOR

A data communications hardware unit which enables several **MESSAGES** propagated at a slow rate to share a channel capable of a high rate. For example six terminals transmitting at 200 band could share a 1,200 band line. Such a relationship represents a key characteristic of a **Multiplexor** in that the high speed channel is allocated to the low speed sources in a fixed fashion—in the example each terminal always has one sixth of the high speed channel allocated. In this respect the **Multiplexor** differs from the **Concentrator**.

MULTITASKING

An IBM term for **Multi-threading**. Used in the literature for IBM's **Real Time** software package CICS.

MULTI-THREADING

The property of a **Real Time** control program which permits the utilization of processor capacity during I/O activity for the purpose of serving additional **EXCHANGES** from other **Terminals** on the system. This property implies the use of input and output queues of **MESSAGES** to decouple processing from receipt and despatch and a scheduling facility to determine what next to process. It is frequently, though not necessarily, accompanied by **Re-entrant** programming to conserve core and channel time.

MULTI-THREAD TESTS

Tests of the ability of a **Real Time** application to handle concurrent executions of the same **EXCHANGE** type. Frequently achieved using a **Test Simulator** to present simulated **ENTRIES** from a serial storage device.

NETWORK MANAGEMENT

A human function by which the network of a **Real Time** system is monitored and adjusted from time to time during the **Real Time** day to keep the system at high efficiency. The function is usually assisted by reserving a number of special **ENTRIES** to the **System Manager** to permit him to monitor throughput or processing and to permit him to react to problems. He may also use special monitoring hardware. His permitted actions may include disabling physical or **Logical Terminals** or lines, disabling **EXCHANGES** or **CONVERSATIONS** by modifying appropriate control tables.

No **Real Time** system design can be considered complete if provision for **Network Management** actions has not been made.

NEXT ENTRY TABLE

Part of a **CONVERSATION CONTROL RECORD** in a conversational system which holds a list of **ENTRY** types permitted to the user associated with the CCR at any stage in his **CONVERSATION**. As a **CONVERSATION** progresses by making **ENTRIES** so the table is altered to reflect dynamically what is next permitted. The permitted **ENTRIES** are deduced from the stage reached in the **CONVERSATION** and any restrictions of **User** authority based on his identity and that of the **Logical Terminal** which he is using.

ONLINE

Processing or files used in the mainline of a computer system or in the line of programs under discussion. Thus in the discussion of a **Real Time** system **Online** programs or files are synonomous with **Real Time** and this sense is used in the book. Some authorities restrict the use of **Real Time** to that class of systems described in this book as **File Updating**, classing less complicated systems as **Online**. The two terms are used interchangeably in this book.

PACKET SWITCHING

A telecommunications technique which permits several **Terminals** to share a high speed channel. The technique differs from **Concentrator** use in that the hardware involved acts as a processor and receives a string of characters (usually a 1,000 bit package) into a buffer and then switches it through a network to the processor via the first available data path. See **Value Added Network**.

The network involved may be private to one large organization or publicly operated by specialized carrier or the common carrier. If a specialized carrier operates such a network then he will normally lease the communication lines from the common carrier and connect them by his own switching centre processors.

PEAK HOUR

The time of day during which **Real Time** system throughput is stabilized at its maximum throughput, variations being only random. This throughput will determine the capacity of the equipment needed to service the system.

There may be different peaks for different components of the system and to determine their separate capacities, their own **Local** peaks should be used. An extreme example is the intercontinental airline whose **Terminal** peaks in different cities round the world will obviously differ.

POLLING

A method of establishing contact between a processor and a **Terminal** in which initiative is taken by the processor. This technique is applicable in systems with a high throughput such that the processor must retain control over when **ENTRIES** are served. In effect part of the potential queueing problem is being moved out of the processor on to the network.

The activity is controlled by a **Polling Table** containing terminal addresses in the sequence in which **Polling** should occur. Either software or specialized hardware will take each address in turn and initiate the appropriate control signal to check whether the **Terminal** is ready to send an **ENTRY**. If it is not the processor will initiate a signal for the next **Terminal** in the table and so on. The first **Terminal** with an **ENTRY** can send it. The next poll may start from that point in the table or from the top.

POLLING TABLE

A list of **Terminal** addresses used to control the sequence of **Polling**. Addresses may be of physical or **Logical Terminals** depending on the software used. Addresses may be repeated if some terminals must be polled more frequently than others.

PRELIMINARY SYSTEMS DESIGN (PSD)

The activity of setting out the major features of an information system in sufficient detail as to be able to evaluate accurately the consequences of installing the system in terms of development effort and time, machine requirements and running time, costs and benefits. To achieve sufficient accuracy in estimating that decisions on proceeding to installation will be valid, it is necessary to develop the systems design to the point of reliably identifying file structures and contents, program identities and synopses.

In a **Real Time** system the design should extend to **EXCHANGES** and to network design, **Terminal** selection and software selection.

PROCEDURE

The sequence of human and computer activities needed in the application to achieve a business function. This concept differs from that of **CONVERSA- TION** in that more than one **CONVERSATION** may be included in a **PROCEDURE** and steps such as filing, form completion, interaction with other people are part of a **PROCEDURE** but not of a **CONVERSATION**. In the context of this book **Task** and **PROCEDURE** differ in concept by virtue of their separation by the act of system design. A **Real Time** system will have more **PROCEDURES** than the previous system had **Tasks**, since some new

PROCEDURES will be needed to support the new system such as **Recovery** procedures of various types—file repair, **Network Management**.

PROJECT DEFINITION AND SURVEY (PDS)

The initial study of an information processing problem to determine the propriety of a computer solution and the appropriate mode of operation. The study is short but intensive and requires experienced analysts familiar with the business environment and with computer technology.

PROTECTED SPACE

A hardware feature of **Visual Display Units** which permits the designation of parts of the display as effectively read-only. In the course of keying an **ENTRY** the occurrence of protected space in the path of the stream of entered characters will cause a skip to occur. A common use of the feature is the display of text, such as field names, which assists in the instruction of the **Terminal User** in the formation of an **ENTRY.**

REAL TIME

A computer processing technique in which the computer reacts to separate events in the real world in time to influence their course. The events are reported by data entered via **Terminals**. Data relating to a single event is processed to completion (partial or total) independently of other data **ENTRIES**.

REAL TIME DAY

The period within one calendar day when a **Real Time** system is open for **Terminal** activity. May be more, less or equal to business hours. The **Real Time Day** of an international or intercontinental organization may be the entire 24 hours. The **Real Time Day** is limited by **Startup** and **Shutdown** activities.

During this period, the controlling batch operating system sees the **Real Time** system as one continuous job albeit frequently interrupted by data transfers on fast and slow peripherals. The **Real Time** job does not terminate between **EXCHANGES** although it might issue a **Wait** macro (IBM) or its equivalent in periods of low activity.

RECOVERY

The actions necessary, whether **User** directed or automatic, to restore an application to a usable condition after **Restart** has restored the system following a failure.

The actions may include bringing the master files or transaction files up to date with the business activity which has occurred during the failure, reloading application files following the replacement of a malfunctioning storage device, restoring updated files to some prior status using a security copy or a log of changes.

RE-ENTRANCE

A property of a program that is absolutely unchanged during and after execution. This quality is achieved by holding all modifiable data, such as switches and addresses in an ECR. The quality is needed when a **Real Time** system is servicing a high enough throughput that not only is **Multi-threading** used but concurrent **Exchanges** of the same type need to use the same physical coding to reduce core occupancy and channel loading.

The exploitation of this quality requires a program management routine to monitor the status of all programs in the system and to decide when to load and when to erase programs.

REMOTE

Distant from a reference point. Usually applied to the separation of a **Terminal** from its processor. Conventionally used when the distance between these units is sufficient to require **Telecommunications** technology.

RESPONSE

A **MESSAGE** transmitted from the central processor of a **Real Time** system to a **Terminal**.

RESPONSE ASSEMBLY

Collecting the data elements needed in the **RESPONSE** from their sources in core work areas or filed records.

RESPONSE EDITING

The conversion of elements from filed form to **MESSAGE** form and the addition of appropriate editorial characters such as currency symbols.

RESPONSE FORMATTING

The arrangement of **Edited** elements in a **RESPONSE** by the addition of spacing symbols such as cursor coordinates, new line symbols.

RESPONSE TIME

The interval between the despatch of an **ENTRY** and the receipt of its consequent **RESPONSE**. A primary characteristic of an **EXCHANGE**. The criticality of **Response Time** requirements of a **Real Time** system will dictate its processor capacity, transmission line speed and backing storage performance.

RESTART

The actions necessary to restore a system to a working condition following a failure. This action precedes the subsequent **Recovery** of an application and includes such matters as reloading software after a processor failure, switching to **Backup** units following any hardware failure, reloading core contents from a **Checkpoint**.

SEQUENCE TESTS
  See **Cycle Tests**.

SERIALLY REUSABLE
  A quality of programs which are unchanged after execution but not during execution. The latter more extreme quality is described as **Re-entrant**. **Serially Reusable** programs may be used in a **Real Time** system which does not permit the concurrent execution of **EXCHANGES** needing a common program, or if it does, ensures that each **EXCHANGE** occurrence uses a physically different copy which is identified with the occurrence.

SHUTDOWN
  The action of making a **Real Time** system unavailable at the end of the **Real Time Day**. It will include disabling all **Terminals** so that no more **ENTRIES** can be made, monitoring the completion of **EXCHANGES** in progress, upon completion closing all files in an orderly fashion and terminating the **Real Time** job.

SIGN-OFF
  Action of a **User** in ending his use of a **Terminal**. This is a special **ENTRY** after which the system can be programmed to accept no other than a **Sign-on ENTRY** thus re-establishing an identity of a **User** who can be associated with any following activity.
  The security of a system requires that **Sign-off** discipline be enforced whenever a **Terminal** is left unattended or **Users** change.

SIGN-ON
  The action of a **User** in first establishing his identity at a **Terminal** which he is planning to use for a number of **CONVERSATIONS**. This is a special **ENTRY** which the system will expect to be entered each time a **Terminal** is activated and contact established. By means of a **CCR** or a **Terminal** control table, the system can be programmed to accept no other type of **ENTRY** until **Sign-on** is achieved. The use of such an **ENTRY** enables the system to associate all following activity with a user identity whose validity will have been checked.

SIMPLEX
  A data transmission line is said to be **Simplex** when it can transmit application data in one direction only. Such a line would be rarely used in a modern **Real Time** system. Its only application could be to serving a 'receive only' **Terminal.**

SIMULATOR
  See **Test Simulator** or **System Simulator**.

STANDARD TERMINAL

A series of standards for forming data strings acceptable to a single (theoretical) **Terminal** type understood by application programs to be the only type in use in the system. The technique is used to avoid the need for application programs to be aware of the characteristics of many, or any, real **Terminal** thus promoting independence of programs from particular terminal hardware.

START-UP

The action of making a **Real Time** system available for use by **Terminals** at the start of the **Real Time Day**. It will include loading resident application programs and tables opening files and perhaps broadcasting to **Terminals**.

SYSTEM MANAGER

The person or department responsible for keeping a **Real Time** system working by **Network Management, Performance Monitoring, Restart, Recovery, Fallback** and **Integrity** actions. The function has operations reporting to it but will be responsible for detecting the need for action and prescribing which action to take. The detailed actions may well be performed by operators.

SYSTEM SIMULATOR

Software whose function is to model the behaviour of the complex queueing system which most large **Real Time** systems are. The behaviour of the system, in terms of such key processor and channel loadings, is predicted. The model will comprise a series of interlinked queues whose behaviour is described in terms of the average rate of demand for service and the average service time, together with indications of the variation of both. Random instances of events drawn from populations whose characteristics correspond to the queueing parameters are then created to give samples of the system's predicted behaviour. Such simulators are used to plan capacity of hardware or to set design objectives for applications.

TASK

(a) A sequence of work steps by which a **User** achieves one instance of a business function. Used during analysis to describe the **User's** pattern of working prior to the introduction of the computer assistance inherent in a new application.

(b) The processing activity included in an **EXCHANGE**. In CICS software this is an elastic concept since an application can 'read' from a **Terminal** thus extending the **Task** beyond the strict limit of an **EXCHANGE**.

TELECOMMUNICATIONS

The practice of transmitting messages whether in digital or analogue form and whether of data or voice, between remote points. The medium of communication may be wire (telephone, telegraph) or radio (microwave, direct or via satellites). The carrier may be the public telephone company or a specialized carrier concentrating on the transmission of data on privately owned facilities or on facilities leased from the common carrier.

TELEPRINTER
In this context, an output **Terminal** only capable of printing **RESPONSES** associated with processing initiated by another input **Terminal**.

TELEPROCESSING
Processing at a distance. A **Real Time** system whose **Terminals** are sufficiently **Remote** from their processor to require the use of data transmission technology.

TELETYPEWRITER (TTY)
A combined input and output **Terminal** providing for keyboard input, locally recorded in print by means of a typewriter mechanism, and printed output, formed one character at a time.

TERMINAL
A computer peripheral capable of input or output of data in a form immediately understandable by its human operators and ordinarily used in an interactive manner compatible with a **Real Time** mode of processing.

TEST DATA GENERATOR
Software for forming test data files holding desired or randomly generated values in nominated fields of nominated records. Most effective if controlled by the record data definitions used in application programs so that fields can be identified by the same symbolic names and test data can be recompiled in the same manner as programs, upon a change of field or record format.

TEST SIMULATOR
Software whose function is to create the appearance of a normal environment to a unit of application program so that the unit's coding may be tested. The unit may be a module and the simulation may be of such functions as linked modules, data management software, core management software, the operating system and the **MESSAGE** which has activated the module. The unit may be a complete library of application programs and service software and the simulation be of the **Terminal** network and the streams of **MESSAGES** apparently coming and going within it.

TRANSACTION
A business event in which the business entity being served by a **Real Time** application interacts with its environment customers, suppliers, employees. The evidence of a **Transaction** is frequently recorded during a **PROCEDURE** (or a **Task**—prior to system installation).

264

TRANSACTION CODE
See **Action Code**.

TURNROUND TIME
The interval between the despatch of a **MESSAGE** from its origin and its receipt at its destination, in a **Message Switching** system. Although clearly related to the concept of **Response Time**, the **Turnround Time** is rarely so critical since the recipient of a **MESSAGE** will rarely be waiting for it—he will only become aware of the **MESSAGE** when it arrives. Although rarely used in any other way, the term could apply to the interval between the receipt of a **RESPONSE** at a **Terminal** and the despatch of its consequent **ENTRY** in an interactive situation. Such a characteristic would dictate many features of the design of a **CONVERSATION**.

UNPACKING
The separation of a string of characters in an **ENTRY** into a series of separate fields or elements.

UNSOLICITED RESPONSE
A **RESPONSE** received at a **Terminal** without a prior **ENTRY** being made. It will be an **Associated Response** from the viewpoint of the initiating **EXCHANGE**.

USER
(a) The terminal operator.
(b) The beneficiary of the computer application.

VALUE ADDED NETWORK
A data communications medium using the technique of **Packet Switching** to offer a service more economically than a private leased line. Economy is achieved by exploiting the line's capacity much more heavily than the individual user of a leased line can achieve, even with line sharing via **Multiplexors** or **Concentrators**.

The technique is to create a network of dedicated high speed lines at whose nodes are small **Message Switching** processors. They receive **MESSAGES** from or to **Terminals** and scan the network for an available path which is not busy. The **MESSAGE** is sent in packets, if long, to avoid dedicating a path to one message for too long.

The network involved may be private to one large organization or publicly operated by a specialized carrier or the common carrier. If a specialized carrier operates the network he will normally lease the lines from the common carrier and connect them by his own switching centre processors. He 'adds value' to the network by utilizing the lines more intensively. A long **MESSAGE** sent via a network may well have its separate packets routed by different paths but this is invisible to the **Terminal** and processor involved.

Another characteristic which might be said to add value is the increased **Integrity** available for the data transmission component of a system using this technique. The network of itself provides several available paths between two points and will automatically select a working path. If the path fails during transmission the node processor has retained a copy of the packet affected and can send it again.

VISUAL DISPLAY UNIT (VDU)

A output **Terminal** usually using cathode ray tube or other technology to form visual symbols from digital signals representing binary coded characters.

VERB

See **Action Code**.

VOLUME TESTS

A test of the ability of a **Real Time** system (applications and software) to handle volumes of **EXCHANGES** up to and beyond the expected live maximum.

WARM START

The **Restart** activity appropriate when a temporary failure has not disturbed back up storage. Current **CONVERSATIONS** can be continued by reading in the last filed version of the **CONVERSATION CONTROL RECORDS** although the interrupted **EXCHANGES** may be lost.